THE RIGHT
TO BE
PEOPLE

Books by Mildred Adams

THE RIGHT TO BE PEOPLE
GETTING AND SPENDING
HISTORY OF THE AMERICAN LEGION AUXILIARY, 1935-1945
BRITAIN'S ROAD TO RECOVERY

Edited by Mildred Adams

REBEL IN BOMBAZINE
LATIN AMERICA: EVOLUTION OR EXPLOSION?

THE
RIGHT
TO BE
PEOPLE

BY
MILDRED
ADAMS

1967
J. B. LIPPINCOTT
COMPANY
PHILADELPHIA
NEW YORK

Remembering
Ray and Gertrude Foster
Brown

CONTENTS

"*The right of citizens of the United States to vote shall not be denied or abridged by the United States or by any State on account of sex.*"

The Constitution

1. BLACKSTONE, ROUSSEAU, AND ALL THAT

"The proper study of mankind is woman, and by common agreement since the time of Adam, it is the most complex and arduous."
Henry Adams

On a ground-floor corridor of the Capitol in Washington stands a marble plinth topped by a tublike construction that embraces the stone busts of three unsmiling females. Portrayed by the sculptor as fully dressed in the fashion of their day, these are three leading pioneers of woman's struggle for the suffrage—Susan B. Anthony, Elizabeth Cady Stanton, Lucretia Mott. A few blocks away a rusty iron fence guards a red brick house, once handsome, now crumbling and ill-kept. This shelters what is left of the Woman's Party. (The building is a national monument, but for other reasons.) Downtown in a modern office structure the League of Women Voters keeps house, and at work throughout the world are the women whom President Johnson, since 1964, has appointed to high political office.

These marble and brick reminders of suffragists and suffragettes, this top level of politically active women, along with women Senators, Congresswomen, and thousands of workers on lower levels, with tons of records in libraries and millions of female voters at polling booths on election day, are the visible vestiges and the living heirs of the woman's suffrage campaign.

Of all the forms that the war between the sexes has taken in our time, this campaign was one of the strangest. In some ways it was funny, and so it seemed to our great-grandfathers. In others it was pathetic. Funny in detail, pathetic that it had to be waged at all, and for so long. Its official life lasted from 1848 to 1920, seventy-two years, but premonitory rumblings began even earlier.

For many of those seven decades the cry for the vote named only one out of a collection of rights that women thought they wanted. As a goal, it was obscured by a tangle of other goals that were urged by women who seemed, at the moment, to think them all of equal importance. The abolition of slavery, temperance, dress reform, the right to rewrite the Bible in women's terms, to keep the money women earned, to wear trousers, to own land in their own names, to govern the upbringing of their children, to divorce errant husbands with reasonable ease—all these confused the suffrage issue. Free love was added by certain spectacular converts. Such demands ran in direct contradiction to Victorian customs. They generated enough emotional heat to divide families and turn supper tables into battlegrounds.

Not only did the demand of women for the vote come awkwardly, but it came at the wrong time (though nobody has yet suggested what would have been the right time). It came late, and as the tag end of a process by which the suffrage was extended from being a limited privilege possessed by white men who held property to being a general right accorded all men. This extension was granted reluctantly, and sometimes after great violence. In the case of Negroes it was granted only after a civil war. But it was done.

Why, then, should the whole atmosphere and temper of society have changed when women, however belatedly, asked the same right? What was there about the combination of the woman and the ballot that seemed so howlingly funny? Our male ancestors in large numbers certainly found it so, and they were not all foolish men. Why should ridicule have alternated with anger?

Yet for more than half a century the conviction that the vote was worth fighting for would be passed on from woman to woman with all the strength of a religious belief. For most of the time the suffragists worked without pay, and without comfort or much encouragement. They had no funds except for occasional gifts and a few small bequests, which came at long intervals. Theirs was largely a pin-money campaign, supported by their own sacrifices and by collections taken up when their lectures had moved a scanty audience to visible approval.

It was a remarkably selfless campaign. The women who spent their lives in it were not working for themselves, but for the common good. They were working for the better status of women in a democracy and for the better conduct of that democracy. They honestly believed that women, then a minority in the adult population, should have the vote because they were citizens, and as a tool with which to improve not only their own legal status, but also the laws and the government of the nation.

Under the circumstances the suffrage campaign inevitably took on the characteristics of a crusade. There is no doubt that most of the crusaders enjoyed it (though sometimes grimly). It gave them a feeling of importance, a great goal, and a purpose held in common with other women. It also gave them heady chances to test their own powers in the larger world. Angels they never were, and at times sharp rivalry appeared between them. But they felt, almost without exception, that they were following a star. That star stood not for individual gain but for a better world.

Legally, the campaign ended on August 26 of 1920, when Mr. Bainbridge Colby of Missouri, Secretary of State in the Cabinet of Woodrow Wilson, reached his office very early on a hot summer morning to sign his name to the Nineteenth Amendment to the Constitution. This had received its final state ratification by the Tennessee legislature on August 18, the state's ratification papers reached Washington at 4 A.M. on the 26th; there were reasons for proclaiming it the law of the land quickly, and before any further political tricks could be played. The wording was simple and direct. The first article said that "The right of citizens of the United States to vote shall not be denied or abridged by the United States or by any State on account of sex" and the second article, that "Congress shall have power to enforce this Article by appropriate legislation." That was all, but the first attempt at a woman's suffrage bill had been introduced into a hostile Congress in 1868. Ten years later this simpler version followed, written by Susan B. Anthony and known by her name. Since then, it had taken countless women endless hours of hard work to get it through. It represented their dreams, their sacrifices, their best legacies to their daughters.

And now, forty-odd years later, what about it? Was it worth the long struggle it cost? Why were women so late in getting at it? Why, once started, did it take so long? What held them back—just men's inertia? Or were there actual enemies behind the scenes? Why was it that sex proved so strong a barrier to the final extension of rights—more powerful than property rights, stronger than race or color? And in these forty years since women have had the vote, how valuable has it been to them? What have they done with it? How does the suffragists' dream look to their granddaughters?

For those of us who were brought up in the last whirlwind years of the campaign these questions continue to bite at the back of the mind and to become more pressing as the years change.

Some of the answers can be dug out of the history books, but not all of them. One has to start far back behind the Declaration of Women's Rights in 1848, and look at the atmosphere in which the three stone-faced pioneers in the Capitol basement were brought up.

The best place to start is with people. Susan B. Anthony was born in 1820, her friend Elizabeth Cady Stanton in 1815, and Lucy Stone of Boston (who became Mrs. Henry Blackwell in fact if not in name) in 1818. Their parents were children of the American Revolution, born and reared in the late eighteenth century, absorbing its attitudes as their own and in turn (in a day when change came slow) passing them on to their children.

That those children should rebel against some of these attitudes may seem less surprising now than it did then. Rebellion was in the air; its success in separating the colonies from England did not by any means satisfy all the feelings of protest and unease that stirred among the people. The history of the time is full of uprisings that were the backwash of the American and the French revolutions—Shays's Rebellion, for instance, the Whiskey Rebellion, the democratic turbulence that swept Massachusetts men out of national power and Andrew Jackson in.

Women were by no means immune to the widespread feeling that wrongs could be righted and old patterns be destroyed in favor of new and fairer ones. Before either Susan, Elizabeth, or Lucy was born, some women spoke up, in the colonies and in England, even in France, but their protests got little hearing. Mary Wollstonecraft, with her pen dipped in acid and anguish, wrote her *Vindication of the Rights of Woman* in 1792, and for her pains was dubbed by Horace Walpole "a hyena in petticoats." Abigail Adams, keeping house and caring for her children in Boston under wartime difficulties, wrote in 1777 to her husband John, "in the new code of laws which I suppose it will be necessary for you to make, I desire you would remember the ladies and be more generous and favorable to them than your ancestors. Do not put such unlimited power into the hands of the husbands. Remember, all men would be tyrants if they could." And then, in what sounded at the moment like a threat more playful that it would seem later, she went on, "If particular care and attention is not paid to the ladies, we are determined to foment a rebellion, and will not hold ourselves bound by any laws in which we have no voice or representation."

The new code of laws that Abigail foresaw for the colonies emerged as a separate work in each of the new states from whence power then stemmed. Matters of property, marriage and divorce, guardianship of children, and all the rest of the rules and orderings of a life that intended to be civilized, except those specifically granted to the new Congress, were set down according to local wishes. This predominating power of the states was to persist, and to cause a great deal of trouble to women as well as to men.

The men who drew up codes in the thirteen original colonies, and in the states that were later to be carved out of the wilderness, leaned heavily on the work of an English lawyer, Sir William Blackstone, whose *Commentaries on the Laws of England* were thought not only to contain the essence of English legal wisdom but also to reflect the true state of English society, moral attitudes, points of view as they then existed. The *Commentaries*, published in 1765, only ten years before the American revolution, is still regarded as a remarkable book; its author was a remarkable man, whose influence lasted.

Sir William was the son (some said illegitimate) of a successful silk merchant. By profession he was a brilliant legal scholar, by instinct and desire a social climber; he was knighted for his efforts. By 1775 the *Commentaries* had gone through seven editions, and as the new United States began setting up the framework for their own laws (based, of course, on the English laws to which the colonies were accustomed) that book became the standard for action and the source of legal wisdom in this country. For nearly a century it was a standard textbook for the training of American lawyers; its influence spread westward as the country grew. Thomas Jefferson said that most people believed that "Everything which is necessary is in him [Blackstone] and what is not in him is not necessary."

Unfortunately what was in Blackstone about women was to cause them much grief and more than a century of trouble. How accurate a reporter he was of the existing state of English (and by extension of American) attitudes toward women, is a matter of argument, but his language is specific. Perhaps because of the property rights involved, the lordly judge was chiefly interested in the rights (if any) and obligations of women who were married.

Among much else, he said,

> By marriage the husband and wife are one person in law, that is, the very being or legal existence of the woman is suspended during the marriage [he does not say whether or not she is legally permitted to keep breathing] or at least is incorporated and consolidated into that of the husband; under whose wing, protection and *cover*, she performs everything. . . . Upon this principle, of a union of persons in husband and wife [and that person the husband] depend almost all the legal rights, duties and disabilities that either of them acquire by the marriage. . . . A man cannot grant anything to his wife, or enter into covenant with her, for to grant would be to suppose her separate existence . . .

Read in the second half of the twentieth century, the sentences sound very different from the way they may have sounded to Abigail Adams. There is, however, reason to suspect that she may have seen in them the very "tyranny" of which she complained to John. The late Mary Beard, a historian who was a most careful student of the subject, said in 1946 that William Blackstone had distorted the actual place of woman in the England of his day. Or, in her more specific language, that his picture "contained a great deal of misleading verbalism, and that in short, it was false."

She may be right. But if things were actually better for women than the writer of the famous *Commentaries* suggests, it also seems certain that the picture his legal phrases present accorded with what his contemporaries thought the status of women *under law* to be. Some of them protested against it but, had there been great discrepancies between the facts and the lawyer's statement of them, the latter would not have been accepted and repeated by generations of his successors at home and abroad. In portraying his age and his country in legal terms he crystallized the structure of society as he portrayed it; this prolonged its life, acted as a brake on change, and provided an image against which rebels focused their protests.

What the social attitudes of that important age were in action, rather than in legal language, has come down in memoirs and essays.

For women, the eighteenth century was apparently a time for private tyranny and public display. In Europe, which set the pace, it was turbulent, expansive, handsome, noisy, full of French theory and British push. In the American colonies, wealthy residents of such cities as Boston, New York, and Philadelphia copied European fashions in ideas as well as in clothes. Women frequently had "vapors," in part because their bodices were laced so tightly that they could not get into their lungs the air that they needed. Men sniffed powdered snuff in order to provode spasms of sneezing that diverted attention, gave them time to think, and were supposed to clear their heads. Women bore children as nature chose—"planned parenthood" would have seemed irrelevant and irreligious. Sanitary standards and medical wisdom were primitive; pigs roamed the streets of New York, and women lost by early death more children than they reared.

Two extraordinary English women of the period spoke out bitterly against prevailing customs. A French writer, Jean Jacques Rousseau, described them as they were and as in his mind they should be. Two Swiss women, mother and daughter, whose gold and purple lives still attract biographers, laid bare the almost unbelievable details. The English women were Mary Wollstonecraft (1759-1797) and, in the next generation, Harriet Martineau (1802-1876). Both of them, in the points they present and the vigor of their language, bring personal testimony to the reality of a social framework grown so tight and so oppressive for women that they would be moved in 1848 to rise against it.

Mary Wollstonecraft's range of protest and invective was the wider of the two; Harriet Martineau, younger and better educated, was the more specific. Born in 1759, Mary was the rebellious daughter of a peripatetic English farmer and an Irish mother. Her father beat her with sticks that hurt her flesh and words that scarred her spirit by making her feel inferior. He also beat her mother; the tomboy Mary sprang between the two and took the blows. At nineteen she left this miserable home and made her way through a series of difficult and badly paid jobs as governess, school mistress, companion, stopping now and then to go home and nurse her mother, a sister, or a friend.

In the process, and perhaps because her personal life held so little satisfaction, she developed ideas and a writing style that attracted attention from the best minds in England. What Mary wanted was to wake up her contemporaries and put an end to the intolerable conditions in which women of spirit and intelligence were forced to live. An original thinker, she proved to be a source of ideas that stirred people far beyond her circle or her time. On the one hand, she was trying to break through the genteel traditions about women that Blackstone was shrewdly building up. (After detailing how the wife had no existence outside her husband, how he might subject her to "domestic chastisement,"* he says smugly that "even the disabilities that the wife lies under are for the most part intended for her protection and benefit." On the other hand, Mary was lashing out against false and sentimental romanticism, and with such effect that political and philosophic reformers like John Stuart Mill picked up her ideas and carried them forward; for the more successful protesters of the nineteenth

---

*Domestic chastisement was by no means rare, then or later, and not only in Mary Wollstonecraft's family. As late as 1848 an American suffragist, Mrs. Emily Collins of South Bristol, New York, remembers that "In those early days a husband's supremacy was reinforced in the rural districts by corporal chastisement, and it was considered by most people as quite right and proper —as much so as the correction of refractory children in like manner. I remember in my own neighborhood a Methodist class-leader and exhorter, esteemed a worthy citizen, who, every few weeks, gave his wife a beating with a horse-whip. He said it was necessary, in older to keep her in subjection, and because she scolded so much." Her scolding may have stemmed from her day's duties, which included caring for "six or seven small children, cooking, cleaning, milking cows, making butter and cheese, spinning, weaving and sewing all the clothes for the family."

and early twentieth centuries they continued to be that flaming spur to the spirit which all reformers, often passionate of mind but poor in words, must have if they are to make their pleas heard.

How much Mary was influenced by Jean Jacques Rousseau (1712-1778) is not known, but although she had little French, she must have met, among the friends attracted by her writings, considerable discussion of his thought. He was forty-seven years old when she was born, a sensual, romantic protester who is still regarded in some circles as the apostle, if not the father, of social rebellion. Those who admire him see in him the great preacher of equality and democracy. He is credited with formulating phrases that fired first the American and then the French Revolutions, and later inspired the South American countries to rebellion against the long rule of Spain. (Bolivar was an admiring disciple; so was Francisco Miranda. Even today their phrases echo in South American talk about the need for "the revolution.")

With his wide-ranging mind and love of the passions—all kinds of passions—Rousseau inevitably occupied himself with the position of women. In his book *Emile*, which was written in 1762 when Mary Wollstonecraft was three years old, he explained that "woman is expressly formed to please the man; if the obligation be reciprocal also, and the man ought to please in his turn, it is not so immediately necessary; his great merit is in his power, and he pleases merely because he is strong." Jean Jacques liked to see himself as binding all women to him with the power of a simper; there is evidence that he was, in his personal habits, rather nasty. From the point of view of the modern woman his attitudes make the flesh crawl. Nevertheless the women of his day forgave that aspect and focused their attention on his glorification of freedom. Freedom of all kinds, free love, an end to the chains of marriage that were a nuisance to men, as well as a cross to women: freedom of speech, freedom of expression, freedom in political affairs.

Later experiences of freedom have made it evident that in some ways Jean Jacques' ideal was a pink-puff anarchy in which everyone was free to call the tune, but no one had to pay the piper. In the late eighteenth century, however, the most serious political thinkers saw his cries as heralding the dawn of a new day; if Blackstone expressed the official legal attitudes that prevailed, Jean Jacques Rousseau inspired stirring ways of saying "Off with such chains!"

The two talented Swiss women whose writings reveal the stark realities that underlay satins and laced-in velvets were Suzanne Curchod Necker and her daughter Germaine. Rebels in spirit and in action as they were, with more enthusiasm than sense of cause and effect, their lives and their writings demonstrate just what it was that happened when ladies of their rank and economic status tried to cast off the chains of convention as Rousseau bade, and to follow his free path to happiness.

Suzanne was a Swiss parson's daughter, born in 1737, brought up in a parsonage in the canton of Vaud. Her father gave her more than the usual book learing allotted to a country girl in those days, but neglected to teach her much about life and birth. Despite the usual Swiss village preoccupation with livestock, the spring process of calving with its coupling preliminaries seems to have escaped her, or to have suggested no likeness in human experience. A pretty girl, but because of her superior learning somewhat formidable, she met the young Edward Gibbon in Lausanne, and fell in love with him. Unfortunately, he needed a rich wife, and this girl had no money. So she lost him. Then, taken to Paris by a pretty young widow as governess and companion, she met and married Jacques Necker, son of a wealthy banker, who became a supplier of funds to Napoleon.

Their only child, Germaine, was born in 1766. Suzanne's pregnancy was a nine months shock which she had somehow not anticipated; she had regarded love as a rare and noble sentiment, having no physical connections. The process of birth was a horror for which she was even less prepared. Madame Necker reported, in terms reflecting both the female ignorance and the medical ineptitude of those days,

I confess that my terrified imagination fell far short of the truth. For three days and nights I suffered the tortures of the damned, and Death was at my bedside, accompanied by his satellites in the shape of a species of men who are still more terrible than the Furies, and who have been invented for the sole purpose of horrifying modesty and scandalizing nature. The word *accoucheur* still makes me shudder. . . . The revolting details of childbirth had been hidden from me with such care that I was as surprised as I was horrified, and I cannot help thinking that the vows most women are made to take are very foolhardy. I doubt whether they would willingly go to the altar to swear that they will allow themselves to be broken on the wheel every nine months.

Once was enough for Madame Necker. But if she learned to avoid eighteenth-century childbirth, she also foreswore the conventional methods of eighteenth-century education that had led her into such a trap. Instead, she brought up her daughter Germaine according to the precepts set by Jean Jacques Rousseau. Rousseau led Suzanne to Diderot, Diderot led to Voltaire. Little Germaine ate her porridge in the midst of philosophic discussions.

At the age of thirteen Suzanne's application of Rousseau's precepts led the thirteen-year-old child into a severe nervous and physical breakdown. She recovered, to become one of the most brilliant, unstable, and notorious women of her period in Europe. As Madame de Staël, she wrote novels that scandalized and delighted society; she traipsed back and forth across Europe, played hostess to kings, loved whom and when she pleased to such an extent that a recent biographer dubbed her "mistress to an age." One of her five children she bore to her legal husband—the other four were offspring of other lovers. She was, in a manner of speaking, not only the ripe fruit of Rousseau's philosophy as applied to woman's place in the world but also a glandular miracle outside the law of God and man.

At the same time, Abigail Adams on the Puritan side of the Atlantic, wife of one President and mother of another, remembered how things were for women when she was young in Massachusetts. Freedom had not entered her life as a personal ideal, nor was there any sign of feminine independence. Even worse, "it was fashionable to ridicule female learning," she wrote. And then, as if mirroring in her own past how life was with young Suzanne Necker in Switzerland, she is quoted (by her grandson) as saying, "I was always sick. Female education, in the best families, went no further than writing and arithmetic: in some few and rare instances, music and dancing."

Abigail went on, of course, to be one of the first ladies in the White House. Between them the able Puritan and the worldly Swiss woman span the arc of women's lives in those days, with Mary Wollstonecraft somewhere in the middle. All of them, for their various reasons and in their various ways, protested vigorously against the public conditions and the private attitudes within which their lives were set.

That sense of protest grew. Taking form, content, and reason, it was reflected back from the new states to England by another extraordinary woman who personified some of the best thinking of her time. Harriet Martineau was born in 1802, after the American revolution and almost sixty years after Abigail's birth date. She sailed to this side of the Atlantic in 1837, a serious, well-educated bundle of British energy, eager to see and to report on life in the rough new United States. She was particularly interested in the way that life affected her own sex. Her books give a vivid picture of the years when women in the United States were making their first attempts at public expression of their points of view. Their first antislavery activities were just beginning: a decade later the Declaration of Women's Rights would be framed and made public at Seneca Falls .

Miss Martineau was observant and reproving. Looking at the new states in the light of their revolutionary proclamations against English rule, she saw that "The Americans have, in the treatment of women, fallen below, not only their own democratic principles, but the practices of some parts of the Old World." She found the familiar political device of giving the shadow while withholding the substance already well intrenched. "While woman's intellect is confined, her morals crushed, her health ruined, her weaknesses encouraged, and her strength punished, she is told that her lot is cast in the paradise of women. And there is no country in the world where there is so much boasting of the 'chivalrous' treatment she enjoys. In short, indulgence is given her as a substitute for justice," and "marriage is the only object left open for women."

Harriet Martineau was not only well read and well traveled, she was also clear sighted. Her comment on the economic situation of this country and its effect on women was made at a time when the young nation felt itself economically depressed; read in the light of modern affluence and its emphasis on the possession of a multitude of objects it is curiously prescient. "The prosperity of America," she says, "is a circumstance unfavorable to its women. It will be long before they are put to the proof as to what they are capable of doing."

The traveler found important differences in the situation of women as between the twenty-odd states then sufficiently settled to be members of the Union. Women in the Northern States at least "have the blessing of work. . . . All married women, except the ladies of rich merchants and others, are liable to have their hands full of household occupations, from the uncertainty of domestic service. . . . Women who do not marry have, in many instances, to work for their own support," though they might find little to do beside teaching school or sewing a fine seam.

Some of her harshest comments on the Northern States were related to the property laws of Massachusetts. Miss Martineau observed that the old Saxon law gave a wife the right to half of her husband's earnings; so does Spanish, French, and Italian law. "Massachusetts," on the other hand, "has copied the faults of the English law, in this particular, and I never," says Miss Martineau emphatically, "met with any lawyer, or other citizen with whom I conversed on the subject, who was not ashamed of the barbarisms of the law under which a woman's property goes into her husband's with herself."

In the Southern States, where Napoleonic law rather than English common law held sway, and women had certain property rights, she shook her head over other conditions. There "the weakest and most ignorant women give up their property to their husbands," and do nothing but produce children who are cared for by slaves. Most Southern women she found pitiable, though the best of them were, to her, remarkable. She paints a picture of the antebellum South that resembles the early days of Elspeth Huxley or the late Isak Dinesen in twentieth-century Africa. Of the ablest plantation mistresses she says,

> Women who have to rule over a barbarous society (small though it may be), to make and enforce laws, provide for all the physical wants, and regulate the entire habits of a number of persons who can in no respect take care of themselves, must be strong and strongly disciplined, if they in any degree discharge their duty. Those who shrink from it become perhaps the weakest women I have anywhere seen; selfishly timid, humblingly dependent, languid in body and with minds of no reach at all.

There were of course many other elements in the Southern picture that affected women—climate and malaria, hookworm and childbearing under circumstances that all too often led to child-burying. Weakness there was not always a matter of spirit.

These, then, were the conditions against which the woman's revolt was brewing—a long tradition of subservience to men's ideal of woman's place as William Blackstone pictured it, a legal structure that froze this tradition into an iron enclosure, a masculine attitude of mind that grew outraged if the justice of the legal structure was questioned, or if its sacredness was for a moment denied. And with that, inadequate education for women and an unwritten body of custom and habit, which assumed that women were frail in mind as in body, and inferior. All this functioned so automatically, among women as among men, that it would take an explosion to break through it.

The situation in the United States was the more complex because the actual conditions of life were more varied here, and demanded of women a more diverse set of skills than did the set and conventional roles allotted to them in Europe. Harriet Martineau was reporting on the countryside and the towns only about fifty years after the colonies had succeeded in freeing themselves from British rule, and while the power of individual states was far more apparent than was that of the new federal government.

Between the Atlantic and the Mississippi this was largely a farming country, sparsely settled, with Boston, New York, and Philadelphia the only towns of real importance. Industry, freed of hampering British regulations, was beginning to compete in importance with agriculture, transportation was moving away from the horse, oxen, and Conestoga wagon days onto the new railroads; but distances still seemed great and communication was slow.

In the older regions, men and women drew their governing techniques from England and their intellectual incitement partly from France. They read and believed the Bible, had enough regard for Greek and Latin to name towns Ithaca, Rome, Athens—and Seneca Falls. Britain was the founding parent, the lawgiver, the pacesetter in custom and fashion, of clothes and of thought in what had been recently the thirteen original colonies. France and Spain held an equal position in certain wide territories of the South and West, which they had occupied, but from which they were receding. (As for the native Indians, reluctantly but surely yielding in person and in land, they had given the settler squash, corn, beans, potatoes, tobacco, and the ways of using them, but their influence, male or female, on his social order was amazingly small.)

Behind the eastern seaboard lay a sparsely settled region, great in extent, but mostly showing the characteristics of a frontier society. Indian wars, repeatedly a part of early eighteenth-century life in the East, had in the nineteenth century been pushed westward;

they were not yet finished. The Louisiana Purchase of 1803 and the short Mexican War had brought land the size of a European empire under United States rule. Most of this land held only its native inhabitants, some of them migratory and warlike as were the Navajos, some of them peaceful and stable like the Hopis, all of then alien to the Puritan tradition and the transplanted English way of life. The Lewis and Clark expedition had told the East something of what these western lands were; the discovery of gold in California in 1848 was attracting wagon trains led by the restless, the ambitious, the land-hungry. Women and their children traveled with the men. Along the way they sowed the seeds of frontier settlements and of frontier law, in which the strongest ruled while the pale shadow of Blackstone's ghost hovered in the wild background. Women who cooked over campfires and helped to fight off Indians could not always wait and "perform everything" under their husband's "wing, protection and *cover*."

All this variety made the mid-nineteenth century an exceedingly vocal time, when people in many countries said what was on their minds and put some of it into action (on both sides of the Atlantic) in the form of rebellions that have not even yet played out their courses. The abortive revolution of 1848 in Europe gave zest to attempts to free the black man in the United States. It sparked, in Seneca Falls, New York, the long-simmering Declaration of the Rights of Women. All these were echoes of that liberalism which flourished in various ways and places between 1830 and 1870—a movement whose central doctrine is described by an historian, the late Carlton Hayes, as "the emancipation of the individual from class or corporate or governmental restraint."

The existence of this trend, both as intellectual doctrine and as a liberal norm of unease toward the usual, goes far to set the stage for the individual protests of women against what they regarded as the injustices of their lot. That stage was peopled with individuals and with ideas, the individuals acting with passion, the ideas passionately held and actively asserted. The person was by no means swallowed up by the movement; the "organization man" or woman had yet to be invented. Leaders led, their faces up, their eyes watching whatever star set their pace. If they stumbled, as many of them certainly did, it was from too much preoccupation with the star, too little watching of the ground over which they moved.

Even the frontier regions were not entirely a free society in the manner urged by Rousseau, nor was the Indian the innocent savage of his dreams. The Indian had very few defenders. In the West he was still regarded as a treacherous fighting man, an enemy. Neither his primary occupancy of the country nor his defense of it on the ground that it was, after all, his homeland and his hunting ground gave him any of the rights of citizenship under English law. Nor did the children of the English colonists waver in the conviction of their own rights to his territory when they replaced English with American citizenship.

The Negro was in a different position. In early days he got not even the fearful respect accorded the fighting enemy. The Negro was a property, a slave, bought and sold as such, and thereby in certain sectors scarcely human.

And the woman?

It would take a brother-against-brother shooting war to get the Negro the right to put his mark on a ballot, but the Negro came first. The Negro man, that is. Negro men, including the mass of ex-slaves, would be given the nominal right to vote in 1868. Negro women would get national suffrage only when white women got it under their own steam, not until 1920.

Women were not the very last. When the Indians had been quite thoroughly conquered and there was deemed to be no further possibility of harm in them (except as some of them might ask exorbitant prices for oil lands), they would be made voters in 1924.

One final detail sets the scene for the social state of mind amid which the women's revolt began. It comes out of a dog-eared copy of *The American Book of Beauty, or A Token of Friendship,* which was published in Hartford, Connecticut, in 1851, just three years after the Seneca Falls protest but before its force began to be felt. Illustrated with ringleted heads of lovely ladies turned coyly to one side and focusing their eyes on flower baskets or on doves, this gem is a fine example of the "gift book" that pretends little and reveals much.

A short essay describes the proper place and demeanor of the socially elect.

A lady should appear to think well of books, rather than to speak well of them. She may show the engaging light that good taste and sensibility always diffuse over conversation; she may give instances of great and affecting passages because they show the fineness of her imagination or the goodness of her heart; but all criticism beyond this sits awkardly upon her. She should, by habit, form her mind to the noble, and pathetic, and she should have an acquaintance with the fine arts, because they enrich and beautify the imagination; but she should carefully keep them out of view in the shape of learning and let them run through the easy vein of unpremeditated thought. For this reason she should seldom use and not always appear to understand the terms of art. The gentleman will occasionally explain them to her.

Undoubtedly the gentlemen did, and perhaps too often. That may have been part of the pattern that led to trouble.

2. REBELLION AND CONFUSION

"For little boys are rancorous
When robbed of any myth
And spiteful, and cantankerous
To all their kin and kith."

Phyllis McGinley—From "What Every Woman Knows"*

Of all the rebellious ideas that buzzed like bees in the heads of men and women of the late eighteenth and early nineteenth centuries, that of equality had the most explosive force. So has it in the twentieth century. By 1776 it had made its way into the American Declaration of Independence, which says specifically, "We hold these truths to be self-evident, that all men are created equal, that they are endowed by their Creator with certain unalienable rights, that among these are Life, Liberty and the pursuit of Happiness" (the pursuit, not necessarily the achievement).

Reading those rolling words, one might think that "men" meant "people," men and women, the part standing for the whole. The eighteenth century did not see it that way. When the founding fathers or the men in village streets looked at the word they saw "men," and "men" was what they were sure was meant. And not all men, but white men. Women? Who said anything about women? Who, for that matter, said anything about slaves?

By the 1830's the Abolitionists were saying things about slaves. So were the women, but in the face of difficulties that today seem incredible. In their demure and bonneted ways they had worked behind the scenes in the antislavery movement from its beginning —a date generally set about 1831, when a few slaves revolted in Virginia and when a young northern reformer, William Lloyd Garrison, started an Abolitionist weekly magazine in Boston. Two years later the North had so many antislavery agitators that they could call a meeting in Philadelphia to form an American Anti-Slavery Society. A few carefully chosen women were allowed to attend, and one or two were allowed the privilege of speaking from the floor, but they could not join the society, nor were they permitted to sign the Declaration of Sentiments and Principles. They did not accept this check meekly. Some twenty women, including the Quaker Lucretia Mott, formed their own group and called it the Philadelphia Female Anti-Slavery Society.

Women in New York, Boston, and other eastern cities followed their example. By 1837, there were eighty-one women from twelve states who met in New York as delegates to the newly born National Female Anti-Slavery Society.

These were exceptional women. Theirs were the first steps into public life that American women had taken since the days of such redoubtable colonial dames as Anne Hutchinson of Boston, who had challenged the Puritan elders to let her have a voice in church affairs, and Margeret Brent of Maryland, who had appeared before the House of Burgesses there. Coming forth not for selfish purposes but in pursuit of a reform such as the antislavery movement, the women sound respectable and harmless, but in the 1830's they set up repercussions for a hundred years or more.

From then on, what came to be known as the woman's movement would, for good or for ill, be linked with the campaign for abolition. A few Negroes, such as the famous Abolitionist orator

Frederick Douglass, spoke up for the women on occasion, but only on occasion, and only in the beginning. As soon as it began to be suggested that the Abolitionists should help the women get the right to vote at the same time that the Negroes were given it, all two-way co-operation ceased. Nor was this strange. Legal slavery, the physical ownership of a black man's body by a white man, was accepted as a greater wrong than the complex legal and social repressions against which women had to struggle. These, in the minds of men, whether reformers or ordinary citizens, constituted the suitable conditions of the weaker sex.

How suitable is suggested by a Pastoral Letter sent out from the Council of Congregational Ministers of Massachusetts in 1836 to warn against allowing women (the Grimké sisters of South Carolina, Angelina and Sarah, were meant but not named) to speak in the churches against slavery. "The appropriate duties and influence of women are clearly stated in the New Testament." (St. Paul had laid down the rules there: "I suffer not a woman to teach, nor to usurp authority over the men, but to be in silence.") "The power of a woman," the letter went on, "is her dependence, flowing from the consciousness of that weakness which God has given her for her protection. . . . But when she assumes the place and tone of man as a public reformer . . . she yields the power which God has given her for her protection, and her character becomes unnatural." And then comes a wonderful sentence foreshadowing those ringleted charmers looking coyly at flowers in *The American Book of Beauty*: "If the vine, whose strength and beauty is to lean on the trellis-work, and half conceal its cluster, thinks to assume the independence and the overshadowing nature of the elm, it will not only cease to bear fruit, but fall in shame and dishonor into the dust." The figure of speech is tortuous, but the intention is clear.

The women replied in many ways, and over many years. In desiring to speak against slavery they were following their consciences. Slavery was, in their minds, an evil, and there was ample biblical authority for doing their best to root evil out. In the process they were also learning skills that they would need for their own purposes and to frame speeches that men and women would listen to, to engage in public debate and win their points, to test strength of mind and power of argument against their brothers. Sarah Grimké, a South Carolinian who had lived with slavery and who loathed it, spoke for them when, in replying to the Pastoral Letter, she said, "I ask no favors for my sex. I surrender not our claim to equality." And then one hears her voice sharpen and her fingers rap the table. "All I ask of our brethren is that they will take their feet from off our necks, and permit us to stand upright on the ground which God has designed us to occupy."

From the 1830's until after the Civil War the antislavery movement and the prowoman movement was interwoven in a fashion that was both troublesome and fortunate. Troublesome for the Abolitionists because, while they needed speakers, the appearance of women in that role brought down on them the added burden of criticism that had to be countered, fortunate for them because these women brought into the campaign a high degree of persuasive emotion and devoted skill. Troublesome for the women because of violent and often rowdy criticism. Fortunate for them, because in working for rights for the Negro they learned their first lessons in political maneuver. The political wisdom they would need came to them the hard way, not only from proslavery adherents who were avowedly their enemies but also from antislavery agitators who, as workers in a common cause, might reasonably be counted as their friends.

All this conflict had been distressing, but mostly unanalyzed in the minds of women until June of 1840 when a World Anti-Slavery Convention was called in London. An American delegation went over, which included a bridge and groom, Henry B. Stanton and his wife, Elizabeth Cady, he an Abolitionist leader and she the young energetic daughter of a New York State judge. They left New York on the sailing ship "Montreal," and the eighteen days of a fine passage to London gave them plenty of time to discuss not only all aspects of the Abolitionist movement but also the women's desire to take part in it.

On the same ship went James G. Birney, nominee of the anti-slavery group for the presidency of the United States. The three did not think alike. Mr. Birney belonged to the old school. Mrs. Stanton was young, vivacious, gay, and intelligent. Mr. Birney reproved her for calling her husband "Henry" in public (instead of "Mr. Stanton"), for persuading the captain to hoist her to the top of the mast in a sailor's sling so she could see far out at sea, and for being so unladylike as to beat the reformer at chess. These were hardly auspicious beginnings for a bride who would need Mr. Birney's good will. While this may not have been the reason why he would find it advisable to support his English brethren in barring women from the convention, it may well have confirmed him in his judgment.

Once ashore, having made their way to London lodgings and hunted out the meeting hall, the visiting delegates found that the first topic for debate was the seating of several women who had come to take part in the convention. This raised voices and tempers. English delegates were fairly agreed that women should be kept off the floor and silent. American opinions were divided. Between them, they debated the issue for an entire day. Mr. Stanton, conscious of his bride's presence, spoke eloquently in favor of the women. Mr. Birney spoke against it.

As Elizabeth Cady Stanton, penned up in a curtained corner of the hall, described it later, "The clerical portion of the convention was most violent in its opposition. The clergymen seemed to have God and his angels especially in their care and keeping, and were in agony lest the women should do or say something to shock the heavenly hosts." After passionate argument, all feminine credentials were refused. The women, safely shut out of sight, listened to "the French, British and American Solons for twelve of the longest days in June."

It was enough to try the patience of a saint, and Mrs. Stanton never laid claim to that status. Instead, long after the first convention sessions were over, she argued the question, and with such emphasis that Mr. Birney, exhausted but unconvinced, sought other lodgings where he could not hear her angry voice.

One of the would-be delegates was of more help. Lucretia Mott, born Lucretia Coffin in Nantucket in 1793, had become a well-known Quaker teacher and the wife of a teacher. The Friends' Meeting in Philadelphia had recognized her rare talents in 1821, when they made her officially a preacher. Twenty-two years older than Mrs. Stanton, she had had twenty-two years more of experience in making her voice heard and her ideas understood. She and Elizabeth walked the London streets, sat in the London parks, arguing, discussing, planning.

These plans would ripen slowly. In the meantime, the young Stantons visited Europe, went home to live in Boston, joined the active liberal group there, took a hand in all sorts of "advanced" activities. Henry was a good and popular speaker and in great demand. He began to study law. "I had never lived in such an enthusiastically literary and reform latitude before," Elizabeth was to write sixty years later, "and my mental powers were kept at the highest tension." So were her physical powers. A baby boy was born, and then another, and another. She learned by trial and error how to care for them: one thing she learned flew in the face of the theory, then current, that babies should be tightly swaddled. Freedom was what she desired, for everyone, and from the cradle up. She freed her babies and taught her practices to other mothers. Her protests against the existing definitions of woman's place were turned into channels other than those she had planned with Lucretia Mott in London.

In the spring of 1847 the Stantons decided that the climate of Boston was too rigorous; they moved West to Seneca Falls, New York, where Judge Cady owned considerable land. Life there was surprisingly different. In Boston there were servants to be had, as well as literary excitement. Seneca Falls had neither. The house that her father gave Elizabeth was on the outskirts of town, the roads were muddy, so were the foot paths. Friends lived nearby, but visiting was limited. Housekeeping without help proved very different from housekeeping with it.

All her life Elizabeth Cady Stanton's temper had a low boiling point. If in London she had wept with frustration over the denial of what she had considered her right to speak in public, in Seneca Falls she simmered over the hard and repetitive tasks that were the common lot of women. For the first time she found herself having to cope with the daily routine of child care, cooking, baking, sewing, washing and ironing. Her restless and eager mind found the situation intolerable. Half a century later she still remembered:

The general discontent I felt with woman's portion as wife, mother, housekeeper, physician and spiritual guide, the chaotic condition into which everything fell without her constant supervision, and the wearied, anxious look of the majority of women, impressed me with the strong feelings that some active measures should be taken to remedy the wrongs of society in general, and of women in particular. My experience at the World Anti-Slavery Convention, all I had read of the legal status of women, and the oppression I saw everywhere, together swept my soul, intensified now by many personal experiences. . . . I could not see what to do or where to begin—my only thought was a public meeting for protest and discussion.

Such a meeting she had discussed eight years earlier in London with Lucretia Mott. Indeed, the two women had planned to meet on their return home, but for various personal reasons had not done so. Now theory was sharpened by experience. In early July of 1848 Mrs. Stanton learned that Mrs. Mott and her husband were to visit Mr. and Mrs. Richard Hunt, at Waterloo, nearby; she drove over to spend the day. There she found four like-minded Quaker women, Mrs. Mott, her sister Martha Wright, her hostess Jane Hunt, and a friend, Mary Jane McClintock. To them she poured out "the torrent of my long accumulating discontent, with such vehemence and indignation that I stirred myself, as well as the rest of the party, to do and dare anything."

The result was the truly daring decision to call a Woman's Rights Convention, not in the future but at once. Its purpose would be "to discuss the social, civil and religious rights of women," its meeting place the Wesleyan Chapel at Seneca Falls on Wednesday and Thursday, July 19 and 20, 1848, commencing at ten in the morning. "During the first day the meeting will be exclusively for women, who are earnestly invited to attend. The public generally are invited to be present on the second day, when Lucretia Mott, of Philadelphia, and other ladies and gentlemen will address the convention." Having drafted their announcement in those terms, the five conspirators sent it by a boy to the Seneca County Courier, which published it on Friday, July 14.

Having begun with that public step, the four Quaker women in gray and white and their firebrand friend, Elizabeth Stanton, in a more fashionable full skirt with a tight basque that must have been hot on a July day, left the leafy lawn and moved indoors for tea. Around a mahogany table (now revered as a historical relic in the Smithsonian Museum) they argued the next step until supper time.

On Sunday morning they met around the same table, to face up to that next step. They had just four days to make their arrangements. They had called a public convention, but in those days such a meeting presupposed a Declaration of Sentiments or Principles. Who would compose it, and how?

Elizabeth Cady Stanton, whose writing style is unmistakable, described their dilemma in the first volume of the famous suffrage history. The ladies had never prepared for such a meeting, "they were quite innocent of the Herculean labors they proposed. On the first attempt to frame a resolution; to crowd a complete thought, clearly and concisely, into three lines; they felt as helpless and hopeless as if they had suddenly been asked to construct a steam engine." They examined reports of peace conventions, temperance conventions, antislavery meetings, but all these seemed too tame to be chosen as models "for the inauguration of a rebellion such as the world had never before seen." Finally someone—the evidence points to Elizabeth herself—took up a copy of the Declaration of Independence, then only seventy-two years old, and read its stirring prologue. With one accord they fell to paraphrasing its sentences for their own purposes. They worked on the draft all day, stopping only for a light lunch. When Elizabeth told them late in the afternoon that she must drive back to Seneca Falls, they gave her the draft and the responsibility of producing a version that could be submitted to the meeting.

Bright and early on Thursday morning her four friends (and James Mott, husband of Lucretia) harnessed the horses and drove to meet her in Seneca Falls for the meeting they had called. The day (July 19, 1848) was clear, and with that fair green freshness which upper New York State presents so vividly at that time of the year. They found the little Wesleyan Chapel locked, but a small Stanton nephew was hoisted through a window to open the door.

The first farm wagon bearing early comers arrived shortly afterward, then others began converging from miles around. July was, to be sure, the haying season, but the good weather promised to hold, and the chance was worth taking, for a meeting called by women to talk about their woes sounded like good entertainment. The fact that the newspaper notice was unsigned and carried as a speaker only the name of the well-known Quaker, Lucretia Mott, increased curiosity. Daniel and Lucy Anthony arrived from Rochester, and with them their daughter Mary. Another daughter, Susan, was teaching school in Canajoharie and could not come, but would hear about it later. Three hundred people finally appeared, some of them from Waterloo, some from Seneca Falls, some from Auburn, some from farms in the district.

The newspaper notice had said that the first day would be exclusively for women, but as more and more men drove their families into the chapel yard a hasty meeting of the organizing committee, held around the alter, had second thoughts. The men might be useful; they should be allowed to stay. Thereupon James Mott was chosen to preside; he was known to be friendly, and no one of the women who had called the convention felt brave enough or experienced enough to take the chair.

For two days there were speeches. Mr. Mott called the meeting to order, Mrs. Mott stated the objects of the Convention, surveyed "the degraded condition of woman the world over," and showed the importance of inaugurating some movement "for her education and elevation." The McClintock sisters and Martha Wright spoke. Frederick Douglass, the ex-slave, and a young law student named Samuel Tillman were invited, along with three other men, to take part in the discussion, and did so with enthusiasm. Mrs. Stanton, curlyheaded, energetic, simmering with the attractive indignation that was to be her lifelong characteristic, made an important speech. Her maiden effort, it began,

I should feel exceedingly diffident to speak before you at this time, having never before spoken in public, were I not nerved by a sense of right and duty, did I not feel that the time had come for the question of woman's wrongs to be laid before the public, did I not believe that woman herself must do this work; for woman alone can understand the height, the depth, the length and breadth of her degradation.

The Declaration of Sentiments was, of course, the central core of all arguments. It was first read as a whole, then its articles were reread one by one, discussed, and put before the audience for their vote. The members of that audience, summoned by an unsigned newspaper notice, had no official status, but they took part as earnestly as though their votes for or against each resolution might sway the course of the country. Solemnly they approved one paragraph after another of the Declaration of Sentiments, most of them with a surprising majority. Only Resolution Number 9 had real trouble; resolving "that it is the sacred duty of the women of this country to secure to themselves their sacred right to the elective franchise," it passed, but only by a hair. At the end, late in the evening of the second day, the Declaration was signed by a hundred earnest men and women.

Mrs. Stanton's Declaration of Sentiments (generally known as the Declaration of Woman's Rights) was published in local papers of the period, and has come down in bits and pieces through innumerable suffrage speeches.* Read today, it sounds like a youthful document, more emotional than logical, not too accurate or well organized, hardly original. The future that lay ahead of it was far more important than the actual fabric of words that she and her friends stitched into place that hot July day.

The fact that it was brought into existence by articulate women who kept the individual's sense of individual responsibility was more important than its actual wording. The public ridiculed it; many of the hundred who had signed it in all earnestness found that they could not stand the jeers of their fellows, and withdrew their names. Its import, if not its phrases, would be dinned into their heads for many years.

The small group of women who had helped in its framing were entirely convinced of its value. Such a stir did their July meeting make in the community that they were invited to go to Rochester two weeks later to repeat their performance. That time a woman, Abigail Bush, presided in place of James Mott. Women were gaining courage.

An isolated rural conference might well have passed without notice. But the times were turbulent, and outcries of this kind attracted wide attention. Recognition of Seneca Falls as the birthplace of a great movement would come later, as women looked back and tried to put a finger on the starting point of

*See the Appendix.

that movement.

Two years after the Seneca Falls meeting and the Rochester sequel, a so-called First National Woman's Rights Convention was called in 1850 at Worcester, Massachusetts. This time the initiators included not only Lucretia Mott but also Lucy Stone of Boston, one of the Grimké sisters of South Carolina, and several other women of growing fame. They did not include Mrs. Stanton or her other rebellious friends of upper New York State. This may have been accidental, but in the light of later events it seems an omen of the differences that were to arise between New York State women and the women of Boston.

For the moment the Boston women led. Conventions under the name of National Woman's Rights followed every year until 1860, and gradually drew to them members of the earlier rebellion. Susan Anthony appeared there at her first convention in 1852. But these meetings, while annual events, retained a sporadic and occasional character. They were not backed by well-organized bodies in which work was being continually planned ahead and done on schedule. On the contrary, their participants were very likely to be speaking more regularly for temperance or for the abolition of slavery. Mrs. Stanton, for instance, a woman of infinite enthusiasms, rushed off after freedom of divorce, the Bloomer dress, or any other reform that caught her fancy.

The result was a movement for women's rights which, until 1890 at least, appeared neither consistent nor united. It suffered from a divergence of goals that distracted the attention of the public and diverted the energies of the reformers.

Nor was confusion of goals the only handicap. Confusion among and between leaders was another. Reform, being the wave of the day, attracted the lively and the lofty, and they in turn became— in a world that still rebelled against letting women emerge from the kitchen and the nursery—individual stars and temperamental prima donnas. Lucy Stone, for example, insisted on keeping her own name after marriage, and with her bridegroom framed a marriage contract that was the scandal of the more conventional ladies of the time. That she was a Quaker was the excuse her friends gave, but the public thought it funny. Yet Lucy's influence would last well into the twentieth century, when energetic young rebels framed similar marriage contracts and joined the Lucy Stone League in their own effort to keep their birth names alive after marriage.

Elizabeth Cady Stanton was frequently at loggerheads with Lucy. Along with Amelia Bloomer she desired to reform woman's dress, and actually wore the Bloomer dress until ridicule drove her back to voluminous skirts. Mrs. Stanton also wanted easier divorce, and her longing to rewrite the Bible so as to give women a fairer deal was so intense that by 1898 she would have two volumes of the Woman's Bible in publishable form. The Quakers, Lydia and Lucretia Mott, the Grimké sisiters, Frances Wright, Antoinette Brown, Abby Kelley Foster, Lydia Child and Maria Chapman of Boston, the lovely Anna Dickinson—the list grew longer. All wrote their papers, all made their speeches, all had their day in print and on the platform.

It is no wonder, given such diversity of individuals with the same complaint, that the public—deeply suspicious of women in this role, and temperamentally opposed to any attempt to stir their wives, their mothers, or their sisters from well-worn attitudes in this deep sector of their lives—responded to feminist agitation chiefly with distrust.

What the movement needed was a slow, steady, determined woman who would go at one thing at a time, get it done, go on to the next, and never get discouraged. It needed Susan B. Anthony.

Susan Brownell Anthony, who would become "Aunt Susan" to generations of younger and frailer feminist workers, was twenty-eight years old when the Declaration of Women's Rights was framed. She did not sign it—she had not been invited to help frame it. Teaching school miles away at Canajoharie, she first learned about the Seneca Falls convention and its declaration from the newspapers, which regarded the whole affair with something less than perfect seriousness. But her father went, so did her mother and her sister Mary. They told her about it in detail. Four years later, in 1852 when she attended the third National Women's Rights Convention, Susan enlisted in the suffrage movement, the woman's revolt (though no one yet called it that), in which she was to spend most of her life.

It is not easy to bring Susan back to life, particularly the Susan of 1852. A Quaker by inheritance and temperament, she was born in 1820 on a farm in the Berkshires, near the northwest corner of Massachusetts and the town of Adams. Nathaniel Hawthorne, visiting her home region when Susan was eighteen, set down something of the closed look of that valley. "These hills, surrounding the town on all sides, give it a snug and insulated air; and viewed from certain points it would be difficult to tell how to get out without climbing over the mountain ridges; but the roads wind away and accomplish the passage without ascending very high." Less romantic observers called it "a dark pocket." Susan's father, Daniel Anthony, was first a farmer there, and then a builder and operator of a textile mill, which did nothing to make the valley lighter.

Emerging from that "snug and insulated air," Susan showed herself to be by nature and training a single-minded, spinsterish reformer with a sense of moral purpose as big as her father's hay barn. Child of a free-born and hard-working Northern society, she would abolish slavery. She would also do away with alcoholic liquors. Tobacco she hated almost as much as she hated alcohol, and lofty language she loved as she loved moral ideas. She had, of course, never tasted alcohol or smoked tobacco, but lofty language was to her as roast beef and fresh milk. Her natural occupation—and in those days the best to which a girl of good family might aspire—was teaching. In 1846 the Academy of Conajoharie, of which her uncle Joshua Anthony was a trustee, offered her "the Female Department, upon the terms which have heretofore been offered to the teachers of that department, viz: the tuition money of the Female Department less 12½ per cent, the teachers collecting their tuition bills." Susan took it.

On the first of March in 1849, six months after the Seneca Falls Convention, a year after the end of the War with Mexico, and a year after James Marshall had discovered gold in Sutter's Creek, California, the Daughters of Temperance in Canajoharie gave a local fair to raise money for the anti-alcohol cause. Susan, who had been teaching there for three years, had become the president of the Daughters; she managed the party, saw her name outlined in evergreens on the wall, and made her first speech. In it, she demanded some means

by which our Brothers and Sons [she had brothers but would never have a son] shall no longer be allured from the *right* by the corrupting influence of the fashionable sippings of wine and brandy, those sure destroyers of Mental and Moral worth, and by which our Sisters and Daughters [she had no daughter] shall no longer be exposed to the vile arts of the gentlemanly-appearing, gallant, but really half-inebriated seducer.

It was strong language for a lady, but more was to come. Susan found it "generally conceded" that women "who are most aggrieved by the foul destroyer's inroads," are the "sex that fashions the Social and Moral State of Society." Therefore women must lead society "to discountenance the use of wine and brandy as beverages at both their private and public parties." If they would do this, "not one of the opposite sex, who has any claim to the title of gentleman, would so insult them as to come into their presence after having quaffed of that foul destroyer of all true delicacy and refinement."

It sounds stilted and unreal, and a generation that lived through prohibition has a right to find it naïve and even absurd. But how was Susan to know that by coming out for temperance (in which she believed with passion) she was contributing to a confusion in issues as great as that which had already begun between women's rights and Negroes' rights, a confusion that would haunt her feminine followers to the very day of the signing of the Suffrage Amendment?

Even had she known, she would not have changed her course.

Her biographer, Katherine Anthony (a distant cousin) describes Aunt Susan as bluntly honest, living her life almost entirely without an eye for beauty, judging novels by their moral or philosophic content, having little craving for the artistic embellishments of life. "She had a fine eye and ear for the beauty of ethical content, but that was all she asked for aesthetic enjoyment." Call her narrow-minded Puritan and have done with it. But one cannot have done with Susan.

Of all that impassioned and demanding group of women reformers who did so much to change the picture of women spread about by Blackstone, Rousseau, and Mme. de Staël, Susan Anthony was the most persistent and the most consistent.

Elizabeth Cady Stanton, who was to become her firm friend, remembered their first meeting on a Seneca Falls street corner. "We met Mrs. Bloomer" (she who was later to give her name to the pleated gymnasium knickerbockers of 1910) "with Miss Anthony at the corner of the street waiting to greet us. There she stood, with her good earnest face and genial smile, dressed in gray delaine, hat and all the same color relieved with pale-blue ribbons, the perfection of neatness and sobriety. I like her thoroughly from the beginning." That liking was mutual; it lasted throughout the century and through a dozen conflicts. But many people did not agree about Susan. Some thought her dangerous. Others thought her dull.

Yet it cannot have been exactly fun, nor the usual role of a dull woman, to have been dragged in 1860 through the streets of Syracuse in effigy, to have seen her image burned in the public square while citizens leaped about the flames like the Indians who had, within a century, pitched their tents and made their bonfires on that same dark and bloody ground. All this because she had come to speak against slavery.

Nor can it have been fun, or dull, to be arrested in Rochester in 1872 for daring, in spite of her sex, to exert the right to vote, to be tried before a judge so complacent and so prejudiced that he directed the jury to find her guilty.

She was an inventive and resourceful woman, our Susan, a woman with an ability to create public excitement about a cause for which she hoped to invoke public sympathy. Starting with a didactic and somewhat fumbling way of speech, she developed a skill in invective that at times curled the beards and soured the mustache cups of her male auditors.

Two chief enemies stood in her path, public apathy and the power of man to beguile woman. The public as a whole was singularly uninterested in her chosen subject. Her best friends got married, acquired households, bore and reared children, had not time enough left in the day for effective indignation against their status. Only the most energetic of them, like Elizabeth Cady Stanton, managed to combine big families and public speeches during a long lifetime.

There is a wonderful letter from Susan to Mrs. Stanton, dated June, 1856, in which Susan, her mind stuck in dead center, begs her lucid and articulate friend to help her with a speech for a teachers' convention so that schoolmasters cannot say, "See, these women can't or won't do anything when we do give them a chance." The pictures she paints of the Stanton household are vivid:

for the love of me and the saving of the reputation of womankind I beg you, with one baby on your knee and another at your feet, and with four boys whistling, buzzing, hallooing "Ma, Ma," set yourself about the work. Now I do pray you to give heed to my prayer—those of you who have the *talent* to do honor to poor, oh, how poor, womanhood, have all given yourselves over to baby making, and left poor brainless me to battle alone.

Susan came to distrust marriage. She did not like it because it distracted the minds and energies of able women. Masculine attention she had, but her standards were exacting. When Mr. Blank walked home with her on a moonlit night, "marvelously attentive," she told her diary that it was "a pity such powers of intellect should lack the moral spine."

She did not trust men, and the more she met them on public platforms, the more that distrust grew.

"I am not complaining or despairing," she wrote to one of her few spinster friends, Lydia Mott, sister-in-law of Lucretia, "but facts are stern realities . . . the twain became one flesh, the woman, 'we'; henceforth she had no separate work. . . . I declare to you that I distrust the power of any woman, even of myself, to withstand the wifely matrimonial maelstrom! . . ." And then, more sharply, "In the depths of my soul there is a continued denial of the self-annihilating spiritual or legal union of two human beings. Such union, in the very nature of things, must bring an end to the free action of one or the other. . . ."

The transition in Susan's life from temperance meetings, attempts as a school teacher to speak on equal terms with men in teachers' meetings (an experience almost as frustrating as the London Anti-Slavery meeting in 1840 had been for Elizabeth Cady Stanton), efforts to take part in abolitionist meetings and to express her active and indignant mind—the transition from this to a growing tide of agitation for women's rights as a separate and primary good was a slow one. No more than the others was Susan immune to the more popular causes of the day.

Until April, 1861, when the attack on Fort Sumter signaled the start of the Civil War, her attempts to stir women to take a hand in the world that was being fashioned around them proceeded by fits and starts. First, she had to learn to make her voice heard; this she did in teachers' meetings and in meetings for temperance. Second, she had to prove that she had something to say that was worth hearing. Of the importance of the causes she championed she never had any doubt.

Women learned to speak and to persuade mostly in the movements for temperance for abolition of slavery. A few women, of whom Susan B. Anthony was the most distinguished, began in the one and moved to the other. A score of able women made their first essays in the antislavery cause. In both of those reform movements their lot was hard. Not only did the preachers, who dominated both in the early days, prefer to do all the speaking themselves, and rely on St. Paul's dictum to keep women at home and off all platforms, but they showed themselves remarkably stubborn. As late as 1852, when Susan in her role as delegate from the Daughters of Temperance rose to speak at a convention of the Sons of Temperance, she was interrupted and told flatly that "Sisters were not invited to speak, but to listen and learn." Thinking, perhaps, that she had learned enough, she walked out and organized the Women's State Temperance Society, which was later infiltrated and scuttled by the men. That was the year she went to the National Woman's Rights Convention in Syracuse. The war between the sexes showed itself early.

In her experience with abolition, she suffered both from prejudices against her sex and public outbreaks against her elected cause. The American Anti-Slavery Society, organized with civilian as well as churchly members and able to collect ample funds, recognized the value of her indomitable soul, and persuaded her in 1855 to become an agent. In 1856, she who had spoken out of conviction and with no reward except the satisfaction of saying what she thought should be said, was paid ten dollars a week and expenses. It sounds like small enough recompense for what she had to endure. Not only were audiences hostile, but they turned violent as passions rose. Being shouted down became a regular experience. She was mobbed in Buffalo, in Rochester, in Port Byron and Utica.

Her own crusade went on spottily. From 1850 to 1861 Woman's Rights Conventions were held, mostly in New York State, to advocate changes in property rights, education, and divorce laws. A loose-jointed central committee ran them, with Lucy Stone as leader and Mrs. Stanton a coruscating speaker. Susan Anthony acted for a while as secretary, but though the vote had been one of many demands at Seneca Falls, now it attracted little attention.

Susan moved in 1854 from this somewhat amorphous organization to a specific campaign for rights. Choosing sixty women to help her, she set out in bonnet and shawl to gather signatures for a petition asking the New York State legislature for control by women of their own earnings, the guardianship of their children in the case of divorce, and the right to vote. For six hard weeks these women trudged from door to door, until they had collected six thousand signatures. The legislature was not impressed. So, thinking six thousand perhaps too few, Susan started out again, this time in the dead of winter. In four months she covered fifty-four of New York's sixty counties with speeches and requests for signatures. The legislature's reply was a heavy-handed bit of humor charging that women "always have the best seat in the cars, carriages and sleighs, the warmest place in the winter and the coolest place in summer. They have their choice on which side of the bed they will lie, front or back." And therefore, "if there is any inequity or oppression in the case, the gentlemen are the sufferers." Susan was neither amused nor impressed, nor discouraged.

Her work was not, however, without result; in 1860, the legislature repented its frivolity and passed an amendment to the existing property law which provided that women should not only control whatever property they inherited, but could also own and control whatever money they themselves earned. They were not earning much in those days, but the principle was revolutionary. In addition, married women were granted the right to make contracts, to sue or be sued, to act with their husbands as joint guardians of their children. This new law, which became a model for other states, must be credited mostly to the hard and unremitting persistence with which Susan B. Anthony held to her path.

She was stopped only by the Civil War, and then only temporarily. For women like Susan with six generations of Quaker ancestry in America behind them, built into the very stuff of the nation, that war, which not only set brother against brother but threatened to split the country into two countries, must have been a daily and a nightly horror.

Other women found new careers in the war; like wars that were to come later, this one called them out of their homes into public life, and by so doing inched forward the cause of women. Dorothea Dix and Clara Barton, following the lead of Florence Nightingale in the Crimean War, busied themselves setting up nursing services for the Northern Armies that made their names famous. One of the first of the women doctors, Elizabeth Blackwell, organized the Women's Sanitary Commission. Her sister-in-law, Lucy Stone, was making surgical dressings and stitching soldier's shirts for the Union Army. But Susan, Quaker to the bone, would have none of war. She went back to her father's farm—planted crops, cultivated them, harvested them, sold them. She also wove twenty yards of rag carpet, cut and sewed pieces for a silk bedspread, and quilted coverlets and petticoats. She even read a novel, and a poem of Browning's "so fitting to our terrible struggle," as well as Buckle's *History of Civilization* and Darwin's *Origin of Species*. Not until autumn did she set foot on a public platform, and then it was to talk on "Emancipation—The Duty of the Government." It was the emancipation of slaves, not of women, that she meant. As long as the rights of Negroes obsessed the nation, her friends persuaded her that it would not be wise even to mention women's rights.

That mid-Victorian forbearance lasted throughout the war. From the spring of 1861 until April of 1865 Susan's speeches were concerned almost entirely with the campaigns of the Abolitionists. They were not easy campaigns nor easy speeches. President Lincoln did not move fast enough to please the Abolitionists, and after Susan became a paid speaker for them she must constantly be calling for quicker and broader action.

Two years of the war she spent in New York City. Early in 1862

Henry Stanton was made Surveyor of the Port of New York, and his wife Elizabeth, eager to knock the dust of Seneca Falls off her feet, persuaded Susan to take the four lively Stanton boys to the city in advance, so that she could arrange in quiet for the moving of the family goods. They went first to Brooklyn, then to a house on 45th Street big enough so that later she could offer Susan a room—at a price.

Meanwhile, Susan returned to home base on her father's farm and to a series of Abolitionist lectures. In September, President Lincoln issued the Emancipation Proclamation, to take effect four months later. It did not go far enough for the Abolitionists. In November, Susan's father fell ill, and died within the month. He had never been a rich man, but he had loved his daughter and supported her causes. Deprived of this backing, she must find some means by which she could pay for food and lodging. It was then that she left the farm to the care of her mother and sister, went back to New York, rented Mrs. Stanton's spare room, and enlisted for pay under the Abolitionist banner. She was to get twelve dollars a week.

Susan arrived in New York May 3, 1863, the day that the highly unpopular draft act was passed, and she lived there through the six-day horror of the July draft riots that killed twelve hundred people and burned both private and public buildings, including a Negro orphan asylum. In May, she set in motion—under Mrs. Stanton's urging and with her leadership—a Women's National Loyal League, of which Susan was made secretary. This was Abolitionist in sympathy and support, but with feminist aspirations hidden under its honest concern for the Negroes. One resolution went so far as to ask equal rights for women as well as for Negroes, but was left as a matter of record rather than an inspiration to activity on that point. The main resolution pledged the "loyal women of the nation . . . to give support to the government in so far as it makes a war for freedom."

The May convention that gave the Loyal League formal status

addressed a petition to Congress asking for the unconditional emancipation of all slaves in the Union: in the full flush of their enthusiasm the members proposed to collect a million signatures. This became Susan's job. Eight months later, in February, 1864, she had her first hundred thousand names on paper, and Senator Sumner of Massachusetts presented the huge pile of signed papers to Congress. By August, Susan had four hundred thousand names, and had made the Women's National Loyal League famous. She also had become a New York office worker, with a changing set of volunteers, and an acquired technique of lunching on less than fifteen cents a day. In the summertime this bought her two "tea rusks" for five cents, a dish of strawberries for five cents, and a glass of milk for three cents. Having no leeway in the budget for transportation, she walked.

Not only did she live on the twelve dollars a week that the Abolitionists paid her, but she had to raise money for office expenses. This she did by lecturing and by the pin-money device of asking one penny from everyone of the four hundred thousand who signed the famous Loyal League petition. Most of them gave it. When she closed her office in August of 1864 it was with an outstanding debt of $4.72. This she paid from her own pocket.

Still the war dragged on, with Susan barred by her conscience from lecturing about anything but abolition. She was forty-five years old, a spinster with no base but the spare room in Mrs. Stanton's house. This refuge had to be paid for. The sure twelve dollars a week had ended. The home farm near Rochester was being sold.

At this point her brother Daniel, who had moved to what was then the frontier town of Leavenworth, Kansas, picked her up out of her despair with the offer of a job and a home. He has prospered in the West. Not only was he a successful investor in Kansas affairs but he was a newspaper publisher, the town's mayor, and its postmaster. Needing competent help, he remembered his sister's demonstrated capabilities; to prove the sincerity of his invitation, he sent her a bank check and a set of railroad tickets.

Susan stopped in Rochester only long enough to bid her mother and sisters farewell and to have a five-dollar silk dress made. Then in the depth of January she started West. Chicago she found cold. The Mississippi River was frozen from bank to bank, and it cost her a dollar to ride across its ice. In Missouri, she boarded a dilapidated train loaded with immigrants headed for free land in the West.

When she reached Leavenworth, unfed, unwarmed, and unwashed, she found a warm welcome, which included a room awaiting her in her brother's new white house, and an immediate job in the editing of her brother's paper. But Daniel had his own ideas as to how he wanted the paper edited. These did not include editorials voicing the Abolitionist point of view or—after the war ended in April—renewed urgings for improvement in the position of women. Susan found herself reduced in rank to the status of a clipping clerk; she salved her soul on Sundays with occasional speeches in Negro churches where she urged the struggle for the vote.

Five months in Kansas were enough. Letters from Elizabeth Cady Stanton, Lydia Mott, Wendell Phillips urged her to come back to the East and go to work more fruitfully.

Three separate frustrations played their part in stirring her to a new part. Kansas in those days was a frontier state, a man's world where women, including her sister-in-law, kept to their interminable housework, and where sudden shots frequently took the place of long legal proceedings. Her brother Daniel, who had been in at least one shooting affray, edited the local newspaper—as he chose to do it. Freedom of speech for his employees, among whom he tacitly included Susan, was not his way. He refused roundly to let her put down for printing a single word about women's rights.

The second frustration was of a similar kind. On July 4 of 1865 Susan, whose reputation as a speaker had traveled that far, was invited to make a patriotic address in the nearby town of Ottawa, Kansas. In her speech she felt free to include what her brother would not print, a good word for woman suffrage. The local Congressman, a Republican, also spoke. The day was fine, the audience appreciative, and after the ceremonies the two speakers traveled back by horse-drawn stage in apparent amity. But when, during supper, it was revealed that the Republican party would like to print the speeches, the Congressman suggested that it might be politic to omit Susan's paragraph about women. When Susan protested, he made it quite clear that her paragraph would not appear.

These two rebuffs were irritating and provocative. The third blew Susan's smoldering indignation into a flame that was to last for the rest of her life. This was the proposal of a Fourteenth Amendment to the Constitution which, like the new Thirteenth, would still be concerned with the voting rights of ex-slaves, but which, in defining them, would for the first time use the word "male."

That the new barrier would be erected with the aid of women's former friends, the Abolitionists, became quickly and painfully clear. Susan, who by this time had worked her way back to the East by giving lectures, had a plan for amalgamating the Anti-Slavery Society with the Women's Rights Society and making out of the merger an American Equal Rights Association pledged to work simultaneously for voting rights for the woman and the Negro. Wendell Phillips, a skilled, charming, and wily speaker, by then leading Abolitionist, refused the plan; the time was ripe for Negro suffrage, but not for woman suffrage, and the women must continue to wait. This was "the Negro's hour." Women would, of course, continue to help. Phillips explained all this in such lofty language that his real meaning was veiled, but not from Susan. She blurted out a flat declaration that she would rather cut off her right hand than ask for suffrage for Negroes and not for women.

That statement was to take its place with the Declaration of Woman's Rights as one that marks a watershed. After it, the women's campaign would lose much of its naïve faith in masculine good will. The way ahead was long, and would continue to be hard, but the facts of political life as men demonstrated them would gradually be woven into the fabric of the campaign techniques that women came to employ.

3. SEX AND COLOR

"The most continuous American revolutionary is the American woman."

Max Lerner

Susan's flat definance of Wendell Phillips—her statement that she would sooner cut off her right hand than ask suffrage for the Negroes and not for women—had behind it almost two decades of co-operation between Abolitionists and the movers for women's rights. Out of their own convictions and the skilful urging of such impassioned leaders as William Lloyd Garrison and Wendell Phillips, Susan and her comrades had selflessly worked, talked, petitioned all that time for the Negro's freedom from slavery. But now the Negroes were, in law at least, as free as the women. The Thirteenth Amendment, declaring that "neither slavery nor involuntary servitude . . . shall exist within the United States" (except on conviction of crime) was passed by the Congress while Susan was playing the part of old-maid aunt and part-time editor at her brother's home in Leavenworth.

To Susan's way of thinking the fact that the long period was over meant that the Anti-Slavery Society could now be dis-

banded and its women workers freed to carry on their own campaign for their own rights. The first part of this, at least, was also
William Lloyd Garrison's idea. But the younger Wendell Phillips,
a fluent, witty, and persuasive speaker, if somewhat less than downright, was by no means ready to give up power and platforms. He
took the ground that the Society's work would not be finished until
the Negroes had the vote. When Garrison, insisting that his work
for the Society was done, resigned the presidency, Phillips was
elected in his place.

Susan's sharp disagreement with the new president freed her for
immediate action. The Woman's Rights Society had not met since
1860; the first thing she did was to gather its members into convention and plan a new campaign. They met in New York, in May
of 1866, directly after a meeting of the Anti-Slavery Society. Susan
had sounded alarm bells, Elizabeth Cady Stanton had drafted petitions asking for the vote for women, ten thousand signatures had
been gathered in preparation for their presentation to Congress.

But the Anti-Slavery Society desired neither to free its workers
and disband nor to join with the Women's Rights Society and
emerge as the American Equal Rights Society. Nor would its
leaders even put their names to the suffrage petition. That these
petitions were presented by loyal friends who had worked with
them for the abolition cause did not move them. "This is the
Negro's hour . . . do not embarrass the Republican Party with any
new issue . . . the Negro once safe, the woman comes next" was the
poor comfort offered those friends.

It was to prove a long "next," the longer because the coming
Fourteenth Amendment, which would enfranchise the Negro,
seemed to make the woman's position even worse. The Amendment defined citizens of the nation (and of the states in which
they lived) as "All persons born or naturalized in the United
States, and subject to the jurisdiction thereof. . . ." Then came a
second article, referring to the way in which representatives shall
be apportioned among the states, and attempting to make quite

sure that Negroes should not be prevented from voting for them. This article fastened on the word "male," and repeated it twice.* The sentence was couched in the negative, and framed so fuzzily that it still causes trouble. The refusal of their Abolitionist friends to sign their suffrage petition or to lift a finger against the needless inclusion of the word "male" in the new amendment taught Susan bitter lessons. Yet in some ways the experience had value. Between the Declaration of Women's Rights in 1848 and Susan's declaration of purpose made to Wendell Phillips in 1866, they all had learned a great deal. By persisting in their determination to take part in the temperance and the antislavery campaigns, women had gained wide experience in public speaking and a notable skill in handling adverse audiences. They had absorbed a certain amount of political wisdom, if not yet enough. They were still too trusting, too confident that moral worth had more power with politicians than did political expediency.

Knowing this, but not yet convinced of all of it, Susan and Elizabeth went to work on a new tack. They would focus all their efforts on the political arena. Their immediate goal was the state of Kansas, young and brash, which had submitted two constitutional amendments to its voters—one that would give the franchise to Negroes, the other that would give it to women. Both were controversial, both gave ample opportunity to talk and be heard. Susan persuaded Lucy Stone (in retirement since the war ended) and her husband Henry Blackwell to go out from Massachusetts, and for two months to campaign for woman suffrage. She and Elizabeth Cady Stanton would then follow.

The Stone-Blackwell expenses were paid by a fund of which

*Sixty years later, Carrie Chapman Catt would write: "To get that word, male, out of the Constitution, cost the women of this country fifty-two years of pauseless campaign; 56 state referendum campaigns; 480 legislative campaigns to get state amendments submitted; 47 state constitutional convention campaigns; 277 state party convention campaigns; 19 campaigns to get suffrage planks in the party platforms; 19 campaigns with 19 successive Congresses to get the federal amendment submitted, and the final ratification campaign." Luckily, it did not look so hard, in 1869, to Miss Anthony or to Mrs. Stanton.

Susan, Lucy Stone, and Wendell Phillips were trustees. The latter lamented this expenditure, but found himself in the minority. He did, however, take pleasure in telling Susan that there would be only enough left in the fund to pay for the first half of the project. Refusing to be daunted, Susan put on her bonnet and went begging from house to house until she had gathered enough to take her and Mrs. Stanton out to Kansas.

There they established headquarters in Lawrence, the capital, and spent two thousand dollars (which Susan had to raise) sending out suffrage pamphlets. Mrs. Stanton toured the state in a carriage drawn by a pair of mules and driven by a friendly ex-governor. Fearing lest she be late for a speaking engagement, Susan was rowed across the wide Missouri by an ex-army captain, and hauled up the muddy bank by the same hero. Her brother Daniel and his newspaper steered clear of her cause during the campaign, but at the last suffrage rally before the election he gathered courage enough to sit on the platform and cheer his sister.

It was a gallant but inauspicious attempt at a state suffrage campaign, the first political campaign ever to be waged by women in the United States. Both referenda lost. The women lost more emphatically than the blacks. Out of thirty thousand men balloting, a third (ten thousand) voted to include Negroes among the voters, while only nine thousand could bring themselves to give women the same right. Susan and Mrs. Stanton declared themselves cheered at getting all of nine thousand votes in the first election in which the question of woman's suffrage had openly appeared. They felt, however, lonely as well as defeated. The eastern Abolitionists had not given them much help. Speaking tours, however long, however eloquent, were not enough. What they needed was a newspaper in which they could continually send their message far and wide. But newspapers, Susan knew from her experience with Daniel's Leavenworth journal, cost money. Where was it to come from?

The need was answered, temporarily, by a curious alliance with a wealthy and persuasive character named George Train (alleged by the Boston group to be a buffoon and a copperhead) who had helped to furnish funds for their Kansas campaign. Eccentric he certainly was, but he was also expansive, energetic, and attractive, Irish in origin, and interested in Irish rebels (then going under the name of Fenians) as well as in women who wanted the vote. He declared himself their supporter, put cash money into their slender store of campaign funds, and then offered to pay the cost of the new tool that they badly needed, a newspaper. They were enchanted and excited. They agreed that the paper should be called *The Revolution.* Its motto would be:

Men, their rights and nothing more;
Women, their rights and nothing less.

Susan Anthony and Mrs. Stanton would be editors and publishers. Train would provide the funds (he wanted to run for the presidency, and he reserved the right to fill a certain amount of space with his own material if he chose to). The first issue appeared on the stands in New York on January 8, 1869. Its masthead motto had been softened to read, "Principle, not policy; Justice, not Favors."

Train argued an unusually trusting financial editor, David Mellis of the *New York World,* into joining him as backer of the new enterprise, a feat of persuasion that makes the capitulation of Mrs. Stanton and Miss Anthony the more comprehensible. He then proved himself as vagrant a character as the Boston ladies had suspected. No sooner had he launched the New York suffragists on their difficult new careers than he took ship and left the country. He had been speaking in New York for the Irish Fenians, and had decided that he must see them on their home ground. His first stop was England, when he made a speech for them. The English police regarded this as treasonable; they arrested him and put him into a British jail where he spent almost a year. Had news reports gone back and forth across the ocean as fast as they do now, the effect on *The Revolution* would have been devastating. As it was, the paper had more trouble with scarcity of money than with its backer's dubious reputation.

Given the financial aid of the loyal David Mellis (who has been too little praised) and the devoted labor of Miss Anthony and Mrs. Stanton, *The Revolution* lasted for two active years. During its short life the paper proved a considerable force. It gave the limping and divided suffrage cause a focus and a direction; its editorials were both brilliant and enlightening, conveying news as well as points of view. It emphasized the major need to make of women voting citizens, but it also advised them to open their windows and let fresh air into their houses, to get more exercise, to wear looser clothes in which they could move about more easily. It spoke up for fairer divorce procedures, equal pay for equal work, and better working conditions. But lacking Train's promised funds and persuasive abilities, it could not pay its way.

The circumstances of the paper's support, its editorial vigor, and the slashing nature of the attacks it launched on various issues stirred the more conservative Boston ladies first to protest, then to action. They were shocked, and they retaliated by producing (on the second birthday of *The Revolution*) a much more discreet and temperate paper, better organized, and financed in a most orderly way. It was called *The Woman's Journal*. Supported not by a wealthy adventurer but by a sound joint-stock company composed of Boston's best, it had a far better chance of enduring, and indeed it was to last for years. The competition it offered proved the last straw for *The Revolution*, which, unable to support itself or to attract more funds, went out of business. This bankruptcy left a debt of $10,000 which Susan assumed as her personal burden, and would pay off bit by bit. It also deepened the quarrel between Boston and New York.

That quarrel, long simmering, and apparent to the women concerned since Susan's sharp words to Wendell Phillips, broke to the surface in May, 1869. That year the Equal Rights Association, to which both men and women belonged, met in New York City. Mrs. Stanton made the keynote speech. Keenly aware that the Fourteenth Amendment giving suffrage to Negroes had just been declared ratified and the Fifteenth Amendment introduced into Congress, she proposed that the Association sponsor a new amendment to the Constitution that should give the women the vote. Highly sensitive on that subject, the Abolitionist members broke into an uproar. The meeting, bitterly divided, adjourned before aroused emotions could stir further damage.

Mrs. Stanton and Miss Anthony left the hall in what can only be described by that Victorian term, high dudgeon. They wasted no time on lamentations, but moved at once to organize a new group, the National Woman Suffrage Association, which should have only women as its members. This was a flat blow at their former men friends among the Abolitionists, who had (or so they firmly believed) maneuvered events within the Equal Rights Association for their own purposes, and without regard to the wishes of the women. It was also a blow at the Abolitionists' friends, the Boston ladies. Those, in turn, and six months later, set up their own group as the American Woman Suffrage Association. They invited men as well as women to join, and made Wendell Phillips their first president.

For a short time there was a pretense of amity and even of cooperation between the two groups, but more trouble was to follow, which deepened the distance between them.

In order to understand the impact on the already divided suffrage movement of such scandals as the Victoria Woodhull campaign for the presidency, the Beecher-Tilton affair, and the arrest and trial of Susan B. Anthony, one must recognize how strong were the conflicting forces of Victorian standards of morality and behavior on the one hand and of post-Civil War turbulence on the other. Each of the American wars has left its aftermath of displacement, if not shattering, of moral standards, but the storm was greater after the Civil War for the very reason that the conservative forces among its victors held desperately to what they believed was the Right. Fearing, and with reason, that orderly society would go down in the North as well as in the South, they clung tightly to the shell as well as the substance of order.

The country was still composed mostly of slow-moving and isolated farming communities, but the relative calm that had reigned during the 1840's had been torn to bits by the struggles between the states to extend or to prevent the spread of slavery, and by the westward movements that were involved. The Mexican War, the discovery of gold in California, the Civil War itself, and the profitable "carpet-bagging" era that followed intensified the violent churning of manners, morals, political ideas, standards of thought and of behavior. If half the country blazed into repeated disturbance, the other half struggled to keep its head clear and its feet on the ground. The shock when elements of the two halves met was such as to set off explosions. Sometimes these explosions were revelations of theft and public immorality on a large scale, sometimes they were merely bizarre. The years 1869-1871 were, after all, the years when the "Tweed ring" flourished in New York politics and is reputed to have taken forty-five million dollars out of the tax money and the city treasury. It was also the period when Anthony Comstock constituted himself as the clamorous guardian of public morals.

Susan B. Anthony, with her honest good sense, got into nothing so spectacularly crooked as the "Tweed ring." That she should have been involved in any situation deserving the adjective "bizarre" seems a contradiction in terms, but there it was. She went where her conscience led her, and if her conscience got her into trouble, so much the worse for the trouble.

Perhaps for the very reason that she was a Quaker and stern of face, she had a weak spot for women who were beautiful, eloquent, and apparently susceptible to the power of reform that she herself advocated. The Victoria Woodhull episode was of that pattern.

Born Victoria Claflin, and with a sister named Tennessee (sometimes written Tennie C.) Mrs. Woodhull had made her first public appearance in Ohio as a professional spiritualist and faith healer. The two sisters held seances, and moved with more or less success and profit from place to place until they reached Pittsburgh. There they met Commodore Cornelius Vanderbilt who, old and sick, came to them for treatment and remained to give them financial advice. So bewitching did they appear to the rich old man that he encouraged them to invade New York. Here they began a new life (with the Commodore's blessing) as Woodhull, Claflin and Co., bankers and brokers. Wall Street responded with outward shock and inward glee. Sirens were what the Street needed. Not only did the sisters prosper in their Broad Street offices, but they flashed into the public eye with a journal called *Woodhull and Claflin's Weekly*.

Control of money, of the spirits, and of the press was intoxicating, but not enough—Victoria Woodhull hungered for greater power. On a day in 1871 when the third National Woman Suffrage Convention was to be held in Washington, she obtained a hearing (but without giving notice to the suffragists) before the Judiciary Committee of Congress in order to present a "Memorial," claiming, that she, as a woman, was enabled to vote by the terms of the Fourteenth Amendment. Sure of her ability to sway men, she had meant to present this in a one-woman appearance, but she had reckoned without Susan. Having come to Washington to attend the suffrage convention, Susan—as was her habit—read the morning paper at breakfast. There she discovered an announcement of Victoria's plan, and recognized its possible importance. At once she put on her bonnet and went forth. Her first move was to find Isabella Beecher Hooker (sister of the famous Henry Ward Beecher) who was managing the convention. Laying the situation before her, she persuaded Mrs. Hooker that it was vitally important to postpone the opening of the meeting until they could find out what it was that this new star in the suffrage firmament had in mind.

Mrs. Hooker made the necessary motions, and the two suffragists hurried to the Senate Committee room. Here they found half a dozen Senators looking with pleasure at the beautiful Mrs. Woodhull, slender and smart in blue broadcloth. With a degree of eloquence hardly less charming than her appearance, Mrs. Woodhull presented her case. The Senators listened, accepted her "Memorial," applauded her speech. They also invited Miss Anthony and Mrs. Hooker to make suffrage speeches—these, of course, had to be impromptu.

Delighted by this unexpected opportunity to plead their own case before Senatorial powers, enchanted by new, young eloquence in a cause that lay so close to their hearts, the two suffragists then invited Victoria to make the same speech at their convention. A hansom cab took the three of them from the Capitol to the hotel, Mrs. Hooker gathered her waiting forces, and the postponed convention was declared open.

In the Assembly Hall Victoria was seated on the platform between two pillars of respectability, Elizabeth Cady Stanton and Lucretia Mott. Her eloquence moved the convention as it had charmed the Senators. It did not, however, cleanse her reputation. By this time Victoria had acquired a second husband, Colonel C. H. Blood, but she still held onto the name of the first. It was also rumored that she also held onto its owner, and that both husbands lived in the same house with her and her sister. To the 1870's this *ménage à quatre* smacked of free love.

The purple glow that surrounded her spread through the suffrage movement and divided its forces. Reporting the anniversary meeting held in Washington in May, 1871, the New York newspapers labeled it as "the Woodhull Convention," and described its purpose not as suffrage but as "free love." Susan, burning with indignation, defended Victoria as a brilliant speaker who was unfairly attacked because she was a woman. The more conservative suffrage group, which had temporarily abandoned Boston to hold a simultaneous meeting in Washington, condemned "free love" in a stately resolution.

Trusting in her spirit "controls" and her magnetic skill with audiences, the dynamic Mrs. Woodhull was neither daunted nor deterred. Instead, she went on developing the idea she had presented to the Senators—that the Fourteenth Amendment, far from making things worse for women, actually made it possible for them as well as for Negroes to vote. Susan, on a speaking tour to the West Coast, delivering 108 lectures on woman suffrage, kept remembering Victoria's argument and trying it on audiences.

Meanwhile Victoria lectured on the East Coast, mixing spiritualism with suffrage, sowing discord. In the process she did her best to take over the suffrage movement and adapt it to her own ends, which grew more and more ambitious as her fortunes prospered. In 1872 she suggested turning the National Woman Suffrage Association into a woman's political party, which would support her desire to run for the presidency of the United States. It is a tribute to the power of her mesmeric skill that she persuaded Mrs. Stanton and three other leading suffragists to agree to back her. The plan was to be ratified at the May suffrage convention in New York.

But for a second time Victoria reckoned without Susan, whose Quaker tolerance went not this far. Having read in a local newspaper of Victoria's new plan, Susan came back from the West in a towering rage and descended on her gullible friends like an avenging angel. Mrs. Stanton, who should have known better, and the somewhat flighty Mrs. Hooker refused to admit that anything was wrong, but they withdrew from the committee that was managing the convention. Susan was left to handle the ambitious Mrs. Woodhull by herself.

This she did in three effective stages. When Victoria and her friends appeared before the first session, declaring they would come and hold a joint meeting with the suffragists, Susan countered by saying that the Convention Hall had been rented in her name, and she would allow its use only by national suffragists. Victoria had to hire another hall.

The next day Victoria appeared on the convention floor and moved that the assembly adjourn to meet the following day in her newly rented Apollo Hall. The audience approved, but Susan declared the whole proceeding out of order on the same ground—that neither Mrs. Woodhull nor her friends who had voted with her were members of the National Woman Suffrage Association. She then declared the convention adjourned for the day. Victoria went on speaking. So Susan, who in leasing the hall had also leased the furnishings, ordered the janitor to turn out the gas lights. The audience also went out.

Strictly speaking, the move may seem unfair, but so was Victoria. Susan's shrewdness saved the National Woman Suffrage Association. It did not, however, end the contest between the two indomitables. Susan, who had admired Victoria's first presentation of her "Memorial" to the Senators, and who was still turning over in her mind the value of Victoria's argument that the Fourteenth Amendment ceded to women, however indirectly, the right to vote, gave full recognition to the uncanny powers of this mesmerizing "siren of Wall Street." Victoria, conscious of the force of her beauty and the power of her words, underestimated the force of Susan's awkward oratory, plain face, and common sense. To her, the suffrage movement was merely a tide of opinion that seemed to be going her way, and that therefore was exploitable for her own purposes; Susan was selfless, and hence unimportant. The suffrage movement, meanwhile, was caught in the middle and dyed an even brighter purple. Victoria, after Susan's rebuff, withdrew from it and formed her own People's Party, which promptly nominated her as its candidate for the presidency of the United States.

The two women would tangle again later in that lively year 1872 when Susan would carry Victoria's arguments about the Fourteenth Amendment into action, and get arrested for her pains. Victoria offered help but got no reply, which was hardly surprising, as she had a few weeks earlier brought the Beecher-Tilton affair out from behind thick veils of secrecy and made out of it a public scandal bent to her own purposes. The modern newspaper reader might not find as exciting as did his great-grandfather the illicit love of a great preacher for his best friend's beautiful wife. But within the close-linked reform group of the 1870's, when the power of a controlling Puritan theocracy was still lively and noble words were expected to be accompanied by proper behavior, the shock amounted to a social earthquake.

The principals were leading intellectuals and churchly figures of more than local fame. The Reverend Henry Ward Beecher was a famous Abolitionist, a beloved reformer, a mighty preacher in the fashionable Plymouth (Congregational) Church of Brooklyn, and by reputation saintly. He had been president of the American Woman Suffrage Association, the Boston group. One of his young lay assistants, a writer and editor of growing fame, was the handsome Theodore Tilton; he was married to a beautiful wife named Elizabeth. Warm-hearted and friendly, these two worshiped the famous preacher, and made their home an informal refuge from the demands that pressed in upon him.

In that bowered garden on Brooklyn Heights the old man fell in love with the young man's wife, and for two delicious and dangerous years the romance blossomed. What happened to break it up is anyone's guess. Perhaps conscience got to work, or age found youth too demanding, or gossip peered over the wall. At any rate, Beecher broke off the relationship.

Had Elizabeth been content to accept the break, the story might have been kept among those private passions that simmer within many families. But she was a highly emotional woman, young, frail, not overbright: she had "no claim to importance except that the great Beecher loved her." Therefore she could not lay aside those exciting years without seeking some recognition. She must tell somone about it; the someone she chose was Susan B. Anthony, come to spend the night, whom she kept awake by pouring details into the spinster ear. At dawn she swore the exhausted Susan to secrecy. Two months later she told her husband, who first decided nobly to forgive her and to leave Beecher to his own conscience; he then fell to bickering with Elizabeth, and finally confided to a friend.

The oaths of secrecy that have been kept under circumstances like this can be counted on the fingers of one hand. Even granitic Susan, shocked to the core by such malfeasance among the saintly, needed someone with whom to share the dreadful weight of Elizabeth's confession. She told her old friend, Mrs. Stanton. Mrs. Stanton told Victoria Woodhull. And late in 1872, Victoria Woodhull told the world.

First, the Wall Street siren tried out the story in the form of an incident that she wrapped within a speech to be delivered before a Boston convention of spiritualists. Coating it all with sugar, she praised the admirable state of broad-mindedness into which the world was moving when three people of the known moral caliber of Beecher and the Tiltons could conduct their love lives together. No reaction followed. The tale had been whispered around newspaper offices for months, but because of the prominence of the people concerned, no editor in New York or Boston would touch it.

Victoria, who lived on publicity, was furious. Also, she needed money. Her next move was more successful. She reprinted the entire address in *Woodhull and Claflin's Weekly*. Funds in the paper's treasury had been low and publication dates irregular, but a scoop on a major scandal will bring the most moribund journal back to life. Eager customers spent as much as $40 for a single copy of that issue of November 2, 1872.

The fat was in a very hot fire. The first people burned were the paper's publishers, Victoria and her sister, Tennessee Claflin, whom Anthony Comstock with his unfailing nose for immorality caused to be arrested and jailed on charges of obscenity.

Then came the long process of charge and countercharge. The Plymouth Church, feeling its very foundations shaken, scandalized by gossip but reluctant to question their great pastor on so vulgar a charge, debated piteously, but was finally forced to call him to account. Sounding remarkably like the late Don Marquis' version of King David's state of mind when caught courting, Beecher denied all charges. Relieved, the elders exonerated him, and after long soul-searching, expelled Mrs. Tilton from membership in Plymouth Church.

Then Tilton, summoning up his public courage, charged Beecher with adultery and sued him for alienating his wife's affections. The public took passionate sides. The newspapers had let Mrs. Woodhull and her sister bear the blame and the punishment for the first public revelation of this sin in saintly places, but once they were sure that there was enough truth in the story to free them from the danger of libel suits, they printed reams about the case, and trebled their circulations. The only legal result was a hung jury.

Other results were harder to measure. The Tilton marriage was ruined, the Beecher reputation stained. The suffrage leaders were inevitably involved, for if Beecher had been president of the Boston association, Tilton was active in the New York group. Mrs. Stanton, who had never forgiven the clergy for their rudeness to her in the London Anti-Slavery Meeting of 1840, wrote widely in defense of Theodore Tilton. Susan refused to talk to anyone about the case (though she had already said too much to Mrs. Stanton). Her sense of justice was outraged when Mrs. Tilton was expelled from the church while Beecher was exonerated. She did write then to Beecher's sister, Isabella Hooker, protesting that "For a cultivated man, at whose feet the whole world of men as well as of women sits in love and reverence, whose moral, intellectual, social resources are without limit—for such a man, so blest to overflowing with *soul food,*—for him to ask or accept the body of one or a dozen of his reverent and revering devotees—*I tell you he is the sinner—if it be a sin—and who shall say it is not?*"

Mrs. Hooker, angry with her brother and ashamed at his refusal to admit responsibility at least equal to that of the unfortunate

Mrs. Tilton, let the *Brooklyn Argus* publish the letter without asking Susan's permission.

How much damage the suffrage cause suffered from this display of clay feet among some of the apostles is debatable. Susan's own incorruptibility was obvious, but Victoria Woodhull did her best to draw other suffragists into the web of her own ambitions. That she succeeded in charming Beecher's sister, Mrs. Hooker, made her famous exposure of the Beecher-Tilton affair on the eve of the presidential election more egregious.

Susan went from the May meeting in New York, where she had momentarily out-maneuvered Victoria, to a set of speaking engagements and her first experience with political party conventions. The situation was electric. General Grant, despite his four disappointing years, was backed by the conservative Republicans for re-election. The disapproving liberal Republicans were joined with the Democrats to run Horace Greeley, famous as an editor but without experience in politics. The newly founded People's Party was running Victoria Woodhull and Frederick Douglass. Susan made it her business to buttonhole delegates at the first two conventions, but paid no attention to the third one. She was instrumental in persuading the Republicans to put into their platform a mild if courteous plank which declared the party "mindful of its obligations to the women of America" and aware that its demands for "equal rights should be treated with respectful consideration." Susan the realist regarded this as a "promise of things not seen," but agreed to campaign for the Republicans. Mindful of her known fame as a speaker, they allotted her a thousand dollars, of which five hundred was to pay the expense of meetings held in New York. She got Mrs. Stanton and two other suffragists to stump the state with her, talked mostly about the suffrage plank, which most suffragists called "a splinter," and wound up with a grand rally at Cooper Union.

Meanwhile, Susan had determined on a spectacular step of her own. Building on her long study of the Fourteenth Amendment, on the mild Republican plan, and on her speeches for that party, she decided the time had come to test just what the woman's status in regard to the vote really was. Later, Susan testified that she had made up her mind three years earlier (in 1869) to test the Fourteenth Amendment at the earliest opportunity.

She embarked on this course only after thought and preparation. Her first biographer, Ida Husted Harper, quotes a pertinent letter from the Civil War General, Benjamin F. Butler, who had become a Congressman. He wrote her,

I do not believe that anybody in Congress doubts that the Constitution authorizes the right of women to vote, precisely as it authorizes trial by jury and many other like rights guaranteed to citizens. But the difficulty is, the courts long since decided that the constitutional provisions do not act upon the citizens except as guarantees, *ex proprio vigore*, and in order to give practical force to them there must be legislation. . . . Therefore the point is for the friends of woman suffrage to get Congressional legislation.

What she remembered, and resolved to test, was the first sentence.

The challenge to a federal amendment could be made only at a federal election. Susan, returned from her speaking tour in the West where she had argued repeatedly that the Fourteenth Amendment had made it possible for women to vote, decided that the moment had come. She persuaded fifty women of stout hearts and good repute in Rochester to attempt to register as voters in advance of the attempt of General Ulysses S. Grant to secure a second term in the White House.

With Susan leading them, fifteen of the fifty—sturdy, determined, and respectable housewives—went to the registration desk in a shoemaker's shop in the Eighth Ward and presented themselves as desiring to register. The inspectors hesitated. Susan had brought along the Fourteenth Amendment and the state election law. These she read aloud. The first article of the Amendment states that "All persons born or naturalized in the United States, and subject to the jurisdiction thereof, are citizens of the United States and of the State wherein they reside. No State shall make or enforce any law which shall abridge the privileges or immunities of citizens of the United States. . . ." Neither this article nor the New York State election law, she pointed out, specifically forbade women to vote. The inspectors in the Eighth Ward were convinced, though those in other wards, where others of the fifty suffragists tried to register, refused to yield.

Everybody knew there would be trouble, but more trouble appeared than Susan had counted on. The very next day, November 2, the heated political atmosphere had its temperature raised still further by the appearance of the November 2 special issue of *Woodhull and Claflin's Weekly* in which Victoria, candidate for the presidency of the People's Party, gave the public her own fevered account of the Beecher-Tilton affair.

For the moment, Susan's defiance was almost forgotten while the public pored eagerly over what the famous principals had said and done individually and to each other. Then the local newspaper, turning back from bedroom farce to political threats, dug out and printed an enforcement act passed by Congress to put teeth into the Fourteenth Amendment. This provided that any person voting without legal right should be deemed guilty of a crime and subject to a fine of not more than $500 or a prison term of not more than three years.

On November 5, 1872, the fifteen who had been registered with Susan B. Anthony at their head went to the polls and voted. The Rochester election officials, respecting Susan but aware of the danger she courted, were cautious and polite. Susan, willing to endure whatever came, but determined that her followers should not suffer, had hired a lawyer on the Saturday before election day, and laid the case before him. Henry R. Selden was an able and thoughtful man who had been a judge in the Court of Appeals. He read the papers that Susan presented, listened to her reasoning, and on Monday morning told her that he not only thought her argument was sound and that women had a right to vote, but added "I will protect you in that right to the best of my ability."

After the day was over, Susan, who was by now fifty-two years of age, wrote gleefully to Mrs. Stanton, "Well, I have been and gone and done it! Positively voted the Republican ticket, straight, this A.M. at 7 o'clock; and swore my vote in at that. . . ."

Judge Selden, who had undertaken in good faith to see Susan through whatever trials awaited her (he was to carry out his promise with a courtesy that never failed and a skill that grew as the case unfolded), had almost a month in which nothing happened. Then, on November 28, 1872, the Republican authorities, convinced that if they did not punish Susan and the fifteen serious housewives who followed her for flouting the law, they would be confronted at the next election by a host of women, sent deputy marshals to arrest the sixteen. It was Thanksgiving Day.

Susan, picked out as the leading offender, heard her doorbell ring and found on the doorstep Chief Marshal Keeney, who took notice of the occasion by presenting himself in top hat and kid gloves. Susan was, he told her, under arrest for a crime against the United States, and he had orders to take her to the courthouse. This was no ordinary crime, Susan no ordinary criminal. Stern and determined, armed with the high consciousness of her mission, she would accept no suggestion from the embarrassed officer that she go by herself, but insisted on being taken to the dingy courthouse by force—a term which in this instance meant that Marshal Keeney accompanied the prisoner through the streets of Rochester. She asked him, in order to make her position clear to passersby, to put handcuffs on her, but this he refused to do.

Susan's fifteen followers were also arrested and sent to the dirty office of the commissioner of elections. They waited all afternoon. Then the commissioner himself appeared and told them that, as the district attorney was not present, they should come back the next morning. They came then, when Susan was examined, and they came back another day when all but Susan pleaded not guilty, and were placed under a bail of five hundred dollars each. Susan asked for a writ of habeas corpus, was refused it, and placed under a bail of a thousand dollars. This, to her fury, Judge Selden put up.

Then began a series of legal moves that were to last for a year and four months. A grand jury indictment charged in Albany that "Susan B. Anthony of Rochester had knowingly, wrongfully and unlawfully voted (the said Susan B. Anthony being then and there a person of the female sex) contrary to the form of the statute and against the peace of the United States of America and their dignity." Susan was put in charge of the marshal and her trial set for the summer term of the Rochester Court.

After the trial date was set, she went on about her usual affairs, the first of which was to attend the annual suffrage convention in Washington—which was scheduled early in January, 1873. At the Rochester railroad station she found Marshal Keeney, who did his duty by protesting against her leaving Rochester, but laid no hand on her. This became a repeated pattern. She was a busy lecturer, and even though, as she told the applauding suffragists, she was "now in custody and not a free person," she saw no reason for curtailing her engagements and plenty of reasons for making her position known wherever possible. Marshal Keeney always appeared at the railroad station when she was about to leave, always protested, always let her go.

Her position was as clear in her own mind as was the indictment against her. She told the suffragists at the Washington convention,

There are three methods of extending suffrage to new classes. The first is for the legislatures of the various states to add women to those already voters. Before the war this was the only way thought of, and during all those years we petitioned the legislatures to submit an amendment striking the word male from the suffrage clauses of the State constitutions. The second method is for Congress to submit to the several legislatures a proposition for a Sixteenth Amendment which shall prohibit the States from depriving women citizens of their right to vote. The third plan is for women to take their right under the Fourteenth Amendment of the National Constitution, which declares that all persons are citizens, and no State shall deny or abridge the privileges of citizens.

She was now adopting the third plan, and not solely for the sake of women. Citizens of the United States have the right to vote, she explained, and "If we once establish the false principle, that United States citizenship does not carry with it the right to vote in every state of this Union, there is no end to the petty freaks and cunning devices that will be resorted to, to exclude one and another class of citizens from the right of suffrage."

To the annoyance of government authorities, Susan drove home this argument in town after town, county after county; in the last months before the trial Matilda Gage of Fayetteville, a poor speaker but a fine thinker, worked with her. Between them they covered every town in Ontario County in a month. Their haste was due to the fact that the trial, set originally for Rochester, had been moved to Canandaigua on pleas that suffrage speeches made in and around Rochester were prejudicing potential jurors. The same protests were made in Canandaigua, but the case had created too much embarrassment among Republican officials to permit further delay.

The actual proceedings in mid-June of 1873 leaned more heavily on politics than on legal niceties meant to safeguard the accused. The presiding justice was J. Ward Hunt, a political hack whom Mrs. Stanton, who attended the trial, described as "A small-brained, prim-looking man, enveloped in a faultless suit of black broadcloth and a snow white necktie." This appearance in the Canandaigua Circuit Court was his first since his appointment. He owed his new office to the powerful New York Senator, Roscoe Conkling, who had made it quite plain that the Anthony case was a political nuisance; she was, after all, a Republican, and too many questions were being asked about her by loyal party members. Justice Hunt was to get the case off the docket quickly and quietly.

The new appointee did the first, but not the second. The hearing took two days, in which the inexperienced Justice Hunt, mindful of his orders and eager to prove his skill, issued a series of rulings so extraordinary that they infuriated Susan's lawyer and disheartened the prosecutor. The second afternoon he rose, drew a piece of paper from his pocket, and read his charge to the jury.

The question, he declared, was simply one of law; the justice, in his wisdom, had decided,

in the first place that under the XIV Amendment, which Miss Anthony claims protects her, she was not protected in a right to vote. And I have decided also that her belief and the advice which she took do not protect her in the act which she committed. If I am right in this, the result must be a verdict on your part of guilty, and I therefore direct that you find a verdict of guilty.

Susan's lawyer protested that no court had the right to behave this way in a criminal case, that Susan had a clear right to jury trial and was not getting it. The jury was too confused to speak up. High-handed, inexperienced, Justice Hunt dismissed them, and except for sentencing the case was over. During the trial, Susan had had no chance to speak a word in her defense, but when she was summoned to stand, Hunt finally gave her one. "Has the prisoner anything to say why sentence should not be pronounced?" The prisoner had plenty; it rang not only in the courtroom but in newspapers all across the country. Their editors might have no sympathy for suffrage, but such high-handed conduct of a court case as fundamental as this one roused their indignation. The comment of the *New York Sun* was typical; if this bypassing of a jury was allowed, "Judge Hunt might on his own *ipse dixit*, and without the intervention of a jury, fine, imprison or hang any man, woman or child in the United States."

Susan was fined $100, which she declared she would never pay. Trial by jury had been denied her. The usual routine would be for her to be sent to jail until she had paid the fine. Then, says her biographer, she could have taken her case to the Supreme Court on a writ of habeas corpus. But the sentence of a fine, unaccompanied by the statement of intent to collect, gave her no further recourse. The case was over except for the echoes. The vital point had been made that women, though citizens, were not to be allowed to vote even though they asserted (and many lawyers agreed with them) that the postwar Fourteenth Admendment in its fuzzy way had enabled them, as well as Negroes, to cast legal ballots. The additional point had been made by Ward Hunt's intransigence that women who disputed this interpretation of the amendment could not expect justice in a federal court, and that even the fundamental right of trial by jury would be denied them.

The importance of the case at the time was great, and references to it still appear in law books. These echoes were important factors in the slow improvement of national attitudes toward women's rights that followed during the last three decades of the nineteenth century. Progress was slow, confused, sometimes arbitrary and unthinking, but it did take place. The territory of Wyoming had given women the right to vote in 1869, and while some argued that this was a joke that the small legislature of that sparsely populated region played on the governor who was a bachelor, the action held. When in 1889 the territory of Wyoming applied to Congress for statehood, its newly adopted state constitution contained provision for full woman suffrage. Southern Democrats, arguing against the Southern grain and habit that a state had no right to determine who should be able to vote within its border, made such a fuss that the Wyoming delegate wired home for instructions as to what to do if it appeared that women suffrage would have to be abandoned as the price of Wyoming's admission to statehood. The legislature, feeling the pressure of the women who had helped to elect it, wired back, "We will remain out of the Union a hundred years rather than come in without the women." The Congress responded meagerly; not until March of 1890 did it vote 139 to 127 to admit Wyoming on its own terms.

The territory of Utah, Mormon in religion and devoted to plural marriage as a way of populating the wilderness, gave the vote to women in 1870. Congress, whose members were outraged by any open exception to monogamy, revoked women suffrage there in 1887 when they passed an act meant to outlaw plural marriage, but Utah held to its convictions; it was admitted as a state in 1896 and came into the Union with woman suffrage imbedded in its constitution. Idaho followed its neighbors.

Those victories were not achieved without effort and anguish. Always there must be campaigns, in which the Eastern stalwarts with experience and some funds from the national organizations came to the aid of energetic local women with less experience but, perhaps, more optimism.

Traveling had become easier than when Susan had started lecturing, but the improvement of railroads in the East and their extension into the West merely meant that she could go farther and find new audiences. The going was still rough. Her biographer describes the conditions of her vain campaign to help Colorado women get the vote in 1877; while the geography was different, the circumstances must have recalled to her the early temperance, antislavery days. Now she was nearing sixty, and the Rocky Mountains were higher than any she had met in the East. Nevertheless, she still had to look after her own transportation, find her own lodging, and her own places to speak: Moreover, as her biographer, Katherine Anthony, tells it, here were "no halls, no schools, no churches available. She spoke in saloons, railroad stations, hotel dining rooms, and general stores. One meeting she conducted from a drygoods box on the courthouse steps. . . ."

She traveled mostly by stagecoach, along rough, pitted, and

perilous mountain roads. "A comfortable night was not to be expected. . . A straw mattress and a separate room were luxuries. In one hotel she slept in a general room with a six-foot-high partition dividing male from female patrons." But she slept, and the next morning she went on. Nor was she utterly alone in the wilderness. Several other volunteers had come from the East, including Lucy Stone and her husband Henry Blackwell. But there was little local response. The Colorado women seemed to be lacking in orators as well as in funds. The press resented the influx of Eastern speakers, the voters were not impressed. The suffrage cause lost at the polls and would be revived in triumph only when a younger speaker, then named Carrie Lane Chapman, invaded the state two decades later.

Meanwhile, despite the fact that speakers from both the American and the National Suffrage Associations appeared in the same state campaigns, the differences that had split them apart in 1869 continued not only to divide and weaken the efforts of their members but also to grow sharper in terms of techniques. The National, to which Miss Anthony and Mrs. Stanton continued their allegiance, did work in state campaigns but believed this to be largely wasted effort. They had been active in getting the first Congressional attention to a proposed national suffrage measure as early as 1868.

In March of 1878, ten years and several local campaigns later, an amendment bearing Susan B. Anthony's name, and expected by her to be the Sixteenth in the Constitution, was presented to Congress by Senator A. A. Sargent of California, an old friend of Miss Anthony. The text, which she herself framed, was utterly simple: "The right of citizens of the United States to vote shall not be denied or abridged by the United States or by any State on account of sex." Susan had learned her lesson, cut her language free from charm of Mrs. Stanton's enthusiastic divagations, and limited herself to an effort to put into the Constitution that vital word which should have been included in the Fifteenth along with "race, color or previous condition of servitude." But Congress would not be convinced of this for three decades and two wars later.

Nor were the Boston ladies and gentlemen of antislavery traditions convinced. While the Anthony Amendment was introduced into Congress year after year, was debated, referred to committees, and to the mercies of such thinkers as Senator West of Missouri (who declared that when he went home he wanted to meet "not the embrace of some female ward politician, but, the earnest loving look and touch of a true woman . . ."),* the Boston group, in the American Association, spent most of its energies in an attempt to amend the constitutions of the individual states. The state-by-state effort was in the main a vain spending. One can, of course, never discount the converting effect of good argument, but between 1870 and 1910 just seventeen state referenda were held; of these, only two were victorious.

Meanwhile the century was moving on, new forces were emerging, famous suffragists were growing older. Mrs. Stanton retired as a professional public speaker in 1880. Limited suffrage was granted to women in Kansas, Michigan, and Minnesota; by 1890 there were nineteen states that had given women local school suffrage. These piecemeal victories were more important as indicating a slow shift in public opinion than as promising full suffrage. They gave politicians a chance to argue that women who did not bother to vote in minor school elections were thereby proving that women did not want the vote. Meanwhile, new colleges were opening to receive the younger ones and to train them as their mothers had never been trained. The tide was rising, though only an occasional ripple slipping farther and farther up the beach made a mark.

Interesting and significant diversions from what was becoming the standard suffrage pattern showed the increasing initiative of

Century of Struggle, by Eleanor Flexner. Harvard University Press, 1959, p. 175.

women in the field of public affairs. The most important of these was the organization, in 1874, of the Woman's Christian Temperance Union. Temperance had been Susan's first crusade, and although she had ceased to speak for it and had steadfastly held to her post-Civil War conviction that she must set aside other reforms until women got the vote, she must have been sorely tempted to join forces with that able temperance crusader, Frances Willard: and this not merely out of her long-held conviction that temperance was greatly to be desired in American society, but also because an organized effort of the liquor interests was marking them as active enemies of the suffrage movement.

This new force was first noted in the Kansas campaign of 1867, when out of thirty thousand votes cast, the suffrage cause got only nine thousand. The suffragists, though glad to get that many, also noted that there might have been more ballots showing crosses for the referendum permitting females to vote had not liquor men appeared "in all parts of the state . . . conspicuous workers against the suffrage amendment." It was not a solitary phenomenon. Five years earlier (1862) the beer makers had gathered to form the United States Brewers Association. Its main object was to be "the political protection of the trade." Its targets would include any group that seemed to threaten its fortunes. It was, perhaps, an indirect compliment to the growing force of women that from 1867 on such dangerous groups would include ladies of high moral purpose who sought either temperance laws or the right to vote.

The Woman's Christian Temperance Union was formed in Cleveland, Ohio, in 1874, in part as an answer to such pressures, and in part as a reaction of orderly women against the effect of raw whiskey in frontier settlements. The Union had strong evangelical overtones but little organizational force until it was captured (in 1879) by the remarkable young educator named Frances Willard. Under her guidance it became a general educational force for women, and it gave valuable aid to the suffrage movement.

Aid was badly needed. The absence among women of political

sense or training, their ignorance of the need for disciplined group action, and for continuing support of an organized program made the efforts of individual suffragists doubly hard. Again and again, in reading their memories and their reports, one finds that in each new campaign they had to start far back of scratch; at the cost of great effort they spurred their inexperienced converts to a high pitch of enthusiasm at election time, only to lose them once the election was over—and lose them with a bump if, as often happened, the opposition won.

In this awkward situation the WCTU became a new source of strength. Miss Willard proved herself not only a magnetic crusader and an able organizer but also a shrewd political strategist. Very early she led women to understand that they could not protect their homes against drunkenness unless they secured a voice in public affairs. In the beginning few of them were suffragists. They were, however, soon led to demand the right to vote for local option in order to control or to prohibit the sale of alcoholic drinks in their own towns. Once they realized the value of the vote in this, they demanded full license to use it. Forty years later Carrie Chapman Catt, the most famous and successful suffragist of the twentieth century, was to credit the WCTU with having trained women for public work more effectively than had any previous movement.

In 1881 the Brewers' Convention adopted an antisuffrage resolution on the curious ground that the brewers would endorse prohibition as less dangerous to the trade than woman suffrage, because "prohibition could be repealed at any time, but woman suffrage would insure the permanency of prohibition." Had the beermakers been clearer of sight, they might have known that this last assumption would not hold. Not all suffragists were prohibitionists, not all prohibitionists were suffragists, nor were memberships in the WCTU and in the suffrage associations interchangeable. Woman suffrage was not going to "insure the permanency of prohibition." Indeed, it would be partly responsible for prohibition's eventual repeal. But the brewers, and later the whiskey men, did not known women very well. They would spend millions of dollars in state campaigns to defeat suffrage referenda, dollars that harassed the suffragists and hardened their determination, but merely prolonged the fight.

The suffragists, meanwhile, would continue to suffer from the tangle caused by their link with temperance, much as they had in earlier days suffered when their orators spoke not only for suffrage but also for Bloomer dresses, Bible reform, abolition of slavery, easier divorce. It was the old trouble of too many goals.

The national scene within which they moved was changing. The country continued to grow, and to grow together. Many people moved westward, a few of them moved south. Transportation improved; so did communication. Boston, which in the 1840's had seemed self-sufficient, superior, far from New York, was now recognizing the growing importance of Washington, and could even contemplate Chicago.

Susan B. Anthony, somewhat to her surprise, came to contemplate Europe.

The circumstances of her first trip abroad say much for the inner warmth of this spare, stern suffragist. Despite her somewhat forbidding exterior (an exterior that lent itself all too well to the skill of cartoonists) she had gained with the years so deep a belief in the moral rightness of her cause that it shone on her plain face and drew to her women of courage and discernment. Our Susan was too downright to be called a saint, and too emphatic of tongue, but as she grew older she developed an inward grace, an illumination of countenance that attracted both the young and the experienced. Also, she was acquiring the attraction that attaches to fame.

In Philadelphia, at the end of the seventies, she met two young women, Rachel and Julia Foster, daughters of a liberal Pittsburgh editor who, at his death two years earlier, had left his wife and children dowered with a comfortable fortune. Rachel, restless and curious, feeling herself modern in the terms of those days, took an immediate liking to the old reformer, joined her workers and planned some lecture tours for her. The two became warm friends. When Mrs. Stanton, who had gone abroad on a holiday, wrote urging Susan to join her, Rachel Foster discovered excellent reasons to second the invitation. She had always wanted to go to Europe, but being a young lady of good family she could not go unaccompanied. What better idea than to persuade Susan to go with her as chaperone and traveling companion?

Left to herself, it is doubtful that Susan would have broken her old habits and embarked on an adventure that must have seemed extravagant in time as well as money. But the Fosters were offering to meet traveling expenses, Susan was dog-tired, and she had the prospect of a long-promised bequest that would enable her to go straight back to suffrage lecturing when she got home. The weariness came in part from the exhausting job of writing the *History of Woman Suffrage* so far as it had developed, a long task to which she had not only to drive herself, but also to drive the gifted and ebullient but erratic Mrs. Stanton.

By this time Susan had become a famous character in many places. People with other convictions still disagreed with her crusade, but something about the selfless and indomitable nature of crusade and crusader caught their respect. When, in the winter of 1883, it became known that she would be traveling abroad there was a wide stirring of interest, and even editorials praising her as a representative American who would be honored in Europe. A hundred dollars came in as a gift from an anonymous friend, receptions were given, and speeches made. Susan responded with the characteristic hope that "while abroad I shall do something to recommend our work here, so as to make them [the Europeans] respect American women and their demand for political equality."

The trip was planned primarily for the education of the young and well-born Miss Foster, but it also fitted the wishes of the older traveler. Susan was determined to get all she could out of what she assumed would be her only foreign trip. She read guidebooks, she made notes in her diary. In February of 1883 the two women headed out across the cold Atlantic (a "beaver-lined satin circular" was Miss Anthony's provision against the weather) and spent a week with Mrs. Stanton in London. She went to Rome, to Switzerland, to Paris. In Paris, Rachel left her for a short time in the home of a hospitable friend of women's rights whose English was as scarce as Susan's French. There, for the first time in her hard-working life, Susan "positively ate my breakfast in bed. What my dear mother would pronounce most lazily."

When, after this mild debauch, she got back to England, it was to plunge into suffrage affairs on another level. By 1883 the English women, whose long campaign for the vote had been started in 1866 by a petition introduced into Parliament by John Stuart Mill, had acquired the vote in municipal elections as well as some property rights. The suffrage movement, however, was split into several parts. Susan found herself welcomed and courted by invitations from many quarters. Even her wardrobe, which she had thought ample, began to seem inadequate and she ordered "a dark garnet velvet dress at Waterloo House." Regarded as an obvious extravagance, it was to serve her as her proudest garment on platforms and receptions for years to come.

Her last point of call was Ireland, to which she was pulled in part by her gratitude to George Train, who had started her career as editor with *The Revolution*. Even though he had left her with promises that were never fulfilled, and that $10,000 debt to pay off at the end, she had never forgotten the lift that his support gave her after the Kansas defeat. In addition to this was a desire to see for herself the home circumstances that thousands of Irish girls, ignorant but determined not to starve, had left to emigrate to domestic jobs in the United States.

What she saw appalled her. Poverty in Ireland in 1883 was neither attractive, romantic, or forgivable. The visible state of the Irish poor so shocked and distressed her that for the first time in her life she failed to complete her schedule and fled from a situation she could not help.

Susan returned to England in October and waited there a month for Mrs. Stanton whose daughter, married to an Englishman, was about to give birth. On the eve of departure from Liverpool she persuaded herself to take a step into the international field that had been in her mind ever since she left the United States. She felt that somehow a link should be established between the suffrage forces at home and those in England. Daunted by the bitter divisions she had found between the English groups, she had withheld her hand. Now she was about to leave; unless she acted at once she must go home with a sense of failure. Braced by Mrs. Stanton's enthusiasm, she proposed to the small group of Liverpool suffragists (reinforced by London friends who had come to see her off) that they form then and there an international committee for women's rights. This proved to be the start of a movement that would circle the globe. The International Council of Women with members in fifty-eight countries would grow from this small seed.

It took five years for the seed to put up a sizable shoot; Susan kept it alive by correspondence with the committee that she and Mrs. Stanton had set up in Liverpool, and by constant mention of it in suffrage conventions in the United States. By 1887 she was able to persuade the National Woman Suffrage Association to sponsor in Washington a meeting of the International Council of Women. It was to be held in 1888, to celebrate the fortieth anniversary of the Declaration of Women's Rights, and to "give women a realizing sense of the power of combination." Suffrage was to be only one of many subjects discussed. It was the subject nearest Susan's heart, but she had become more and more a realist. Remembering from her travels in Europe how little support woman suffrage had on the continent, and how divided the English women were, she recognized that if she gave her desire for the vote too much prominence in Washington, she might alienate some of the visitors she most valued. To get them to come, and then to persuade them of the importance of her cause—that was the strategy.

The International Council met with flags, speeches, and a more substantial public success than its best wishers could have expected. Albaugh's opera house, famous in 1888 as the largest public meeting place in Washington, was crowded for eight afternoons and evenings. Forty-nine nations were represented, and fifty-three American organizations. Among the latter was the American Woman Suffrage Association of the Boston ladies estranged for years from the National, but yielding to the drawing power of those forty-nine foreign states. Representing it were Susan's well-known and now elderly rivals, Lucy Stone and her husband Henry Blackwell, Julia Ward Howe, Mary Livermore. They all had honored places on the program, they all made speeches.

With them came a woman who had made a rare place for herself in both the church and the medical worlds, Anna Howard Shaw, ordained by the Methodist Protestant Church in 1880 (the first woman to be so honored) and granted a medical degree in Boston in 1885. She was scheduled to preach a sermon at the Council meeting on Sunday; so powerful an orator did she prove, with so firm a belief in woman suffrage, that Susan, always on the alert for able younger converts, marked her for fine work ahead.

The International Council of Women was at that meeting made a permanent organization. Its meetings would take Susan to Europe again and again, until her somewhat hazy dream in 1883 of alerting the world to women's protests against repression and women's demands for the vote would take form and force.

By 1890 Susan B. Anthony was seventy years old, Elizabeth Cady Stanton was seventy-five, Lucy Stone was seventy-two (and to die three years later). The old fires that had kept hot the differences between them were dying down. A younger generation was stirring, better educated and showing signs of bringing new points of view to bear on old problems.

The suffrage movement, unlike certain other reform movements that flourished in the nineteenth century, was fortunate in that it had continued to develop an active interest among the younger generation. And this in spite (or perhaps because) of the powerful old personalities that led it. Miss Anthony, Mrs. Stanton, Lucy Stone were women of force, intelligence, and persistence who brooked little interference with what experience had taught them. They might easily have laid too heavy a hand on the young.

Fortunately Lucy Stone had a daughter, Alice Stone Blackwell, who was both gentle and firm, a peacemaker by nature, and a poet. She had been active in the delicate task of taking the Boston ladies to the meeting of the International Council of Women in 1888. By putting the warring old leaders in the limelight on the same platform, that meeting had brought them international recognition; the heat of applause had melted some of the ice between them. It was Alice who proposed to follow up with plans for a truce and then for a design that, recognizing both the independence and the interdependence of the two suffrage groups, would reunite them. It was time to forget differences, to put aside rivalries, and to work for the goal that was emerging bit by bit as the one in which they all believed. If they could once get the vote, they could use it to get other reforms. They had begun to realize the broad implications of their impotence without it.

Convinced of the need, though clinging to their differences, they agreed in February to Alice Blackwell's plan. They would combine their names and make of themselves the single National American Woman Suffrage Association.

After that major decision, the matter of officers practically settled itself. Lucy Stone was too frail, Susan B. Anthony refused to be considered. The third of the famous triumvirate, that coruscating old orator Elizabeth Cady Stanton, accepted the office, held it for two years, and then handed it over to Miss Anthony, who by then was seventy-two but still indomitable. The younger generation wandered restless in the wings. The power of the old, though fading, was not yet ready to yield command. It would hold until the new century came in.

4. TOWARD MASS MOVEMENT

"All the tensions of society seemed to come to a focus in the Woman Question."

Ernest Samuels

Newspaper reports of New Year's Day, 1900, say that the people who toasted each other at midnight in Delmonico's of New York or the Palace Hotel in San Francisco sensed for the moment not only the end of the nineteenth century, but also the thrust and challenge that would characterize the twentieth.

In the suffrage movement, determined if still minute, Susan B. Anthony, grown almost mellow in her old age, was resigning from active service as second president of the merged National American Woman Suffrage Association. (The merger of the American with the National had taken place in 1890.) She was eighty years old. Anna Howard Shaw, with her red apple cheeks, her snow-white hair, her "mind like a man's" (to this compliment she habitually retorted, "But which man's?"), yearned to succeed her old friend.

At first sight the succession look inevitable. Dr. Shaw was of the Anthony type, a spinster, but warmer and more human, a physician and an educator. Twenty-seven years younger than

Susan, built of the same sturdy stuff, she had a gift of language the like of which Susan had struggled for all her life. Born in England in 1847, Dr. Shaw had come to the United States with her parents at the age of four. They were poor and hard-working, and only too pleased to let their ambitious daughter do what she wanted as long as she could find ways to pay for it. Her dearest wish was to get a good education. With a budget so small as to be almost at the starvation level, she persuaded Albion College in Michigan to accept her; then, deeply religious, she moved to the Theological School of Boston University and was graduated from it in 1878. She had paid her way through college by preaching and lecturing.

Carrie Chapman Catt, twelve years younger, used to tell a story about Dr. Shaw's school days that sets the picture of the place and the person. Young Anna had so little money that she chose the cheapest room in the college. This was up steep stairs under the roof, with a single dormer window, a bed, a chest, and one small rocking chair. The only light was a candle that she brought in from the hall, and by this small flame she did all her studying. The room was cheap because everyone else had shunned it; a former student, a lonesome little Quaker girl, had died there, and students spread a rumor that she came back to haunt the place. Dr. Shaw could not afford to be superstitious. She laughed and asked what ghost would want to do any harm to a poor, hard-working student.

Nevertheless, as the term went on she became aware that there was something strange about the room. More than once she turned the doorknob with a feeling of arriving on the very heels of someone who was just going out. Yet going out how? There was only the one door, and the dormer window.

One evening, she climbed the stairs late, very silently, and without the lighted candle. A full moon made every detail visible. Anna Shaw stopped on the threshold. The little rocking chair, her study chair, was moving, back and forth, back and forth.

She looked again. The chair was undoubtedly moving, as if some-one had just left it. She could see no one. But was it empty? And if not, what moved it, and why?

Astonishment, fear, curiosity, swept through her mind. Finally, in the ghost's own plain language, she asked gently, "Is thee lonely?"

The little chair gave a jerk, as if its invisible occupant had been surprised, and then it moved quickly back and forth like a nodding head. "Shall I read to thee?" Again the chair nodded. So Anna Shaw got out her lessons for the next day, perched herself on the bed, and went over them, reading and explaining in a low voice. At the end the little chair stood quiet. Anna Shaw undressed, said her prayers, and went to bed.

Was it a ghost? Or a vagrant breeze? Was it all in the imagination of a girl who too often went to bed hungry? All that term the little ghost kept coming, but at infrequent intervals, and with more and more time between visits. There was about it an air of friendliness, even of gratitude, but it never came when there were other girls in the room. Toward the end of the term its visits ceased. The little chair stood quiet, leaving Anna Shaw to study by herself.

Taught by the ghost or not, she proved so eloquent as a preacher that two Methodist Episcopal churches on Cape Cod, one at Hingham and the other at East Dennis, asked for her services. The pay was minute, but for two years as a supply pastor she preached in both towns. Then the Northeast Conference of the Methodist Episcopal Church refused (in 1880) to ordain her because she was a woman. Competing Methodists who belonged to the Methodist Protestant Church came to her rescue. On October 12 of that same year they gave her formal ordination; this was the first time that they had broken through the long tradition that souls were to be cared for only by a man.

Five years later, finding in the Boston slums that souls had a harder time if bodies were uncared for, Dr. Shaw added a medical degree from Boston University to her rare churchly recognition, and worked in the poorest parts of Boston. Hers were paid posts— she had no money except what she earned, and she earned it at jobs for which few women in those days were either trained or acceptable.

Such a woman was, in theory, the perfect successor to Miss Anthony. Ten years earlier there would have been no doubt about it. But the younger generation in the wings of the suffrage movement had had enough of her kind of excellence. They wanted a new type of leader. Anna Howard Shaw was an orator in the great tradition. But oratory, overused in the past hundred years, practiced too much in politics by William Jennings Bryan and in educational and cultural matters by the Chautauqua speakers, was going out of style. Dr. Shaw was of the stuff of pioneers, but pioneers with their country ways and their hard-won knowledge were going out of style, too.

What was important in 1900 was not the past but the present and the future. Organizing the country, which by now was fully explored and becoming widely settled. Organizing industry, building good roads, laying out towns, getting the practical things done. Theodore Roosevelt had his eye on the White House; his abundant energy, his reforming zeal, his flair for the emphatic gesture and the picturesque phrase swept the country into his train.

Theodore Roosevelt had no personal interest in woman suffrage, but he did like change and action. A practical man, he was also a romantic. His image and his attitude set the national tone, and at the same time reflected the national temper. It was a practical moment; it was also a romantic moment. The desire to get things done was at the same time in many quarters infused with high aspirations and fine ideals. *Ad astra per aspera* was the motto that more than one schoolgirl wrote in her school books; some of them rendered it, "to the stars, but up through thistles."

Given this attitude in the country, it was not to Anna Howard Shaw, the aging preacher, that suffragists turned at this moment, but to Carrie Chapman Catt, the analyst and the doer. They would come back to Dr. Shaw later, after the new winds had blown through the old fabric, after the mechanics had been improved and the system modernized. She would have her wish, and be president of the National American Woman Suffrage Association from 1904 to 1915, but for the moment it was young blood that was wanted.

Carrie Lane Chapman Catt, Mrs. Chapman Catt as the South Americans would call her later, was the chosen candidate. She was not as young as she seemed, but forty looks young when the lookers are twenty years older. A vigorous and experienced woman, with two decades of hard work in the suffrage cause to her credit, she was by temperament and training a leader. Tall and handsome, with bright blue eyes set wide apart, hair white as new snow, back straight and speech both downright and eloquent—that is the way she looked in the 1920's, the way most people now remember her. She was born in 1859, so those are gone who could remember her as a young, chestnut-haired, high-spirited daughter of an Iowa farmer, but that was what she was in bone and in essence, and what she continued to be.

One of the secrets of her power was the fact that in addition to being an excellent organizer she was gifted with intelligence, analytical ability, and a high degree of common sense. Almost as magnetic as the half-forgotten "siren of Wall Street" (who had married a wealthy Englishman and left the United States in peace), she had enough oratorical skill to inspire women, enough drive to lead them straight to carefully chosen goals. In contrast to Susan B. Anthony, she liked men, liked them well enough to marry two; her confidence in them was not, however, unlimited.

There is evidence that a mainspring in her ambition for women, including herself, lay in a deep resentment of the way her father and her father's hearty farmer friends had roared with laughter when her mother expressed any political idea. Her mother, who was a quiet thinker, shut her mouth in a straight line and went about her housework, but young Carrie fired up, not content to be laughed at for no better reason than that, like her mother, she was female.

Resentment was one thing, distrust was another. There is every evidence that her childhood was happy. Her biographer records only the usual young battles with her brothers, the flying arguments, the country tricks played and played back. Her own writings about her life stress her activities in the public rather than the private sphere. She belonged to that vanishing type that thinks a private life is a private life, and no affair of other people.

Neither Susan B. Anthony nor Elizabeth Cady Stanton had attended college, but in 1877, when they were trying to convert the sparsely settled Western states to suffrage, Carrie Lane entered Iowa State College at Ames as a sophomore. (She had previously taught school at $20 a month for spring and fall, and $28 a month in the winter.) In 1880 she was graduated with a B.S. degree, and got a job in a lawyer's office where she proposed to study law, but a year was enough. In 1881 she was persuaded to become principal of the high school in Mason City. Two years later (in 1883) she was made superintendent of the Mason City schools, a rise that must be counted rapid even in those free-moving days. In 1884 she met an attractive young newspaper man, Leo Chapman, married him six months later, took a turn at editorial work on his paper, and got her first taste of suffrage work in a campaign to get for women the municipal vote. She met Lucy Stone at a suffrage convention, and was captivated.

But first came tragedy. Her engaging young husband sold his newspaper in the spring of 1886 and set out by train for San Francisco, where he believed that opportunities would be better than they were in Iowa. His wife was to follow with their new housekeeping equipment. Instead, she got word that he had been taken ill on the train with typhoid fever. He died before she could reach him.

Widowed at twenty-seven, after only two years of marriage,

Carrie Lane Chapman had few resources except her own brains and her short periods of working experience. She had tossed away a sure career in education when she married. She was fifteen hundred miles away from home, almost without friends, caught in a moment of great grief. The unfortunate Chapman was too young to have left her well endowed. They had all their lives ahead of them. She had fallen in love with him suddenly, she had loved him well. That is all that most of her New York friends ever knew. When she married again she would discard her own name, and keep his as a second name.

The period after 1886, when Leo Chapman died of typhoid fever in San Francisco, the four years that intervened before his young widow married again, may provide a clue to the somewhat skeptical eye with which she would regard men in later life. Young Carrie Lane Chapman was an exceedingly handsome woman. Magnetic and shapely, dowered with a fine fair skin, bright chestnut hair, and those lively sky-blue eyes, she must have attracted any man's gaze. That in some instances she attracted more than a look was obvious in the distaste with which she spoke of job-hunting up and down San Francisco hills. Women in the 1880's were not commonly seen in offices, but Carrie Lane Chapman had taught school and worked in an editorial office in Iowa. She regarded herself as experienced and competent. What it was that happened to her in San Francisco offices where she sought work after her husband's death she may have confided long afterward, but if so, the confidante never told. She hated tobacco, she hated liquor, and while she never said that many men were, in the Victorian phrase, "brutish beasts," it was quite clear that at some time that was the way they had looked to her.

If as a child she had resented the mocking laughter with which her father and his friends greeted her mother's ideas, as a young widow she distrusted the masculine advances that made her feel no more than a man's prize. Later she came to trust no politician's word, and as all politicians were men in those days, her innate distrust of the masculine sex reached through the world of public affairs. Promises, proclamations, noble speeches of intent she received with interest and an open mind, but always with a measuring look, as of one who will accept the promise only when she sees it kept.

Sometimes skepticism is a crippling thing that so cramps the mind as to inhibit creed or action, but Carrie's was not of that kind. She believed deeply in God, in the ideals of the founding fathers, and in the moral superiority of women. She also recognized that human beings are fallible and that some of them, particularly in the liquor business and in politics, might be more fallible than others.

Ever since 1882, when she first met the Iowa Woman Suffrage Association, Carrie had been thinking about suffrage, and taking small parts in local struggles. After Lee Chapman's sudden death she was to devote most of her life to it. (Thirty-eight constant years was the way she counted it.)

Her first notable assignment came to her in 1887, when she had returned from her California tragedy. The Iowa Suffrage Association gave her the job of organizer. Here she showed that inventive quality that was to prove so welcome. Her first move was simple: a new system of pledges and enrollments which, adding both to membership and to income, made it possible to keep accurate records for the first time. She also worked out for the Iowa suffragists a simple teaching course in American political institutions that was to be the forerunner of many such teaching plans in later years. This new energy, applied with hard thought behind it, delighted the Iowa women; when they were asked to supply state delegates for the national suffrage convention called in 1890 in Washington—the one that was to unite the two organizations, the American and the National—young Carrie Lane Chapman was named to represent Iowa.

Her sympathies were with Lucy Stone and the more conservative American Suffrage Association, but Lucy Stone was ill in Boston.

Elizabeth Cady Stanton, that intermittent firebrand, with her curled white hair and her rolling oratory, had come to Washington. Susan B. Anthony, seventy years old and straight as a vaulting pole, was there; so was Julia Ward Howe in a gray silk dress and a lace cap. These women, with their history of long hard campaigns, called up the past for the young delegate; their presence inspired her to a speech that would catch and hold their attention. Hers was to be a paid speech, though not paid much; young Carrie promptly donated the fee to the cause. She also promised to campaign for suffrage from the first of August until election.

This latter promise was to cost her more than the gift of her lecture fee. After her husband had died in San Francisco, she had stayed there, working at various jobs under various circumstances, for a year. Walking up hill one day, still in mourning, she heard her name called, and turning, saw a fellow student of her college days at Ames. This was George Catt, now a bridge-building engineer whose headquarters were in San Francisco but whose business was spread across the West.

The two friends talked on the street, talked over a dinner table. The widow was lonely, if plucky. The engineer remembered her young vigor in college, and determined to make her laugh again. He had to follow her to Iowa to do it. He did not find the winning easy, but he was a determined man, used to analyzing problems and planning ways to solve them. Her sense of shock at the sudden death of Leo Chapman was still too acute to be conquered by any appeal to her affections, so George Catt put his plea on grounds of intelligence. She was a vulnerable young widow whose deepest vow, now that she had lost her husband, was given to the cause of getting suffrage for women. This was commendable, but not a very good way of earning her living. He, on the other hand, had been an advocate of woman's suffrage since he was eight years old; he was also a good money-maker. As her biographer explains it, "He would earn the living for both of them, and she would render the public service for both." Together they drew, as Lucy Stone and Henry Blackwell had done, a written contract. Signed and sealed before they were married, it contained their agreement that she was to have two months off from matrimonial obligations in the spring and two months in the fall for suffrage speaking and organizing. He would be away from home during those periods overseeing his bridges.

In June Carrie Lane Chapman married George Catt; they went at once to a new home in Seattle. Here the first project of this Iowa farm girl was to set out eighty rose bushes. In August she left Seattle to spend the first pair of suffrage months agreed to in her marriage contract by campaigning for the vote in South Dakota.

This was to prove a hard struggle in a desperately poor state. Mrs. Catt was to learn by personal experience much that she had thus far known only by hearing the suffrage pioneers talk. She also would learn some of the reasons why they had failed so often. In addition, she would have her first personal collision with the organized liquor lords.

The start of the campaign was not auspicious. The energetic bride went from cool Seattle to South Dakota in the hot month of August, planning to meet Susan B. Anthony in Huron. Here she was brought face to face with reality, and told that funds for the campaign were very scarce. Because she was young and strong, she was given the central plain to cover, a region that had been cursed by drought for five straight years, where farmers were gaunt and cattle were dying. She traveled from one sun-baked crossroads to another, meeting poverty, desperation, endurance, but little encouragement. Not only were funds lacking; so also were party support and political organization. Thirty or forty farmers and their families would drive into a meager station to see her and hear her talk from an improvised platform set on the ground floor of a grain elevator. The only seats were backless boards laid across nail kegs. Babies, swaddled like Indian papooses, were laid in a corner on the floor. People showed themselves silent, kindly, uncertain; after she stopped speaking they would drift out without comment to their wagons and start home across the plains in the dry and empty night.

It took only a little of this, only a few visits to the spare and comfortless houses to persuade Carrie Chapman Catt that this kind of campaigning, which was in substance a western repetition of the more easterly pioneer pattern, was mostly a sad waste of energy.

"We have opposed to us the most powerful political elements in the state," she wrote to suffrage headquarters with a frankness that must have been as refreshing as it was startling. "Continuing as we are, we cannot poll 20,000 votes. We are converting women to want to vote by the hundreds, but we are having no appreciable effect on the men. . . . we need some kind of a political mustard plaster to make things lively."

The bride underestimated her own effectiveness. After her prodding, South Dakota gave suffrage twenty-two thousand votes that year—and forty-five thousand against it. Beaten but not daunted, Mrs. Catt went home to her bridegroom in Seattle, traveled with him on a business trip to San Francisco, developed typhoid fever, and almost died. There must have been dark hours when she remembered the fate of her first husband in the same city.

She was, however, a woman who could learn from experience and analyze what she had learned. While she was convalescing, she made for herself a pertinent list of political essentials for future suffrage campaigns: first, a referendum cannot possibly be won unless it is endorsed by large and effective citizen organizations, and by at least one of the influential political parties; second, it must have behind it an adequate campaign fund; third, it must have campaign forces that are organized and energetic. The beginning of political sophistication was entering the suffrage world.

Her next campaign was three years later, in Colorado where Susan had vainly campaigned in 1887. The first move came from the state suffragists. Unlike the ineffective women in South Dakota, the women in Colorado had learned what organization could do, and had built one which for those days was good. What they then decided they needed was a leader who had had experience in other states, who would come in with authority, and give them that extra lift which could mean victory.

News of Mrs. Catt's ability had reached them. They found her in Chicago, where she was managing a series of lectures on civil law and government at the World's Fair of 1893. They told her the state legislature of Colorado had been persuaded to give women the vote, provided they could get the voters to approve this in a referendum. A nationwide depression had brought the Populists into power there, and that party was in favor of woman suffrage. The women had an alert campaign committee, funds that they hoped would be adequate, and a large body of citizens behind them. Mrs. Catt listened and recognized that her first essentials for a campaign had been met. She agreed to go west and help.

Her first act was to address a huge Labor Day mass meeting that had been arranged in Denver. Her second was to hold a session with the suffrage campaign committee and plan a program that would reach every county in the state. The campaign was to be conducted without undue fanfare (these were days before Madison Avenue had convinced nearly everybody that fanfare always helps) in order not to awaken the fears of the liquor interests. Mrs. Catt's own assignment included speaking in the large towns and the mining centers, as well as at local party conventions.

It was to be, as South Dakota had been, a grueling campaign. Mining towns were rough, but they were also lively and full of fun. The Iowa girl found very quickly that she enjoyed the lusty humor of mining audiences; the mining audiences responded to the Iowa girl's energy, her good temper, her young magnetism.

Moving around that mountainous state in those pre-automobile days was very different from getting around the flat central plain of South Dakota. Colorado was fairly well laced with railroads, most of them narrow gauge, individually owned, and built primarily for hauling ore. Passenger schedules seldom provided transfer arrangements that were convenient, or that paid any attention to customary sleeping hours. Ore had the first claim; accidents on mountain slopes were frequent.

The mining town of Durango had arranged a two-day meeting, but the Iowan's part in it had to be interrupted by a promised speech in Silverton. The distance between the two towns does not look so great on the map as to make such a schedule impossible, but these are vertical, not horizontal miles. She left Durango on schedule, got up to Silverton, made her speech, spent the night, arrived at the station to go back. There she learned that because there had been a bad wreck halfway down the long grade, no trains were running.

By the time I heard the story of what happened next, Mrs. Catt must have been nearing eighty, but the twinkle in her eye and the gayety in her voice were ageless. I am sure the story had gained in the telling. She told the station agent that she must get to Durango that very day, and why. A handcar, known as a pushcar, was found; she was told that if she could slide downhill on that as far as the wreck, she could then walk around it, and find a wrecking train on the other side which would take her the rest of the way to Durango. Always sure of herself, she agreed.

Comfort was, of course, nonexistent. Safety was minimal. So she tied her voluminous skirts around her ankles, pinned her hat firmly on her head, took a box of sandwiches in one hand and grasped the edge of the car tightly with the other. Her feet she fixed on a rope slung under the front edge. There were no sides to the car, and no cover, no power but gravity, no brake but a board that could be thrust through a hole in the floor and held hard against the wheels when gravity pulled too fast.

As I heard the story, Mrs. Catt had started on the perilous trip by herself, with the president of the road that owned the handcar giving the first push, the miners cheering as the car started down the slope, and the skill of manipulating the life-saving board brake still to be learned. She lost her hat as she rounded the first curve, and her box of sandwiches as she approached the second. After a journey that was literally hair-raising she arrived at the wreck, breathless, hatless, luncheonless, but safe.

Her biographer and friend, Mary Gray Peck, tells the same story, but with variations. She has the Catt hat clutched to her bosom and saved. Also, perhaps because she heard an earlier version, she notes that Mrs. Catt did have with her an old workman who had lost an arm, and was to manipulate the board brake with his remaining hand. His ideas of desirable speed were excessive; he never applied the brake except at the last moment, but "after several miles of mad descent the screech of the board-brake and the smell of scorching wood announced that they were slowing down."

The wrecking gang, to whom this arrival must have looked like an apparition from another world, cheered loudly and conducted the young campaigner on foot around the wreck. Then she learned that the wrecking train could not leave for Durango until the day's work was done. There was nothing to do but wait. She finally arrived at nine o'clock that night, and went at once to speak to the patiently waiting audience. After she finished, she was taken home by a considerate hostess who, learning that her guest had had nothing to eat since early breakfast, cooked at midnight the steak dinner that had been planned for six o'clock. At four in the morning the speaker took another train to her next assignment.

Mrs. Catt never forgot that hair-raising ride. Neither did Colorado. In 1893 it was a sparsely settled mining state but its people spread the news of her spunk, and responded to her speeches with a rousing vote for woman suffrage.

The Colorado victory of 1893 marked a change in attitude that spread far beyond local boundaries. Colorado was the first state where men actually went to the polls to vote for woman suffrage and won it. The Wyoming victory of 1869, the short-lived Utah triumph, were won by a handful of pioneer legislators. Neither the

Colorado political bosses nor the liquor interests that had been active in the Kansas referendum of 1867 believed that the miners would do so strange a thing as vote for woman's suffrage. How much the state's action was a vote for Carrie Chapman Catt, tearing down hill on her handcar, no one will ever know.

Nor is it easy to tell how much effect this Colorado victory had on the minds of eastern feminists. Even though the East considered the West of little importance, and much too wild to imitate, the fact of a second state won under the inspiration of new young leaders must have made its impression.

The moment of victory in Colorado was sweeter in contrast with the South Dakota debacle of 1890, and from the fact that two other states, Utah and Idaho, followed Colorado's brave example. Utah had made a first try at giving women suffrage in the early 1870's while it was still a territory, but this move, along with plural marriage, had been expunged by Congress. Now, in 1895, Utah gained acceptance as a state, with the right of women to vote embedded firmly in its constitution. Idaho granted suffrage to women in 1896, after Mrs. Catt had set up for the workers a plan of campaign that included organizing suffrage forces in every precinct of every city. This was the tryout of a pattern that was to be repeated again and again over the next three decades.

Mrs. Catt's experience as a field worker, her skill in analysis and organization of state campaigns were making their marks. Such skills were also badly needed at central headquarters. The celebrated welding together of the two nationwide suffrage organizations—the American and the National—that had taken place in 1890 had not been followed by co-operation in methods, nor by the process of tightening and reform that was obviously required.

Old as they were, the pioneers were still in command, and all of them were individualists. Mrs. Stanton served as president for two years (1890-92) but she was much more interested in writing her Woman's Bible than in overhauling the organization of the reconciled suffrage forces. Susan B. Anthony followed her in office, and functioned as president of the merged organization from 1892 to 1900, but Susan, while not temperamentally adverse to organization, had worked too long in her own patterns to think out new ones for the new need.

It was the younger and more energetic Carrie Chapman Catt who recognized most clearly how heavy a drag on the suffrage efforts was the prevailing lack of orderly procedures. At the NAWSA convention in 1895 she had shocked the older suffragists and delighted some of the younger ones by saying flatly that although they had been agitating for forty years, and had stirred prosuffrage sentiment all over the country, they had failed to transform sentiment into power. She called on them to provide proper correlation of national, state, and local branches, to create a program of concrete aims, to set up a finance committee to finance properly the work that was essential. She recommended a standing committee on organization to map out work across the nation, and then to put organizers in the field whose job it would be raise the needed money. To knit the loose-jointed state organizations into a firmer fabric, she would have four regional conventions meeting midway between the national conventions. And to educate the local clubs, she proposed a stiff study course in politics and government.

The plan sounds obvious today, but in 1895 it was little short of revolutionary. The convention, dazed by so much young efficiency, accepted its main lines. An Organization Committee was appointed, and the woman who had called for it was made its chairman.

What Mrs. Catt found when she surveyed her field intensively was even worse than she had foreseen. Ten states had no suffrage organizations of any kind, and no known friend to turn to. No list of local suffrage clubs existed, no roster of local officers. When she set about compiling a club directory (a job that took the better part of a year) she found eight hundred separate suffrage clubs proceeding in their separate ways. Her first remedy for this chaos was to recommend to existing clubs a standard form of constitution that would also serve new clubs as they were set up. She invited the aid of state presidents and found only two who were willing to give her full co-operation.

Mrs. Catt's skill as an organizer was based on an instinctive love for orderly methods, an educated ability to analyze the problem and the situation in hand, and the opportunity to draw advice and help from George Catt's engineering skills and experience. She had difficult material to work with. Few women were (or are) as neat-minded as she; many of her contemporaries were amateur enthusiasts, fond of their own ways and impatient with the rules she made for them. Her efforts as chairman did result in an important new step, the creation of a workable skeleton for the NAWSA, with the states linked to the national organization, and usable channels of communication forged between the head and the more distant members. She could not, however, overcome the divisive tendencies that seemed then (and seem now) to flourish in any lively body of workers, male or female, in the political field. Old jealousies, new ambitions were to plague the suffragists in the years that lay ahead, even more spectacularly than in the years behind.

Yet the wiser of the pioneers recognized that times and needs were changing, and women becoming more impatient. When the suffrage convention of 1900 met it was with the warning that Susan B. Anthony would not stand for re-election. Instead, the old pioneer led Carrie Chapman Catt to the front of the platform and recommended her as the ideal leader for them all. The Convention cheered, and voted her their new president.

The lady from Iowa had experience, she had made her analysis, she had her plan. Also she had ahead of her difficulties that were enormous. Old habits, old prejudices, a tradition of defeat, and the innate frivolity of most feminine minds all lay in wait to trip her.

There was in the first place the old argument, sharpened during twenty years of split endeavor, as to whether major efforts should be directed toward Congress or toward the individual states. Forty-odd states had, by that time, state suffrage organizations, and these repeatedly called for help. Ever since Susan B. Anthony had started on her long speaking trips, much, perhaps too much, of the suffrage energy had gone into state campaigns that had been coopered together hastily by local women with assistance from one of the famous pioneers, if one could be lured that way.

It is true that the Anthony Amendment was first introduced into Congress in 1878, following one a decade earlier that won no attention whatsoever. It may also be true, as one historian says, that Miss Anthony and Mrs. Stanton "kept their main fire concentrated on Congress," though in view of Miss Anthony's travel record, the minority fire directed at the states was considerable. Certainly much grass-roots work was lavished on the state-by-state method. A suffrage referendum would sooner or later be introduced in a state legislature, a campaign set up, grueling work done by women totally unaccustomed to the ways or the arguments of politics. Meantime, word would be passed from the functioning headquarters of the ruling political party that a bunch of silly women were on the rampage and were, of course, to be voted down. A *pro forma* election would be held, and when the votes were counted the women would find themselves on the losing end.

The old suffragists were indomitable and the habit of loss dulled their imaginations. Between 1870 and 1910 seventeen suffrage referenda were held in eleven states, most of them located west of the Mississippi and populated by more animals than people. The women won only two. They got out of the experience a certain education in political affairs as conducted, and a certain disillusionment with windy promises, but the price was heavy and what was bought was often put to little use. Only after 1895 was an adequate and continuing suffrage organization built to keep devoted women in training and to capitalize on the experience gained in these lonely treks from farm to farm.

As the new suffrage chief for the new century, Mrs. Catt proved a hard driver. When the old officers met in midyear at Miss Anthony's Rochester home, they found that the new president had prepared for them a completely new survey of the national organization as it was then constituted: its membership, its finances, its leadership. In addition, she had ransacked the state constitutions for methods best suited to each in winning the vote. For each state she had outlined what was then the political situation and analyzed the prospects.

This startling innovation, like Mrs. Catt's Organization Committee with its analysis and its plans, was a triumph of the new element in the old suffrage job, the college-trained mind against the instinctive and traditional worker. It appeared to some of these instinctive ones as a process of trying to teach grandmothers how to suck eggs. Somewhat grudgingly, and over a period of time, the grandmothers admitted that the effort was well organized and admirable. The granddaughters were the ones who would find in it a valuable blueprint for the future.

Despite the grumblings of the elders, the merged suffrage organizations underwent during the next four years a combination of earthquake and house-cleaning. Its component parts had been built up on high ideals, individual stubbornness, pertinacious work, but it suffered from conflict within and without. There had been so much to do, so many battles to win, that no one had had time to sit down and work out a farsighted plan of campaign. Such a plan was one of Mrs. Catt's great contributions. She had been thinking about it, working on its structure and its details long before she moved into the president's chair.

For four years as president of the National American Suffrage Association, Mrs. Catt tried to educate her followers up to her own high standards. She hammered away at the incorrigible casualness of mind and diversity of spirit that was and is, the mark of too many women. Trained by centuries of pressure to believe that their most important job if not their only real one is to be a wife and a mother, they can be enlisted in other work and educated to perform it, but always there is deep within them a hidden alarm bell waiting to be rung by the voices of the husband, the child, the household demand, or the personal whim that takes precedence over an outside duty. The "so sorry not to be here, but I had to take my husband's suit to the tailor's," "my child to her dancing lesson," "my son to his Scout meeting," "my hair to be done"— these phrases are modern only in their wording. The theater alone, with its insistence that "the show must go on," has been able to break through this conditioning without leaving behind in the feminine mind a feeling of guilt.

Mrs. Catt was attempting to buck this ancient tide in order to weld the suffragists into a team that would have a professional attitude toward their work, but the going was very tough. To give women a sense of the political implications of their cause, to teach them how to plan ahead, and how to earn money with which to pay the expenses of campaigning, these were three of her primary tasks.

The fourth task was a matter not of tactics but of strategy. In 1884 Miss Anthony and Mrs. Stanton had laid in Liverpool the first foundations for an International Council of Women, but when its first meeting was called in 1888 it was composed of organizations in many fields. The Council adopted a broad general program, but did not lend itself to woman suffrage propaganda. What Mrs. Catt proposed, in a day when only four American states (Wyoming, Colorado, Utah, Idaho) had yielded to the pleas of suffragists, was that an International Woman's Suffrage Alliance should be created in which American suffragists, whatever their local affiliations, would appear as a single unit. This, she believed, was a step that would add to the strength of the movement everywhere. If successful, it would certainly fortify the American association. The first step would be to issue invitations to an international conference to be held in Washington, when the NAWSA met in February, 1902.

Once this plan was accepted, Mrs. Catt spent an entire year

assembling the names of known women leaders from around the world. There were only five national suffrage associations known to be in existence, British, Australian, Norwegian, Dutch, and American. To get names of influential women in other countries she questioned diplomats, American officers stationed abroad, friends of friends in other countries. She persuaded nine women to come, from Britian, Germany, Norway, Sweden, Denmark, Turkey, Russia, Australia, and Chile.

The meeting was carefully planned, and staged to be impressive as well as interesting. In addition to the suffrage convention itself, the delegates attended two Congressional hearings, and were received by President Theodore Roosevelt at the White House. A planning committee was set up. After days of work the delegates decided not only to create a permanent organization, but also to hold a first meeting in Berlin in 1904 as an adjunct to the International Council of Women, which was due to meet there at that time. Mrs. Catt, as might have been expected, as asked to organize it. Miss Anthony promised to act as its presiding officer.

Having sowed these international seeds, having attracted to the National American Woman Suffrage Association a sizable corps of young officers, better trained than their elders and feeling quite capable of carrying on without those elders, having amassed $12,000 in the suffrage treasury (an unprecedented act), Mrs. Catt again surprised her followers, this time by letting it be known that she was about to resign from the presidency. She said is was because she found that "rest from the responsibilities of the office had become essential," and there is reason to believe her. What she did not say was that the new blood in the organization was being accused of moving too fast, that the older officers were still urging Anna Howard Shaw's candidacy, that a fund had been collected by the president of Bryn Mawr College which would make it possible for Dr. Shaw to take the job, and that she herself had worries of health and home which demanded attention.

Mrs. Catt had given those worries some attention in 1903, when for the first time in her life she gave herself a vacation and went with her husband on a trip to France and Italy. Now (after her resignation in January of 1904) she took a whole month of leisure. Then she began on her new tasks. The first step was to attend in Berlin the 1904 meeting of the new International Suffrage Alliance for which she had already laid precise plans.

In a day when international conferences of women for various purposes are as common as the airplane flights that take delegates to and fro, this first International Woman Suffrage Alliance may not sound like much of an accomplishment, but in those early days of the century it did; its existence was to hearten women in many countries for decades to come. Why certain women want to reach out across the oceans to touch the women of other countries who have the same interests and the same aspirations may be a mystery to the home-loving, but that they do is as certain as that they reap from the process a tremendous stimulus.

A long account of that meeting, as of any other, would make dull reading, but certain details do reveal the relative innocence of women of the time about public functions of that kind. There was the matter of the reporters, enough to surround a big table; these were unexpected, and to many delegates undesired. Journalism had a bad name in Europe. The accuracy of the press was suspect, and its employees were assumed to be venal. Dr. Aletta Jacobs of Holland moved that reporters be banned from the hall. The presiding officer, eighty-four-year-old Miss Anthony, whose knowledge of the place of publicity in promoting a cause was longer and more realistic, intervened. With a sweeping gesture she welcomed "All reporters who want to come! Let all we say and do here be told far and wide." Having for two years worked on a newspaper, she had learned the importance of courting publicity. Offered it now, she was too wise to turn it down.

The second pertinent detail concerned a gavel, made of Wyoming cedar and silver at the order of Wyoming women who were the first in the United States to have full voting privileges; they had sent it by Mrs. Catt's hand, to be presented publicly to Miss Anthony as a token of their esteem. The German customs officers inspected Mrs. Catt's luggage when she landed at Hamburg. They found the gavel and almost took it away from her as a dangerous weapon; in Europe, meetings were called to order with a polite bell. She finally persuaded them to admit her and the gavel, and made of the incident a story to tell when she presented it.

The other thing she brought with her was a copy of Roberts' *Rules of Order*, that extraordinarily useful guide for the conduct of meetings which most Americans first meet in grade school. In 1904 this was a complete novelty to the European women, whom Mrs. Catt found "innocent as the fowls of the air" of its sheperding techniques and procedures. Not only were they ignorant of any accepted technique of order, but they treated meetings as social occasions. The fact that the meetings were conducted in three languages slowed down formal debate; it also provided time for informal conversations—even the cedar and silver gavel could hardly restrain the buzz. In all this Mrs. Catt was learner as well as teacher. What she learned about the difficulties created by the need for translations she was to apply in international meetings all the rest of her life.

Her zest for such wide contacts was never to leave her, but first she went through a dark brace of years when death dogged her footsteps and modified her life. George Catt had been meticulous in his support of all her efforts. From the point of view of hearth and home-keeping theirs was not a model marriage: they moved from Seattle to a house in Bensonhurst, overlooking New York harbor, and much too often that house stood empty while his bridge-building activities were taking him one way and she was traveling another. In suffrage circles it was a common saying that the two must make breakfast dates with each other on odd Thursdays in June and December. But underneath this apparently vagrant relationship lay a solid level of confidence, mutual admiration, and affection. This second marriage was far more important in Carrie Catt's scheme of things than her most devoted followers knew.

When in October, 1905, George Catt fell ill, suffered an operation for gallstones, and died, a major light went out of his wife's active life. He had supported her in physical comfort, with sound advice and with moral backing, for fifteen years. Now he was gone, at the age of forty-five. He left her the fortune built up by his skills in engineering and business; it would prove large enough to keep her the rest of her life, pleasantly housed, adequately fed and clad, and with extra money for her travels and her causes.

Nor was George Catt's death to be the only blow. Four months later, in February, 1906, Susan B. Anthony, who had been Mrs. Catt's first sponsor in the national field, who had given her the kind of backing that comes with repeated demands for service to a cause jointly held and mutually valued, died at the ripe age of eighty-six. The following year, 1907, Mrs. Catt's mother and her younger brother died.

Deprived of four persons who were at once sources of affection, of inspiration, and of responsibility, the suffrage leader turned back to the one specific and recognized reason for living that was left to her.

She had been out of the National Association since her resignation from the presidency in 1904; it was natural that she should turn first to the International Woman Suffrage Alliance, which badly need her skill. In 1906 she toured Europe, presiding at suffrage meetings in Copenhagen and Vienna, Prague and Budapest. In 1908, while keeping in touch with the Alliance through an active correspondence, she was persuaded to take hold of the confused New York situation.

The New York situation deserves a chapter in itself. For two years it profited from Mrs. Catt's organizing skill and experience, then from 1910 to 1912 it moved ahead under its own steam and with the impetus of individual leaders, some of whom she had trained and others who came out of the blue.

But Mrs. Catt, who had brought to suffrage so much dynamism and intelligence, was ill.

In April, 1910, at the age of fifty-one she collapsed. In June her doctor sent her to a hospital for a critical operation. A month later, mending but still frail, she summoned grit enough to write a friend, "I always have had nerves, and naturally they have not been improved by the continual pain of the last three or four years. The form of nervous display I manifest is excitement, but I hope that by going slow and keeping quiet I shall escape the lunatic asylum." And then, with a flash of her old humor, ". . . I am in doubt whether my wits will return, or indeed if I ever possessed any. The weaker minded I grow, the more I aspire to be thought wise. If I go clear off the bat, I will be one of the type who imagine themselves Napoleon or Jesus Christ."

She gave her recuperative powers too little credit. In September she was well enough to resume her duties as chairman of the Woman Suffrage Party in New York. Even then she continued to look too white, too frail. Not even the suffrage victory in the state of Washington, adding a fifth state to the famous four, restored her bounce. Her doctor kept urging her to take a vacation.

In 1911 she obeyed him, but in a characteristic fashion. The International Alliance was doing so well in Europe that women in other continents besought its counsel. Mrs. Catt persuaded the Woman Suffrage Party of New York to give her a leave of absence, and to appoint Mrs. W. W. Penfield as acting chairman. She placated her worried doctor by telling him that a Dutch physician, Dr. Aletta Jacobs, would travel with her.

The third in the party was Mrs. Catt's salty friend, Mary Garrett Hay of Indiana, to whom the give and take of politics was the breath of life. Quick witted, sharp of tongue, she was as warm-hearted as she was downright; her flashes of sidewalk humor offended some of Mrs. Catt's more elegant friends, who shook their heads over her influence. But it was not hard to see between the two women a close and mutually valued friendship of the rare kind that includes instant comprehension and complete trust.

The two sailed in April to attend a meeting of the International Alliance, which was to be held in Stockholm in June. Then Miss Hay returned to New York, Dr. Aletta Jacobs of Holland took her place as Mrs. Catt's companion for the rest of the trip, and two other women, Miss Amelia Cameron of New York and Mrs. Boersma of The Hague, traveled with them as far as South Africa.

That trip around the world laid the basis for lifelong friendships, for innumerable speeches, for conferences, for sprigs of interest in problems and possibilities that would grow into lively movements directed toward getting for veiled women in Egypt, for foot-bound women in China, for dutiful hausfrauen in South Africa the equivalents of rights that American women were demanding for themselves. Also, the journey resulted in a vast broadening of Mrs. Catt's own horizon. The reception given her wherever she went showed that the movement of feminine protest she was leading went far beyond the United States, far beyond Western Europe. She found herself received as though she had ambassadorial rank—unofficial, of course, but genuine. Rulers who welcomed her were sometimes not quite sure why she had come, but they recognized that this tall, white-haired woman from America represented a force that called for honor. They did not always welcome her questions, but at least they listened, and sometimes asked their own.

Along with understanding, she brought back ivories, silks, and bronzes, embossed scrolls and bits of intricately worked silver, gifts presented by admirers around the world. In later years, a question about any one of them would bring forth a smile, a quick phrase, or a short tale, to be followed by "But I sound like the Ancient Mariner. What was it you were saying?"

5. CONVERTS
BY FIRE
AND PARADES

"Out in the middle of Fifth Avenue's width we felt a heap isolated . . . tagging after the girls, that's what we were doing and nobody would let us forget it."

Ray Brown

In the last half of the nineteenth century New York seemed farther from the Mississippi than it now does from the moon. Nothing that the West did was important to the eastern metropolis; nothing that the West said influenced its fashions or its thinking. Nevertheless, there was for some of the women of a state that considered itself the most important, the richest, the most influential in the country, a tinge of reproach if not of shame in the fact that four rough and graceless Western states had been the first to give women the vote.

In 1910 a dinner party on Long Island, which was amiably discussing President Taft's conservatism and wondering if Theodore Roosevelt was beginning to get restless, gathered itself together after dessert to let the ladies leave the table. Guests were startled to hear the hostess ask the guest of honor, "Judge, do you think women ought to vote?" The judge, who had been silent all during dinner, came suddenly to life. "Think they ought to vote?" he repeated vigorously. "Of course I do, and they would have voted years ago if they hadn't been such damn fools."

At that moment the hostess rose and let the bombshell lie. The men turned to port and cigars, and subjects of more masculine interest. The women, rustling out to powder their noses and discuss the newest item of gossip, seemed equally unmoved. As my handsome aunt, Gertrude Foster Brown, reported later in a private account (which unfortunately did not name the catalytic judge), "There was not one strong-minded female present." Professional though she was, a concert pianist trained in Europe and with wide experience in the United States, this was the first time in her life that she had heard anyone mention woman suffrage.

She herself was stirred to further argument. Going home that night she asked her husband if he agreed with the judge. Ray Brown hesitated for a moment, then, with a characteristic willingness to think about any subject brought to him, said slowly, "Yes, I believe I do. We've been trying for two thousand years to run the world with only half of our available human power, and nobody likes it. The half that is unenfranchised is supposed to have at least a good share of the sweetness and kindliness in the world, and to be largely concerned with and responsible for the care of humanity. Yes—I think women ought to vote; and I believe they ought to vote whether they want to or not, whether the vote will do them any good or not, and whether they will do any good with it or not."

This private and highly individualistic opinion was to have a considerable effect on the suffrage movement, and not only in New York. Ray Brown had been a newspaper man in Chicago. He was also an artist, and later the art editor for a group of publications that included *Everybody's Magazine*, then one of the most popular crusading monthlies in the country. In the early days of the automobile *Everybody's* campaigned for public funds to be spent on improving muddy country roads with paving that would speed harvests to market. It published an exposé of Wall Street practices written by Thomas Lawson and called "Frenzied Finance." It laid bare conditions in the stockyards, scandals in the oil industry and in Chicago politics. It was brash, vivid, popular, and a power for reform. If Ray Brown should take a vigorous interest in woman suffrage, that interest would begin to show itself in the magazines he helped to produce. And so it did. It was also to show itself in his designing of better suffrage literature, in picturesque publicity, in a general modernizing of the old and by now threateningly stodgy theme of votes for women.

Like Will Irwin, James Lees Laidlaw, and other husbands of suffragists, Ray Brown was one of the unsung heroes of the suffrage movement. His wide-ranging reply on the way home from that suburban dinner party took his musician wife out of the business of giving lecture-recitals about Wagner's music dramas and set her to work on the suffrage circuit. This activity was to deprive him of her company for most of the next ten years, to lead him to membership in the much derided Men's League for Woman Suffrage, and to set him to marching up Fifth Avenue in suffrage parades. But first his wife (who since childhood had, like Carrie Lane Chapman Catt, been quite sure that anything men could do, she could do better) began to inquire further into the suffrage question. Her first moves were to look about for other likeminded women and to see what kind of an organization there was to work with.

"I remember the mingled sense of daring and trepidation with which two of us hunted for suffrage headquarters in New York City," she wrote years later. Their first find was the head office of the New York State Suffrage Association, almost empty at that moment, but in charge of a dowdy little woman in very old-fashioned clothes and frizzed grey hair. "We considered ourselves as smart young things," Gertrude Brown remembered, "and I confess our enthusiasm was more than a little dampened. Could this be the center of the cause that seemed to us so momentous?"

This was the same frame of mind with which young suffragists in 1900 had welcomed the young Carrie Chapman Catt and defeated the older Anna Howard Shaw. But Anna Shaw came back in 1904. A pioneer, a fine speaker, an admirable character, she was not an organizer but a lone worker whose ability to inspire did not include the techniques of effective leadership. The almost empty office of the New York State Suffrage Association was all too symbolic of her lack of practical influence.

Yet at the same time, Dr. Shaw in person could still inspire the young. Gertrude Brown's friends were largely professional women, musicians and artists. When she asked them, "Do *you* believe in woman suffrage?" their answers were mostly fumbling and hesitant. They had not thought about it. She invited them to her apartment one afternoon to talk about suffrage, and got Dr. Shaw to come. So vigorous and challenging did the old preacher prove herself that on the spot and at the moment a Woman Suffrage Study Club took shape.

Gertrude Brown by instinct was an organizer. Her study club met regularly, and she conducted it with such zest that it attracted members who were equally active and intelligent. Discussions thrived; so did the membership list. Writing of the project years later, Mrs. Brown remembered it as holding real excitement: "We discussed suffrage from every angle, we studied many problems of government, especially city affairs; city officials often came to discuss them with us, and it was so unusual for women to express interest in city affairs that the newspapers gave much publicity to our meetings." When it grew too big and too powerful to meet in a private home, the Woman Suffrage Study Club was to merge with the Woman Suffrage Party that Mrs. Catt had organized two years earlier.

Nor were these two the only new organizations in the suffrage field. The moment was propitious. If the little old office secretary with her dowdy clothes and frizzed hair was a vestige of the generation that was gone, Mrs. Brown and her friends represented the new one that was coming into power. With the deaths of Lucy Stone, Elizabeth Cady Stanton, and Susan B. Anthony, and with the resignation of Mrs. Catt in 1904 from the presidency of the National American Woman Suffrage Association, the movement as such had suffered a slump in personnel. But not in the force of the ideas that the old pioneers had spent such devoted time pounding into the heads of the young: these ideas were flourishing; they needed only new leaders to carry them forward.

These leaders came partly out of sectors of society that had hitherto seemed impervious to the appeal of the suffrage cause. Some of them had been brought up in the early suffrage atmosphere: for instance, Harriet Stanton Blatch (daughter of Elizabeth Cady Stanton), who, having married an Englishman, had worked with the British suffrage movement in London. Widowed, she came back to New York in 1907 expecting to find her mother's influence still active. Indignant at the state of doldrums that confronted her, she moved at once into action and organized the Equality League of Self-Supporting Women. Later, this somewhat awkward title was exchanged for one more concise and pertinent, the Women's Political Union.

Other new recruits showed the growing effect of college education for women: in New York City and several towns a Collegiate Equal Suffrage League came into being. One group after another took fire, and by the time Mrs. Catt returned from her first successful European tour for the International Woman Suffrage Alliance, she found waiting for her the task of welding jostling and competitive groups into the Interurban Suffrage Council for Greater New York. This Council became the parent of the Women Suffrage Party, which held its first convention in Carnegie Hall in October of 1909.

This meeting represented the complete acceptance of the principles of organization that Mrs. Catt had been developing since the young days of her Organization Committee in the NAWSA of the late 1890's. The old pioneers were gone, the better educated young were in command. Here, for the first time in suffrage history, women came together to form an avowedly political party, for the purpose of getting the vote. They proposed to organize New York City "from the sidewalks up," appointing captains and workers for every Assembly district. The aim was to out-Tammany Tammany Hall, but honestly; Carrie Chapman Catt, growing daily in persuasive grace and political sophistication, was elected chairman.

All this energy was infectious, especially among women with more energy than outlet for it. Suffrage even began to acquire a certain tinge of fashion. Mrs. Clarence Mackay, the beautiful and wealthy wife of a copper baron, had become a convert, and had organized the Equal Franchise Society, with handsome offices high up in what was then the marvelous Metropolitan Tower on Twenty-third Street. Newspapers, impressed with her wealth and her daring, printed photographs of her, her office, her house, and her butler. Then came Mrs. O. H. P. Belmont, divorced wife of William K. Vanderbilt, mother of Consuelo, Duchess of Marlborough. Consuelo had been invited to give a reception for visiting delegates to the 1909 International Suffrage Convention in London, a group that attracted women of wealth and position. Consuelo said she would; papa Vanderbilt, who held the purse strings that governed what his titled daughter did, said she would not. Consuelo bowed to the power of her father's money, but her mother, divorced, remarried, and free to make her own decisions, thereupon announced that for her part she was converted to the suffrage cause and would do everything she could to encourage it.

Mrs. Belmont was no idle convert. She took an entire floor in a new office building on Fifth Avenue near Forty-second Street, installed a suffrage press bureau, and welcomed not only the National American Woman Suffrage Association (which at that time had its headquarters in the Ohio home of its treasurer) but also the New York State Association. Later, Mrs. Belmont was to separate from these groups and support the National Woman's Party, which still lives on her bounty, but those schisms were veiled.

With the new and fashionable guise came new and fashionable money. The older generation of pioneers had expected no pay for their services, and they received none. The newer generation, however, working in a wider field, found that they could at least count on travel money. Katherine Bell Lewis of Baltimore gave the National Association $10,000 in honor of Susan B. Anthony. M. Carey Thomas, President of Bryn Mawr College, raised a substantial fund for the support of Dr. Shaw. Suffrage was suddenly fashionable. Suffrage was news.

It was news in places other than New York. Especially it was news on the Pacific Coast. The state of Washington, under the leadership of Mrs. Emma De Voe who had been trained in thorough methods of organization under Mrs. Catt during the days of her National Organization Committee of the NAWSA, was persuaded to grant the vote to women by a majority of almost two to one. That was November 9, 1910. A year later, California, which had refused to vote for woman suffrage in 1896, granted it on referendum by the narrow margin of 3,587 ballots; most of those were rural ballots that came in late because they had been cast in solitary country districts without telephone. (They also came from regions where the liquor interests had less influence than they had in the cities.) The California campaign was brilliantly conceived and conducted. It reached even into the lower grades of the public schools, where more than one energetic child, being by instinct sure that girls were as bright as boys, did her own small bit by summoning the courage to stand up and debate for women's rights in the classroom.

The next year suffrage for women became news in Kansas, where Susan B. Anthony and Elizabeth Cady Stanton had labored so hard and so vainly. Kansas gave its women the vote in 1912. So did Oregon, completing the Pacific Coast roll call. So did Arizona.

In 1913 suffrage became news in Illinois. During the campaign "Mr. Dooley" was stirred to friendly comment in the Chicago press. "Molly Donahue wants a vote," he reported gravely, "but though she could bound Kamchatka as aisily as ye cud this precinct, she ain't qualified f'r it. It's meant for great sturdy American patriots like the Pollacky down th' street. He don't know yet that he ain't votin' f'r the King of Poland.'"

Molly Donahue would get her vote, and more quickly than Mr. Dooley could have foreseen. She would get it because the Illinois women, who had tried in vain for twenty years to get a state constitutional amendment through the Illinois legislature, had learned from Mrs. Catt's teaching to change their tactics, and organize the cities precinct by precinct. She would get it because a quiet and friendly little woman named Elizabeth K. Booth invented a legislative card index system with which she could make lobbying in the state capitol a highly personal and individual campaign. (That card index system became a major political tool for suffragists in many states.) She would get it because Catherine Waugh McCullough was a good enough lawyer to draw a bill that, once past the legislature, would stand under heavy attack when it reached the Supreme Court. Because Ruth Hanna McCormick, daughter of the politician Mark Hanna and wife of the Harvester heir, Medill McCormick, took the press in hand. Because the leader of the Chicago Democrats who had earlier opposed suffrage was also a man who kept his word when he gave it, even to a suffragist.

Earlier Western campaigns had been harbingers that the East could overlook. The Illinois campaign of 1913 marked an important watershed that could not be disregarded. Up to that point, women, for all their campaign drudgery, their speaking trips, their eloquence, their lonely travels and persistent courage, their growing political skill, had won the vote in only nine states, and all those lay west of the Mississippi. Illinois, while in and of the Middle West, lay east of the river. It could hold up its head and make its voice heard on the Eastern seaboard. Here, for the first time, women as a body appeared in new roles that were politically significant. No longer content to act merely as polite pleaders, they began to show themselves wise in political techniques and astute in matters of political strategy. Bribery, all too familiar a political tool among men, was to these women beyond the pale—never in the history of the suffrage movement did they use it as a weapon— but pressure and individual persuasion of almost every other kind were marshaled and applied to the individual members of the Illinois legislature. Profiting by the lessons that Mrs. Catt had developed for suffragists while she was president of the NAWSA, the Illinois workers concentrated their shrewd political skill on the legislative chamber itself. When Mrs. Booth's personal card file of Springfield legislators showed more than the seven extra promises of "aye" needed to ensure victory and the suffrage measure came to the moment of debate, the House was scattered with women "captains," all of them staying through five hours of oratory, each one watching a certain number of friendly legislators, to be sure that they were in their seats to vote, each making sure their quota voted as promised. At the critical moment the psychological force of the coming victory took hold and the "ayes" outpaced the prophecy of the well-thumbed card index; the final affirming vote was 83 to 58.

This, though hailed across the country as an important victory, was not a complete one. It gave Illinois women only partial suffrage: the right to vote in municipal elections and for presidential electors, but no more.

Their political enemies—and there was no doubt that they had developed a seasoned and bitter set of such enemies—could salve their wounds with the fact that the women of Illinois could not yet vote for state officers or for federal Congressmen or Senators. The state machine was still intact.

However, partial though the Illinois victory was, it spread among women a knowledge of the kind of tactics that could win. If Illinois with its long tradition of heavy-handed bosses, wealthy liquor interests, and known political corruption could, by shrewd political manipulation, be made to yield even part way, why not New York?

This aim was logical; it was also more ambitious than the cold facts warranted. Two passionate suffrage campaigns and the first of the World Wars would shake the state before women could break the hold of New York politicians on the voting structure. It would take parades, open police brutality, strikes, the emotion sparked by a tragic fire, the news of women chaining themselves to the White House fence. It would take the development and practice of a complex political astuteness, linked with a determination to break through the combination of traditional inertia and well-financed opposition.

In the process, powerful industrial and commercial interests would make themselves felt because they thought they were threatened by the possibility that women might be added to the voting lists. Chief among these were the liquor interests. New Yorkers knew that in one Western state after another the liquor men had shown their intent to defeat suffrage, and that they had been successful again and again.

All this the women knew, but they refused to be discouraged. A lively determination to win and to have done once and for all with the old campaign method became a tonic force that carried them well beyond what they thought in the beginning was their immediate goal. In the process of struggling for the vote they learned what kind of a world they lived in as they had never learned before. The suffrage campaigns of the decade 1910-1920 brought these daughters of the Victorians out of their overstuffed, overheated, and overcurtained houses into the streets, the slums, the factories, the political clubrooms where decisions are made on the lowest level, and into the state and national capitals where some of those decisions are (one hopes) made on the highest levels. Women broke through class barriers, they moved across economic barriers. They learned that they had fellow women in places very different from their pleasant homes—in garment factories, hospitals, vaudeville houses, academic halls—and they learned how these fellow women worked, what they were paid, how they lived. As a widespread exercise in democracy, there was nothing between Jackson's mob and the social consciences of the New Deal that could equal the 1910-1920 woman suffrage campaigns. Those campaigns became an educational force of lasting value. The effect of that force is by no means spent.

In the main, the first two New York campaigns in 1915 and then in 1917 were middle-class exercises, revolts of ladies against the smothering privileges that surrounded their sex and class. Like suffrage campaigns in other states, these represented a revolt on the part of the comfortable and well-fed, and insistence of these middle-class women (more and more of whom were college graduates) that they be allowed to share in the responsibilities and opportunities of adult citizenship. The working women came in more slowly. They became a symbol of economic and social wrongs to be redressed and of oppressions to be lifted by means of the voting power. Their plight challenged the sensitive reforming instincts of the suffrage leaders and led their followers into what were, in suffrage terms, the side issues of the labor movement. In turn the workers themselves moved into the suffrage ranks, and added strength to them.

It was, however, the middle-class women who first faced the challenge of borrowing or inventing political tactics that could move their husbands and brothers—uninterested, lethargic, content with the *status quo*—to cast their ballots so as to change the status of women within the body politics. This was not an easy challenge. In the first place, political tactics were in sharp contrast with the social ideals of the parlors in which these women had been trained. These polite and well-bred ladies must learn how to appeal to perfect strangers, without the shield of a previous introduction. They must come out from the shelter of their houses and mingle with the crowds, no matter how raucous. They must learn to speak on street corners and to march in parades.

The speaking was harder than the marching, partly because it had to be done by the individual, and without help. Ladies of that day were expected to be quiet and retiring, with voices ever soft, gentle, "an excellent thing in women." Such voices do not carry well, and modern electronic aids had not been invented. The suffragists set up courses in public speaking, both to train their volunteers in effective argument and to help them overcome the verbal handicaps of being a lady.

Gertrude Foster Brown describes in an unpublished manuscript just how it felt to make her first street speech. A musician and lecturer, used to facing audiences on public platforms, she found street corners very different.

"With legs trembling so I could hardly keep from tottering," she wrote, "I stood on the back seat of our motor car, on the most crowded corner of 125th Street, and in a quavering voice I began to call out to the passers-by. The spectacle was so unusual in those days that from all directions men and women came running, curious to see what was happening." Mrs. Brown went on to say,

The difficulties of reaching voters in those days can hardly be imagined now. We had no radios, no loud-speakers, no effective talking pictures, and women were timid. For centuries, they had been taught that self-distrust, a shrinking from public gaze, were the most admirable of womanly qualities. Womanly modesty was the word that covered it all, and it was the supreme feminine quality. The suffrage movement was now demanding a startling change. Millions of men stood between us and our goal. Some of them were bitterly opposed, but most of them were indifferent, or regarded it as a huge joke. For more than fifty years suffragists had been trying in vain to get men to listen to them. Now they were determined to make it impossible for men to escape. . . .

Frightened or not, the women learned as they went along.

It was sometimes difficult to begin to orate when there was only a small boy, a dog, and perhaps one loafer as audience, but however small at the beginning, the crowd would always materialize. Sooner or later, in spite of themselves, men listened to suffrage arguments on the street, and they seemed to enjoy it. Many of the suffragists were beautiful women, they dressed well, and the large picture hats of that time made a fetching frame for the face of an eager, enthusiastic speaker.

Nor were polite and well-dressed women the only lure. The earlier days of picturesque political manifestations when torch-light parades and chowder-and-marching parties were expected of men had slipped away. And club house politics were mostly dingy. The women changed that. They brought back a political excitement, a vigorous enthusiasm that made their demand for the vote beguiling and exciting. They had artists and actresses in their ranks, designers and experts in pageantry; their leaders seized on such talents and made the most of them. Their mass meetings were colorful and enticing, they invented new kinds of parades that brought out crowds to watch them from the sidewalks.

The amateur spirit that characterized them was helped, not quenched, by professional expertise; the two types of women worked together in unexampled harmony, perhaps because neither was making any money out of the performances, but both were working for a common cause. In New York in 1910 the amateur spirit triumphed in a suffrage bazaar, a glorified copy of the familiar church bazaar held in towns and villages before industry had taken over so many of the household arts.

This one was, as such bazaars have always been, held to raise money. But it also had a new professional sense of its own publicity value. Set in the handsome old Madison Square Garden on Madison Square, it displayed for sale the proud products of each state as set forth by the local suffrage associations. Florida sent citrus fruits; it also sent alligators. Utah, more surprisingly, sent bales of native silk—the Mormons must have had a hopeful silkworm industry that has since died. Idaho sent Indian antiques. Kansas sent a carload of flour and two hundred pounds of butter;

day after day the devoted Kansas suffragists made the flour into fresh bread and spread the butter on its slices. There was a doll booth, which included an Indian doll made by a Sioux squaw, its hair fashioned from a scalplock torn from a Crow enemy. (The frontier was still that close and that vivid.) There were millinery booths, book and picture booths, and a "handsome $700 automobile" contributed by a Tarrytown dealer in which Mrs. Catt accompanied distinguished visitors around the hall. When the week was over, the amateur efforts had netted $10,000 for the suffrage cause. That was, in those days, a great deal of money.

Then the women went back to speaking from street corners, to speaking between the acts in theaters, in vaudeville houses; they were invited to speak in pulpits; they spoke wherever a crowd had been gathered for whatever purpose, and whenever that purpose could be interrupted. They were urged to take part in the new moving pictures, still in their infancy, but here they had very little luck. They were better at parades.

Into those parades they gathered a few of the working women, but only after the horror of the Triangle Fire had burned away class barriers on both sides.

While middle-class women had been working to get the vote, learning what weapons to use against the prevailing inertia and how best to use them, working women had been making their way timidly into positions of some influence in the labor movement. Between 1903 and 1917 they took part in the formation of unions that were composed largely of women. This was a new thing. Within their own groups they were subject to the same tabus and the same restrictive and repressive traditions that controlled many members of the middle class. But this did not lead them early to the suffrage ranks. Their first efforts went toward improving their standing as members of the work force, rather than as citizens.

The struggle of the working women for any recognition, except as semislaves, was complex and difficult. They had to establish the power for which their brother workers also clamored.

That the broader vision which would win their interest in the crusade for women's rights developed slowly results from many factors that did not hamper other suffragists. Most of the factory workers were recent immigrants, unused to American political ways, ignorant of the implications of the Bill of Rights. Many of them worked twelve hours a day for wages only half those paid to men in equivalent jobs. Equal rights within the labor world appeared to such women as matters of life or death. Equal rights outside—they had little time or energy to think that far.

The first enlistments came from the garment workers, but at a truly fearful cost. A decade earlier the task of sewing had been parceled out to families that labored at home, but under the drive of a budding social conscience protests rose that these homes were unsanitary slum dwellings. The work "sweatshop" was fastened on them, and by extension to those who worked in them.

The word and the connotations were unlovely. People were moved to protest, and "sweatshop" garments began to be refused in the stores. The contractors, fearing loss of trade or the imposition of new laws that would cut into profits, hunted a new scheme of manufacture. New sewing machines were offered them, run by electricity instead of by foot pedal. These were faster than the old ones, but so expensive that private families could not afford them. The brighter contractors figured that with these machines work could be done more efficiently in factories.

Pushed by one force, pulled by another, the contractors moved to end the family system and start the garment factories. Mothers and daughters were invited into loft buildings, light and seeming airy, where space was cheap and many workers could be crowded around the new machines.

Most of these garment workers were Jewish, Russian, and Italian immigrants; many spoke no English. Docile by training, they were used to hard words from harsh bosses, and an absence of comforts. In the new factories they discovered that working with strangers, freed in part from the pressures of the family unit, had its advantages. For the first time they found themselves free to compare wages, exchange complaints, spur each other to speak up to the bosses. The younger ones began to develop a new resistance to low pay and harsh working conditions.

Their organized center for defense was the International Ladies Garment Workers Union, then young and far from strong. Outside help and sympathy came to them from the National Women's Trade Union League, formed in 1904 under the stimulus of Jane Addams of Chicago, and her New York disciple, Lillian Wald of Henry Street. But neither the Union nor the League was yet strong enough to force real changes. In 1909 the girls working in the Triangle Shirtwaist Factory, just off Washington Square, decided to take matters into their own hands. They would go on strike.

This was a phenomenon worth watching. Women in labor circles had no reputation for courage, but were reputed to be timid, helpless, easily pushed around. Never before had they undertaken a large strike. Would they carry it through? Could they hold their members in check for the long, hard weeks of a winter without work?

The test was severe. The girls were plucky, but their backing was insufficient, and their strike benefits scanty. As the winter wore on their hearts and their funds began to fail.

Help came from an unexpected source. The strike caught the attention of women who had been feeling the great feminine surge for a better position in the then modern world. Social figures whose names made headlines gave money and made speeches for the strikers. Mrs. O. H. P. Belmont, Miss Anne Morgan, Mrs. J. Borden Harriman (later to be Minister to Norway), all of them women of wealth and position, called a meeting at the fashionable Colony Club in New York, and collected over a thousand dollars for the strikers, a sum more notable for the gesture than for the amount.

Part of this was genuine sympathy, but part of it was surely a liking for drama. Mrs. Belmont, for example, wrapped in furs and wearing a fashionable hat so huge that it had to be anchored to her abundant hair with six jeweled hatpins, appeared in court one Sunday afternoon to stand bail for four strikers who had been arrested for disturbing the peace. She put up as security the Belmont house on Madison Avenue. It was valued at $400,000 (the bail asked was $800) and, said Mrs. Belmont, "There is a mortgage of $100,000 on it which I placed to help the cause of the shirtwaist makers and the women's suffrage movement." Society women were not then accustomed to upholding the cause of working women. The point was made, the headlines won. Mrs. Belmont was new in suffrage, and the gesture created a sensation. It helped the strikers for a moment; it helped the suffrage cause, and if cynics now smile they can be referred to certain money-raising gestures of the present days.

As for the strikers, the times were against them. Despite their courage and the new support they received from women outside the labor group, the strike was lost. Conditions in the Triangle Shirtwaist Factory were not improved, but the girls who had struck needed their jobs. They went back to work for two years longer.

This factory occupied the eighth, ninth, and tenth floors of a loft building just off Washington Square. The building was only about ten years old, and fireproof according to the legal standards of that day. But if the shell was supposed to resist flame, the piles of rags and cuttings allowed to accumulate in the process of manufacture were not. Kept in corners until a ton of them had piled up and could be sold profitably, these materials were highly combustible.

On March 25, 1911, at 4:30 in the afternoon, one of those piles caught fire. Nobody ever knew how, nobody knows even now whether the spark came from worn wiring, or a hot iron, or a careless cigarette. (Later it would be agreed that factory supervision was lax, and that neither state laws nor city regulations had caught up with requirements of safety in the garment factories.) The fire spread to the ninth floor and the tenth. The girl workers panicked. Elevator service was inadequate, and could not possibly get them all out at once. They ran for the stairs. Some found the doors were locked. The open staircases clogged with frantic, screaming humans. The fireescape, which ended on a glass skylight a full story above the street, broke under human weight. The glass skylight crashed, and dropped girls to the ground.

The fire department came quickly and did their best, but their tallest ladders reached only to the sixth floor. Spreading flames drove the frightened girls to the windows, and out of them. Screaming bodies began hurtling to the payment.

Even when nets were spread they did not hold—the girls' bodies came too fast. When the flaming afternoon was done, a hundred and forty-six workers—mostly young girls, many of them the former strikers—were burned to death, broken as their bodies hit the paving, or were impaled on an iron fence.

Horror at the tragedy swept through the city and across the nation. Who was to blame? Everybody and nobody. Hearings were held, consciences examined. The owners of the Triangle Factory, Max Blanck and Isaac Harris (known to have been demanding the last ounce of effort from the workers while refusing to improve conditions, raise wages, or allow union organization), were indicted by the Grand Jury. After a bitter trial, and with the aid of their lawyer, the powerful Max Steuer, they were acquitted of any legal responsibility for the holocaust.

Frances Perkins, then a young social worker, and two decades later to be Secretary of Labor under President Franklin D. Roosevelt, was visiting in the neighborhood and saw the tragedy. She never forgot. Afterward, she told a reporter:

There was stricken consciousness of public guilt, and we all felt that we had been wrong, that something was wrong with that building which we had accepted, or the tragedy would never have happened. Moved by this sense of stricken guilt, we banded ourselves together to find a way by law to prevent this kind of disaster.

And so it was that the Factory Commission that sprang out of the ashes of the tragedy made an investigation that took four years to complete, four years of searching, of public hearings, of legislative formulations, of pressuring through the legislature the greatest battery of bills to prevent disasters and hardships affecting working people. . . . They did not die in vain, and we will never forget them.

The resulting New York factory laws came too late to save the shirtwaist girls, but they saved others. In their day, the laws ranked as models for the nation. Women pressed hard for their adoption. Indignation at the refusal of the courts to hold the Triangle owners guilty then took another form, and one that helped the suffragists. The cry rose that if acquittal of these men was the kind of justice that women could expect, it was time to step up the forces of rebellion and reform. Susan B. Anthony had felt the same way when, at her trial for illegal voting, the judge had brushed aside her plea and instructed the jury to find her guilty. The Triangle Fire case weighed more heavily on consciences, but the cry of protest among women had the veritable Anthony ring. With this terrible example as a weapon, women stirred up women; workers who had felt themselves submerged and disregarded found themselves heroines, courted in circles they had thought oblivious to their needs. They, in turn, partly out of gratitude and partly out of a growing perception of common interest, began to enlist in the suffrage struggle. By 1912, a few of them were marching in parades and working in the suffrage forces.

Exactly what it was about these parades that caught the imagination and made them popular, both with spectators and with marchers, the contemporary accounts do not attempt to say, but the records report the excitement they created. Perhaps it was women's appearance in such numbers that carried a new conviction. They came out of their homes, their offices, their factories, and for the first time made their plea visible. Parades had started as early as 1910. There is reason to believe that the first one was organized by Harriet Stanton Blatch's Equality League and the Collegiate Equal Suffrage League; the latter marched in the long skirts of the period, with academic gowns blowing loose, and mortar board hats skewered to long hair. That same year Mrs. James Lee Laidlaw of the Woman Suffrage Party organized a night parade, which she set marching up Fifth Avenue with red flares and Chinese lanterns. It attracted such a crowd that the women were encouraged to march again.

In 1911, on the first Sunday in May, a few of them enlisted their husbands. That time three thousand women and eighty-nine brave men marched up Fifth Avenue, the women in white and gold, handsome in the brilliant sunshine, the men a small minority. Jeers and hoots greeted the male handful. Facing an articulate wall of hostility, they set their jaws and marched straight ahead. "But don't you think for a moment," Ray Brown, who was one of them, wrote later, "that the forlorn little corporal's guard marching at the tail end of the first suffrage parade up Fifth Avenue didn't feel acutely every hostile taunt. It takes a good deal better man than I've met to face the mirth of a mob without some of it getting under his skin.

"Out in the middle of Fifth Avenue's width we felt a heap isolated; it even went farther than that . . . we felt ostracized. Tagging after the girls, that's what we were doing; and nobody would let us forget it. . . . unchaperoned, entirely surrounded by empty asphalt, with two or three hundred people earnestly cracking their larynxes calling us 'sis' or 'henpecked.' "

Some of the small corporal's guard took it even harder. One husky young redhead with football shoulders stepped out of his place among the marchers to deliver taunt for taunt. "Yes, laugh!" he roared at the sidewalk crowd. "How many of your wives have got jobs, and your mothers, and your sisters? What wages do they get? Don't you know why these women are marching? It's for better hours, and fairer wages for your own folks . . . and you stand there and jeer. Yes, it's funny, isn't it? Laugh! Laugh!" For a moment the crowd was silent, then they broke into loud applause. In the next parade the corporal's guard had grown in number, and while the onlookers still jeered, the tone was softer.

In 1912 a torchlight parade in New York enlisted ten thousand women to march in order to celebrate the addition of Kansas, Oregon, and Arizona to the suffrage states. This was led by handsome Inez Milholland, riding a white horse and followed by fifty young women dressed in white togas, blowing golden trumpets. Victory floats and chariots, each drawn by four white horses, were driven by women from the enfranchised West. Five thousand golden paper lanterns imported from Paris lit the pavement for them.

In 1913 there were forty thousand women marching.

These parades were large-scale productions. As Gertrude Brown remembered, they were planned a year in advance, the marchers organized and trained. "Banners and pennants were made by the thousands, captains and sergeants took their marchers to the armories where they were drilled by captains of the National Guards. It was a matter of pride to make a fine showing, not only of numbers, but of orderliness and discipline." The parades were headed by the handsomest women in the movement, and they started at the appointed minute.

On each corner, from the side streets, a special contingent, with its band, would wheel into line with military precision. There were squads of women on horseback. There were women who had no one at home with whom to leave the baby, and who pushed the baby carriage all the way. There were lovely young girls and women in fashionable clothes, others in well-worn garments. Mothers brought their young daughters, and daughters took care of old mothers. There were groups of women architects, typists, explorers, aviators, physicians, lawyers, nurses, painters, writers, editors, actresses, chauffeurs, real estate and insurance agents, decorators, teachers, farmers, milliners, dressmakers, librarians, even pilots, and the trade union girls . . . hat makers, shirtwaist makers and glove makers, laundry workers, all marching in military order to the music of many brass bands, Scotch pipers or women trumpeters. Multitudes of fluttering flags and pennants. Slogans in big letters, some of them gently satirical. "This comes of Teaching Girls to Read," one assured the onlookers, and another, "No Nation Can Rise Higher Than Its Women."

Nor was New York the only parade city. The fever spread to Boston and to Chicago, where on a bitter day of rain and wind the women staged a parade to coincide with the Republican National Convention. And to St. Louis, where delegates going from their hotels to the Democratic National Convention had to run the gauntlet of the "Walkless Parade," with women in white and gold lining the sidewalk on both sides of the street, suffrage banners held high, their challenging slogans gleaming in the sunshine. These suffragists had their share of wit and inventiveness as well as determination. Finally, the fever spread to Washington in 1913 on the day before Woodrow Wilson was to be inaugurated.

This Washington show was planned as a parade to end all parades. It was designed to persuade the nation's capital not only that women across the country wanted to vote, but that all kinds and classes of women wanted the vote. Its organization was entrusted to the Congressional Committee of the NAWSA, then headed by a new chairman. Alice Paul was a young Quaker with dramatic ideas who had spent three years in England learning the more extreme suffragette techniques. (She imported the term "suffragette" along with the techniques.) This was her first big show in the United States, but not her last. Preparations went on for weeks. A model of the Liberty Bell arrived from Philadelphia, a set of golden chariots from Baltimore; women farmers came in sunbonnets, university graduates in cap and gown, Mrs. Catt's Woman Suffrage Party in white with gay yellow sashes. Large groups from the International Woman Suffrage Alliance represented countries where women already had the vote.

Everything started on Capitol Hill with what had become the familiar suffrage precision, but when the paraders reached Pennsylvania Avenue they found the street blocked by a mob of jeering men. This sent a shock of surprise and indignation through the ranks. Jeering was not new to suffragists but here in the nation's capital they met for the first time with mass force and violence. They had police permits to hold the parade, but the police stood by making no attempt to restrain the mob. It seemed as though all the hoodlums in the country were massed for the specific purpose of breaking up the suffrage parade, and as though the police force were in league with them. The crowd crushed in, men and women fainted, and were crushed by the crowd. Ambulances fought their way through to reach the injured and take them out. Hospitals filled, cots lined the corridors. Finally, the U.S. Cavalry, summoned from Fort Myer, charged the crowds and restored order.

The reaction came swift and indignant. Favorite daughters told their stories at home and showed their bruises; angry fathers and husbands wrote their Congressman to demand the reason for such shabby treatment. Thus prodded, Senators roared their indignation and promised an investigation. No one admitted responsibility and everyone pointed to someone else. Suspicion gathered chiefly around the liquor industry, known to be pouring money into the opposition, capable of making its wishes clear to the local Washington government. The police repeated plaintively that every precaution had been taken. The facts were against them. The net result was an amount of advertising for the suffrage cause and of sympathy for the suffragists that no orderly parade could possibly have roused.

6. NEW YORK FOR SUFFRAGE —
A FORTUNE, A FIGHT,
AND A WAR

"Woman is a very curious people:
Maybe that is why she is so nice.
Never saw two alike any onetime,
Never saw one alike twice."

The news of the Washington parade and its aftermath of protest undoubtedly created additional sympathy for the suffrage cause in New York, but the tide was not yet ready to turn.

Suffrage forces had been divided before, but never in quite as spectacular a fashion. The old division between Boston and New York, with Lucy Stone and her American Suffrage Association on one side, and on the other Susan B. Anthony with the National Woman Suffrage Association that she and Elizabeth Cady Stanton had fashioned, had been sharp and at times bitter. It had not, however, done the suffrage cause measurable harm. This new break between moderates and extremists, suffragists and suffragettes was more dangerous.

At no time could the seventy years of the suffrage campaign be called a monolithic effort. Most of the time action came from a host of individual groups. Counties and towns had their own suffrage societies, tied loosely or not at all to a state organization. Neither of the early national organizations was ever more than an informal holding company, so to speak, co-ordinating campaigns as best they could, but always dependent on local enthusiasts. Not until the two national organizations merged in 1890 was there any possibility of co-ordinated effort.

Mrs. Catt had won for them a modest degree of unity that was beginning to show results, but not quickly enough for the extremist suffragettes. The latter group had its inception in England, where the radical young had, about 1910, become convinced that the polite petitions and ladylike speeches of the older suffragists were producing very little effect. The young rebels wanted results. Something must be done to stir the public and the politicians, something to dramatize the cause. A journalist, seeing how very young the new crusaders looked, dubbed them "suffragettes" (little suffragists) and the name stuck. It also invited publicity.

Under the leadership of Emmeline Pankhurst, a small and slender woman who hid a will of iron beneath a gentle voice, the new suffrage wing invented militant tactics. The young British rebels besieged the Prime Minister, harassed Parliament, cast themselves under the feet of police horses, courted arrest, and created riots when they got it. Jailed for disturbing the peace, they went on hunger strikes and threatened to starve themselves to death. Forcibly fed, their suffering faces aroused wide sympathy at home and in the United States, but no softening on the part of Parliament.

These British suffragettes attracted American followers, among them red-headed Alice Paul, and another young woman of good family who was blessed with swift grace, Miss Lucy Burns. It was these two who, back in the United States, met to talk with Dr. Anna Howard Shaw and to offer their services in persuading Congress to pass the Susan B. Anthony amendment.

The old leader was impressed with their beauty, their energy, and their determination. She persuaded the National American

Woman Suffrage Association to make Miss Paul the chairman of its Congressional Committee. It was in that post that the young firebrand and her friend decided that what Washington needed was a parade of the type that had been successful in New York, and offered to organize it. This was the 1913 parade that was mobbed and that stirred a flood of angry letters to Congress.

The amount of publicity this Washington spectacle attracted for suffrage and the praise that came to Miss Paul apparently convinced the ambitious leader that the bounds of the NAWSA were too narrow for her abilities. Still keeping her post as chairman of that organization's Congressional Committee, she set up a new Congressional Union on her own initiative. This was to have as its sole purpose a campaign to get through Congress the Anthony amendment, first proposed in 1878, and offered vainly every year since then.

In this new departure Miss Paul had Dr. Shaw's blessing, but not for long. Half a year after the Washington parade the Congressional union launched its own magazine, *The Suffragist:* this moved into direct competition with the venerated and official *Woman's Journal,* started long ago by Lucy Stone and actively supported by the NAWSA. That bit of insubordination, together with an insistence that the only proper policy for the suffrage forces was to besiege Congress, and combined with a tendency to mix the Congressional Committee funds of the NAWSA with those of Miss Paul's Congressional Union, aroused the older suffragists and alienated even the grandmotherly Dr. Shaw. After a thoroughly unpleasant series of meetings with the national board of the NAWSA Miss Paul was pried loose from her post as head of the organization's Congressional Committee. Mrs. Medill McCormick of Chicago was installed in her place. Lucy Burns resigned to follow Miss Paul.

The first effect of the break was to give the new Congressional Union complete freedom of action. In addition, it began to attract money. Mrs. O. H. P. Belmont loved action, publicity, excitement. Irked by the reluctance of the suffragists to take her seriously and give her sufficient credit, she joined the suffragettes and showered them with contributions. With Belmont gold to aid them, they plunged ahead with tremendous energy. By 1915 they were organizing suffrage groups in every state. In June of 1916 they held a meeting of delegates in Chicago and turned themselves into the Woman's Party (adapting the name from Mrs. Catt's powerful Woman Suffrage Party in New York); in this guise its members again pledged themselves to work solely for a national woman suffrage amendment. Toward that end they would campaign for whichever political party showed itself most friendly.

The more moderate and experienced suffragists were startled by this new competitive force. Lulled too long by the charm and the oratory of Dr. Anna Howard Shaw, they now found themselves in danger of losing what they considered their own cause, and with it their position as leaders of the suffrage movement. The public did not discriminate between two groups of women asking for the vote. They did not like women who screamed, and they tended to put all suffragists under that heading. Suffrage funds began falling off; suffrage workers demanded that the vigorous new competition be met by more energetic measures on the part of the older organization.

The result was a call for Mrs. Catt. She had been working hard and effectively in the New York campaign, but now she was persuaded that it was her duty to leave the work of that single state for the bigger (and in many minds the more important) job of putting the national organization into fighting form. Coming as this demand did on the eve of the 1915 state elections, it presented no easy decision for her. Nor was it an easy one for the New York suffragists. With considerable grief on both sides, the draft of the great leader was accepted. Mrs. Catt went to Washington, and Gertrude Foster Brown agreed to carry on the presidency of the New York State Suffrage Association.

Mrs. Catt, who when she was young had had her own moments of rebellion against the old and conservative elements, was wise enough in the beginning to recognize the values that the suffragettes, full of youthful energy and imagination, were bringing to the suffrage cause. She recognized in their "new broom" techniques a likeness to some that she herself had urged twenty years earlier. But while acknowledging the publicity value of this rebel action she also understood its perils. For a couple of years she and other leaders tried to persuade the militants to temper their tactics and to come back into the NAWSA fold. But the differences in temperament and ambition were too great. After a joint luncheon, held on April 2, 1917, to celebrate the election of Jeanette Rankin of Wyoming as the first woman in the House of Representatives, the two organizations went their separate ways. But this gets ahead of the story.

Whether or not Mrs. Catt's decision to accept the draft from the national organization at the very moment when the New York suffrage campaign of 1915 was coming to a head meant certain defeat for the New York suffragists is a question that was bitterly argued. She was chairman of an Empire State Campaign Committee, to which most of the local (and frequently warring) organizations adhered, thus putting their forces under her leadership. She had begun her work by advertising a campaign workers' school to be held in the Woman Suffrage Party headquarters in New York City. Expecting two or three dozen students, all New Yorkers, she got a hundred and fifty of them from eighteen different states. To these women she taught the reasons why the only sure way to get the vote was through a political campaign such as New York women were waging, what the techniques of such a campaign were, what challenges it offered, and what opportunities. She conveyed to them as much as she could of her own hard-won and thorough knowledge of the techniques of political maneuvering. With this went an abiding and inspiring sense of what their grandmothers had gone through in earlier suffrage campaigns, and how vital it was to continue until the vote was won.

That 1915 campaign in New York with its lines thus laid down before Mrs. Catt was drafted for national duty was a highly important one. It was also a good one, and well waged. Thorough, vivid, and picturesque, it included what were by now familiar techniques of popular appeal. It made many converts, but not enough. Neither the parades nor the street speaking from motor cars nor the hard work of Mrs. Catt's lieutenants stirred enough of the Irish, the Germans, or the Italians to get a majority vote for suffrage. It was no comfort that suffrage amendments in Massachusetts, New Jersey, and Pennsylvania also lost.

Mrs. Catt, who had come back to state headquarters for the actual voting day, conceded defeat at midnight. But word went out at once that the defeat was only temporary. Mrs. Norman deR. Whitehouse, one of her handsome workers who had headed the publicity subcommittee, gathered friends into her car. They toured the city announcing to election crowds that the second New York suffrage campaign would start within forty-eight hours. It did. In a mass meeting held two days later at Cooper Union the suffragists undertook to raise $100,000 toward the costs of the new campaign. When the checks and the cash were counted, the leaders found that they had raised $115,000.

Suffrage had taken on new dimensions. It was a far cry from the days when Susan B. Anthony arranged her own speaking tours, hired her own halls, collected with her own hands the slender offerings that would, she hoped, pay her modest expenses. The change had been slow and hard over the years. Financial help for campaigns had come mostly in pin-money lots—a dime here, a dollar there, the hoarded pennies of women who walked to work for a week or a month and gave to the cause what would have been their carfare. In the 1880's, a bequest of $50,000 was left by Eliza Eddy to Lucy Stone and Susan B. Anthony: part of this had paid for the publication of early volumes of the *History of Woman Suffrage*, a work which, for all its faults of commission and omission, is still a primary source of information as to what actually happened in all those years of effort. In the early 1900's, a fund of $60,000 was gathered by M. Carey Thomas, president of Bryn Mawr College, and her friend Mary Garrett, at the express urging of Susan B. Anthony. This was to make it possible for Dr. Anna Howard Shaw to give all her time to the presidency of the National American Woman Suffrage Association. Presidents had hitherto never been paid for their services, but Dr. Shaw had no income other than what she earned by preaching and lecturing. By 1904, the post had become a full-time job. The $60,000 was meant to last for five years. A thrifty woman, with long practice in personal economies, Dr. Shaw stretched it more than twice that far.

By 1916 suffrage costs and suffrage contributions were moving into the thousands. Then, on February 1, 1917, Mrs. Catt was handed a check for half a million dollars. This was the first installment of an inheritance left to her personally, for suffrage purposes, by an extraordinary woman who bore the then famous name of Mrs. Frank Leslie.

The story of the woman and the money is told in a report published in 1929 by the Leslie Woman Suffrage Commission (created by Mrs. Catt to receive and distribute the fund) when it finished doling out the funds in accordance with Mrs. Leslie's wish. This account begins with a picture taken in 1880 after her husband's death, showing Mrs. Leslie standing in a photographer's snowstorm. Her hour-glass figure is draped in ruffled black taffeta, her hands are hidden in a muff shaped like a black rose, her handsome face is topped by a Mary Stuart bonnet that supports a long mourning veil. A widow indubitably, but white ruching edges the hat, and a gaze resembling that of a startled fawn distracts attention from a remarkably firm chin.

Mrs. Leslie, so runs the tale, had shrunk from publicity since her husband's death, but a moment came when she consented to see both a photographer and a reporter. She told the latter that her husband had bidden her (presumably on his deathbed) to "go down and rescue the business, pay the creditors, and manage the establishment." This rather large order seems not to have daunted the widow. As she explained the situation, "the whole concern was in the hands of a receiver. The creditors were clamorous, and naturally they did not want a woman to have the management." To this the reporter made complimentary noises; Mrs. Leslie responded by announcing that she had just finished the accounts for her first year, and found "that the establishment has made $60,000 more in clear profit than it ever made in a year before, under any management." That firm chin, those intelligent eyes, were doing their work. The business was publishing, and its most famous product was *Leslie's Weekly*, which ranked as the *Time, Life, Look* of its day.

This handsome genius was a heroine straight out of the dime novels. Her birth in New Orleans and her family were shrouded in some mystery, but over the years her brains and her beauty had had the usual expansive effect. She rose out of poverty and acquired a succession of husbands. (Among them was a brother of Oscar Wilde.) The first substantial one was Ephraim J. Squier, an archaeologist and a man of some means, who became associated with the Leslie publications. His handsome young wife met Frank J. Leslie, the publisher, and was made fashion editor of the *Weekly*. The result, after a suitable interval, was a divorce. Mrs. Squier became Mrs. Frank Leslie.

She and her new husband seem to have enjoyed each other immensely. They traveled widely, they entertained lavishly, and Mrs. Leslie, who had a lush and vivid gift for writing, turned everything they did into literary grist for the Leslie magazines. The great public was delighted to be taken into her confidence on all sorts of human questions, including love and the problems that arise between men and women. The Leslie publications profited accordingly.

After her husband's death, and apparently at his request, she took legal steps to take his name, Frank Leslie, as her own, and she so signed herself. Twenty years later, when she retired from business, she invoked the name of a supposed Huguenot ancestor and called herself the Baroness de Bazus.

A friend, whom she named executor of her will, testified that by the time Mrs. Leslie died, "Through the world-wide circulation of her various publications, by her constant association with literati, by her own literary works and by her constant appearance before the public eye, she was probably the most talked of and most photographed woman in America. . . . She spoke several languages, and possessed more than usual mental attainments. . . . Few women were ever so well known."

It may be difficult today to see why a Victorian beauty possessed of such extraordinary attainments, a woman so popular and so glamourous, should have left her money to the leader of the suffrage cause. One can only assume that the barriers she met and largely surmounted during her working lifetime created in her a resolution to do away with them insofar as she could.

Power she loved, intelligence she had, and with these an exceptionally sane balance. This was no flighty Victoria Woodhull, but a beautiful and charming woman of proved intellectual and managerial ability, living in a period when those abilities were supposed to be confined to the male sex.

For whatever reasons, she did admire both Susan B. Anthony and Carrie Chapman Catt, she did during her active lifetime contribute an occasional hundred dollars to the suffrage fund, always with a personal note, and she did write Mrs. Catt in 1913 that "when I come to die you will find that, like yourself, I am interested in woman's advancement." To prove this, she left the bulk of her estate to Mrs. Catt in person, making her the residuary legatee, and laying on her this obligation: "It is my expectation and wish that she turn all of my residuary estate into cash, and apply the whole thereof as she shall think most advisable to the furtherance of the cause of Woman Suffrage. . . ."

Mrs. Frank Leslie, the self-styled Baroness de Bazus, died

September 19, 1914. A swarm of people who were or pretended to be relatives buzzed forward to claim her money. Two and a half years of legal infighting followed. Mrs. Catt refused to yield, and early in 1917 she received a check for $500,000, representing the first payment from the inheritance. Five days later a suitcase was delivered to her office, which contained a second payment. This came in the form of the famous Leslie jewels. Complete with tiara, they were poured in a glittering stream across her desk.

Mrs. Catt loved handsome clothes, preferably blue. She would have been less than human, much less than feminine, had she not lingered over the pool of precious stones. She called in her assistants to gloat with her over the fabulous pile, and one of them went so far as to perch the diamond tiara on Mrs. Catt's crisp white hair. But that was all. The glittering interlude was only a single bright moment in a busy day. The jewels went back into their cases and were sent immediately to be sold. The proceeds were added to the very welcome Leslie fund.

Meanwhile, Mrs. Catt, shrewd as well as wise, had taken steps to safeguard the fund in case she should be kicked by a horse or knocked down by a trolley car. She named a Leslie Woman Suffrage Commission, Inc., composed of suffrage friends in whose honesty and dispassionate judgment she had complete confidence, and to them she entrusted the burden of administering the Leslie funds in accordance with Mrs. Leslie's wishes. They received the equivalent of $977,875.02 in cash, jewels, securities, and real estate, a gift unprecedented in suffrage history.

The first expenditure took the form of contributions to the crucial second New York campaign, then shaping up. Ten thousand dollars went to the New York State campaign, fifteen thousand to the key campaign in New York City. The rest of the Leslie money was distributed over the next twelve years. Including the $25,000 given to the 1917 campaign in New York City and State, only $80,691.23 went to "State referenda and ratification campaigns, and to the National American Woman Suffrage

Association." For one thing the inheritance came late in the long fight. For another, the technique of money-raising for regular expenses in the states and in the national organization was so well embedded in suffrage practices that the Leslie Commission agreed not to disturb it with too much of Mrs. Leslie's money. On the other hand, the task of educating women in the duties of citizenship, of making sure that the *History of Woman Suffrage* was finished and properly distributed, of aiding suffrage ambitions in other countries—these were deemed proper goals, proper uses. The Bureau of Suffrage Education was, in twelve years, given $282,398. The League of Women Voters received $47,100 in its earliest years, and $116,180.97 was given to responsible representatives of the International Woman Suffrage Alliance. The whole record of receipts and disbursements would be set down and published after the Leslie Commission held its last meeting on July 17, 1929.

In spite of that golden shower the year 1917 proved a very difficult one for the suffrage forces. They went from high expectations in February to the depths of despair in April, when Congress voted the United States into World War I (the only woman member Jeannette Rankin, Congresswoman from Wyoming, voted "No," weeping as she did so) and then to elation in November, when New York State voted an amendment to its constitution that gave New York women the vote.

During all this period decisions had to be made that tested the caliber of suffrage leadership. The first question after the April vote for war was whether or not the women would give up their work for suffrage and devote all their time, money, and attention to war needs. Their campaigns had been doing very well and they thought they could see victory just over the horizon. Twelve states had by this time yielded (Montana and Nevada in 1914), and given their woman citizens the right to vote in some form, national, state, local or all three. Sentiment in Congress was swinging their way, and they could not in honor withdraw or desert their amendment. Yet the nation was at war. Could they, as an organization, disregard the war and continue to campaign for the vote? After long discussion and in the face of much heavy criticism they decided to continue their work for suffrage and at the same time engage in work work.

This decision widened the split between suffragists and suffragettes. The suffragettes determined to focus solely on the vote. They began by picketing the White House, at first standing silent at the gates, so politely that in the beginning President Wilson raised his hat to them as he went by. Soon their continued presence and their challenging banners began to irritate the public. As war sentiment mounted, riots flared around them. The pickets were arrested and jailed. For Alice Paul, who had been jailed years earlier in Britain, this was the way to martyrdom and the front page, but for her less experienced followers, many of them Quakers of good families, the conditions in the Occoquan workhouse in Virginia where they were sent to serve their sentences must have seemed appalling. These conditions and the ensuing hunger strike got them ample attention in the press.

The suffragists were disapproving, and annoyed by what they considered an unwarranted and violent bid for publicity. The suffragettes were unrepentant and persistent. They chained themselves to the iron fence around the White House and dared the police to cut them loose. They even went so far as to burn President Wilson in effigy; like the riots, this incited popular reproaches that were leveled against all suffragists rather than just against the exhibitionists.

Yet in the long run, who can say that this left-wing campaign of dramatic protest was a mistake or that it did, as was often claimed by the irritated right wing, "set the cause back"? That much-quoted statement of P. T. Barnum that "it doesn't matter what they say about us as long as they keep talking about us" was as true for suffrage as for circuses. The important thing was to keep the campaign before the public eye and the public mind.

Keep the mass of Americans from forgetting what was wanted, keep the voters and the politicians from sinking back into their old lethargy. This the spectacular campaign of the Woman's Party certainly did: irritating as Mrs. Catt's followers found it, they had reason to be grateful.

If it was the Illinois victory of 1913 that took suffrage forces eastward across the vital watershed of the Mississippi, it was the second New York State campaign in 1916-17, with its extra lift from the Leslie funds, that really pulled the long campaign over its hardest hills. It was not easy to isolate the effect of those funds, but Rose Young, who was press chairman for the suffragists as well as Mrs. Leslie's biographer, admitted dryly that "The campaign did fly faster from that date, and in November came a glorious victory . . . certainly to that triumph was due the speedy submission of the federal suffrage amendment two years later."

In the light of the hard work done in 1915, the result of the second campaign could hardly be called surprising. The only thing that made it seem so was that the suffrage workers were long accustomed to defeat. When the result of the vote was sure beyond any doubt, the women gathered in Carnegie Hall to celebrate. It was a particularly feminine celebration. No liquor, no long speeches, but with tears running down their faces all the women who could crowd into the hall stood and sang the Doxology. They were celebrating not only that single campaign but long years of grueling work, and they all knew it.

The 1917 vote was even more important for the country as a whole than for the State of New York. Up to that moment, votes for women had spread among the Western states but the Mississippi River was a wide moat cutting the movement off from the East until 1913. Then Illinois yielded reluctantly, and only in part, granting national suffrage, but reserving state votes for the uses of state politicians who knew how to handle their men. Early in that historic year of 1917, little Rhode Island had preceded New York as the first Atlantic Coast state to drop the bars and allow women to express their will at the polls—but only in presidential elections.

Nebraska, North Dakota, and Arkansas joined the 1917 procession. Now sixteen states (without New York) meant thirty-two prosuffrage Senators out of ninety-six in Washington. Of the sixteen, only Illinois was heavily populated, so that the suffrage bloc in the House of Representatives showed a smaller proportion than in the Senate. In a day when political power in the national sense rested with New York, Ohio, and Pennsylvania, the sixteen suffrage states had only eighty-four out of some four hundred and twenty representatives in Congress.

But when New York, so long besieged, so long paraded, so long talked to on street corners, in kitchens, parlors, lecture halls, high schools and auditoriums, ballrooms and barrooms, finally threw up its hands, the picture changed in proportion vastly more than sixteen plus one.

New York had forty-two representatives, all of them now bound to vote for the Anthony amendment when it came up in Congress. Also, all of them had friends in Congress from other states. The political weight of New York went far beyond the actual votes its representatives cast. It reached throughout the states on both sides of the Appalachians, it set the tone for 1920.

Meanwhile, the United States had gone to war. After long discussion the NAWSA decided to undertake a project that would both contribute to the war effort and make clear the abilities of women to play a worthy role in the world about them. Florence Nightingale of the Crimean War, Dorothea Dix and Clara Barton of the Civil War were their models. They would raise the funds needed to purchase and equip ambulance units that should be organized and trained by the New York Infirmary for Women and Children, and staffed by women doctors and nurses. The Unit would then be offered to the American Army, and sent wherever ordered. With the determination that had now become a suffragist habit they did this, only to learn that the Armed Forces of the United States had no desire for women's help. The high command was horrified at the idea of sending women to war in any capacity. The Red Cross did not agree, but sympathy with the suffrage demonstration was all they could offer. They had their own staff and their own equipment, needed no outsiders, and could not afford to become involved in an argument.

For a couple of weeks that seemed like a couple of years, the suffragists, with Gertrude Foster Brown as their representative in charge, were left with trained and equipped ambulance units staffed by women from drivers and mechanics to doctors, and no one to use them. Then word came that the French Army, to which these units had been offered after the Americans had refused their aid, would be delighted to accept them. The French were low in morale and materials; any new equipment of any kind seemed a gift from heaven, even though manned (and the verb is ironic) by women.

Once the French invitation reached Washington and was cleared, the suffrage ambulances with their staffs were loaded on a French ship and in February of 1918 were unloaded at Le Havre. What happened after that, Mrs. Brown reported to the convention of the National American Woman Suffrage Association meeting in St. Louis in March of 1919. The women, she said, had reached France in the midst of a German *putsch*, and two successive sets of villages to which they had been assigned were captured before they could go to work. One group under Dr. Caroline Finley was installed in Chateau Ognon, north of Senlis on the main road between Paris and Compiegne. Almost before their equipment was set up they found their quarters flooded with wounded: 630 men in 36 hours needed attention. That unit was hit three times by German bombs, once with severe loss of life; the bravery of nurses and doctors under fire won them the *Croix de Guerre*. As the war moved over France they were ordered to Metz and then to Cambrai to help deal with the mass of refugees.

Another unit under Dr. Alice Gregory was sent to Labouheyre, in the Department of the Landes, to run a twenty-five-bed hospital for refugees coming down from the battered northern regions. Later, a unit was trained and equipped to deal with the effects of poison gas; then in May of 1918 the women were asked by the French Service de Santé to organize a three-hundred-bed hospital for men who had been wounded in gas attacks. The suffrage ambulance groups also played an important part in restoring civilian morale. They set up dispensaries in Luneville, they organized a hospital in Nancy, they worked in the provincial capital of Soissons, which had been shelled and bombed first by one side and then by the other.

Much of the work of the ambulance units with civilians, for whom they set up clinics to help sick women, injured children, starving babies, lasted long after the war ended. From the beginning the American women had worked with French liaison aides. One of these, a professor's vivid daughter named Charlotte Pressoir, persuaded one of the ambulance captains to come in December, 1918, to her own village of Acy-le-Haut. This is a hilltop town between Soissons and Rheims, a small settlement mediaeval in shape, looking from a distance like a single castle. Because of the way the land lies in the valley of the Aisne the village is a natural strong point for defenders, a natural target for any invading army's land-based guns. It had been shelled, half destroyed, and rebuilt in its traditional shape in 1870. Between 1914 and 1918 it had been battered almost to its foundations by the great guns that moved back and forth along the Chemin des Dames on the other side of the valley.

Christmas, 1918. The two hundred fifty residents of little Acy were making their way back from parts of France where they had taken shelter. For the sake of the village and its morale there had to be a celebration—but where? The gray old stone church with its candle-snuffer tower had been hit too many times to be safe;

the *Mairie* was battered. Finally the women of the ambulance unit were shown a farm yard with a big stone sheepfold that had enough of its roof intact to provide shelter. This they seized on as a proper place to celebrate Christmas. The village was invited to come there and sing Christmas songs with the Americans.

First a tree had to be dressed, and where, in that landscape shattered by shell fire, could be found a whole green tree? Not finding it, they made one, out of branches lashed together. And there must be decorations. This was a country that war had devastated; supplies were very scarce. The ambulance girls wheedled a supply of popcorn from an American Army mess sergeant who had a kind heart and no objection at all to women. Then they built a small fire, popped the corn, strung it on thread, and looped the long white strands around the tree.

Certainly there had to be presents, not for the adults, but for every child. There were no toys to be had in Rheims or Soissons or Laon. The population, half starving, was rich only in victory and hope, which are hardly satisfying for children. The ambulance girls took all their own rationed chocolate, added all they could get from the Army mess sergeant. Somehow they found sugar, somehow they made fudge over small fires, shaped it and tied it in bits of bright paper cut from medical supply packages. Somehow they made a winged angel out of gauze and cotton, and fastened it firmly at the tree's top. Somehow they gathered candle bits, very precious in those lightless days, to light their fete.

The girls had learned to sing "*Noel*" in French, and "*Frère Jacques,*" which is not a Christmas song but will do as an expression of friendliness. As they started singing the line of little children started coming, so painfully patched and scrubbed and shy, little human scraps, born and kept alive in war, hidden in caves, taught to fear light lest the enemy find them. And as they came into the candlelight of the shadowed sheepfold, heard the voices and saw the tree, a little moan ran through them, of pleasure, and pain, and disbelief. For a moment the song broke.

Who could sing in the face of these children? Their short lives had known no Christmases, no presents. They had to be urged to move forward and take the small but precious sacks of candies. It was in very truth their first Christmas, and no one who was there could ever forget it.

The ambulance units did many other things—set up a permanent hospital for women and children in Reims, established clinics, trained French civilian aides, formed friendships that lasted for a lifetime.

In retrospect, and measured by modern costs, their funds seem incredibly small. They had raised only $114,486.50 when Mrs. Brown came back to make her report to the suffrage convention. Yet out of this they had not only provided seventy-four doctors and the necessary complement of nurses, aides, drivers, and plumbers, but they had proved that women could fill a brave, honorable, and useful place even in the world of war. They had won the high regard of the grateful French and had inspired second thoughts among their own countrymen as to the emerging value of women in the working world.

Compared to the much more considerable work of women in the Armed Forces during the Second World War, this pilot project in the first war appears as a small effort, but as an element in the long campaign to get the vote for women its attention value was out of all proportion to its size. Women had come out of sheltered homes to demand the vote on public platforms, they had organized meetings, sidewalk speeches, great parades to dramatize their plea. They had shown themselves in the working garb of a multitude of occupations, they had set in motion political campaigns that caught the admiration of veteran politicians. But war? War was a man's job, and in the romantic tradition a man's glory. What could women do in that field? So they proved that women could doctor not only in maternity hospitals but in camps under battlefield conditions, that they could not only drive motored ambulances but mend them under fire, that they could even fathom the mysteries of plumbing. Then, with a sense of "mission accomplished," they came home to resume their different and still difficult battles for the right to vote.

What they found at home raised blood pressures and stirred these veterans to new activity. New York had been won for suffrage while they were away, and one by one other states were yielding, but the national amendment was still bogged down in Congress. This was no moment to rest on their war records. Indeed, those very records were under attack. In November, 1917, shortly after the Armistice was signed, Mrs. Catt reported to the Board of the National American Woman Suffrage Association that

The work of the past two years has been the most trying and difficult of my experience. All anti-suffragists in the country did their utmost to make the public believe that suffragists were traitors to their country since they did not lay down their work when the U.S.A. went to war. They had an extensive press bureau which advertised this theory from the Atlantic to the Pacific. It appeared in the most subtle way, in speeches, articles and all other means of spreading propaganda. . . . To have held the work in the middle of the road [supporting ambulance units abroad and working for suffrage at home] has been a . . . stupendous undertaking.

The special war session of Congress, which ran from April to October, 1917, had agreed to consider only war measures. But when the 65th Congress met in regular session on January 2, 1918, they would be free to consider other matters.

7· CLIMAX
AND
ANTICLIMAX

"In Tennessee whiskey and legislation go hand in hand, especially when controversial questions are urged."

Carrie Chapman Catt

The Amendment to the Constitution that was to give all American women the right to vote was a dry and precise measure containing only two articles and not an unnecessary word. When in 1878 Susan Anthony entrusted her amendment to Senator A. A. Sargent of California, it was meant to be the Sixteenth. Early that year he introduced it into the Senate, and until 1918 it was introduced into one Congress after another. In the early days it usually died in Committee. In 1887 it was debated on the floor of the Senate, but voted down; it did not reach that eminence again until 1914, when it was defeated. In 1915 the Anthony Amendment came to a vote in the House; it was defeated by a vote of 204 to 174.

Meanwhile a Sixteenth Amendment giving Congress the right to impose income taxes had been ratified in 1913 as a part of Woodrow Wilson's reform program. So had a Seventeenth Amendment whereby Senators were to be elected by the people instead of by the legislatures of their various states. The famous Eighteenth Amendment, which prohibited the "manufacture, sale, or transportation of intoxicating liquors," was passed by Congress in 1917 and declared in effect in 1920.

The progress of the Anthony Amendment, once it began to move through the Congressional machinery, was a combination of high drama and grudging anticlimax. In 1914 it was brought out of Committee and taken to a vote on the floor of the Senate. In 1915 it achieved for the first time a similar distinction on the floor of the House. From then on it became a subject of active and acrimonious dispute. The story of its repeated appearances on the floor of the Senate and the House, the oratory for and against it, the defeats, the reappearances, the lobbying and the lobbyists, from part of the legislative history of the United States—important in its unfolding, quickly forgotten when its end is achieved.

As the women learned their lessons in practical politics, so did some of the Congressmen. To block the suffrage amendment in appropriate committees of the House or the Senate (or both) was a simple game that had been carried on year after year. A freshman Congressman could play it as well as a veteran. The real trick was to get the measure out from behind the block and bring it to a vote. The women tried reason, persuasion, drama. None of them worked. Alice Paul's young Congressional Union in 1915 organized an automobile pilgrimage from San Francisco to Washington (automobiles were new, roads were poor; meetings were held in between changing tires and being pulled out of mud holes). They collected half a million signatures on a suffrage petition. The amendment was again blocked in the Rules Committee, the Judiciary Committee, the Woman Suffrage Committee of the House and Senate. The women were persistant, the Congressmen were unconvinced. The struggle became a political chess game that took time, wit, and patience on the part of devoted workers.

A major share of the credit for successful use of those virtues goes to the famous "fourfold plan" that Mrs. Catt had presented in

1916 to the Executive Committee of the NAWSA. This was, in the Catt fashion, a reasoned and logical blueprint for speeding the suffrage fight in the states and in Congress. The white-haired leader repeated what she had said before: that for too many years the suffrage forces had divided their energies, choosing to concentrate on state or on nation as suited the moment's need. The time had come, despite schisms within the suffrage forces and the looming threat that the country might become involved in the European struggle, to make a concerted drive on both the state and the national fronts.

Much of the responsibility for the campaign in Washington was placed on the shoulders of the National Association's Congressional Committee, which Mrs. Catt had originally organized and where Miss Paul had played cowbird in the nest. Now that that intransigent redhead was out and preoccupied with her own Congressional Union, the NAWSA Committee was to be enlarged and a house provided near the Capitol for its activities; Mrs. Maud Wood Park of Boston became its chairman.

Mrs. Park, even more than Mrs. Catt, was in her own person the perfect representative of the suffragist ideals. In training and appearance the approved model of a gentlewoman, she had a charmingly balanced figure and a serenely beautiful face. Her head was crowned by wide braids. Too much intelligence, perhaps, looked out of level eyes, but this she kept in check. Her voice was low, and the steel persistence that kept her at her ungrateful job was hidden under a velvet surface that children, suffragists, and Congressmen all felt they could trust.

She confesses in her memoirs that she was appalled when Mrs. Catt named her for the job, but her response was direct and unquestioning. She would do the best she could. It was to prove a very good best. She learned that a first duty was to call on all Senators in the hope of finding one or two who could be added to the slender number of suffrage friends. Senator Henry Cabot Lodge of Massachusetts seemed, to her Boston mind, a good man to start with. He was known to be typical of the unfriends. "You'll *never* get another state," he told the novice shrilly. "Look at your defeats in Massachusetts and New York and New Jersey and Pennsylvania last year. I tell you, you're done. Illinois is the only place east of the Mississippi where there will ever be women voting." Senator Lodge was a poor prophet, but as a leader of Senate opposition he was powerful.

Day after industrious day the new chairman and her NAWSA Congressional Committee worked to sort out the Senators and the Representatives, to get their attitudes and their prejudices clear, their friends and their hobbies carded, along with the pressures they could withstand and the ones they might accept. To keep the NAWSA aware of what was going on the Committee published a paper, which they called *Searchlight on Congress.* In the goldfish bowl of Washington these devoted, polite, and intelligent women began to attract attention as a new type of lobbyist. They were not looking for jobs or for financial gain. Their tactics were open, their appeals honest, their skill abundant. A friendly newspaperman dubbed them the Front Door Lobby.

From the women's point of view, to work in that lobby was a thorough education in the political machinery and the convolutions of the American Congress. The goal was to muster a two-thirds majority of the votes in the House and in the Senate in favor of whatever bill was introduced for the passage of the Anthony Amendment. There were at that time 435 members in the house, 96 in the Senate. If the full membership was present the women must have 290 sure "yeas" in the House, 64 in the Senate.

The tallies that the lobby made from time to time tell part of the story. The Senate was the more obdurate body, the House, elected anew each two years, the more responsive to changes in political climates. In February, 1917, the tally showed this probable picture in the House if the amendment were brought to a vote: 182 yeas, 178 nays, 75 doubtful. On November 30, 1917, after the New York victory, 195 yeas, 163 nays, 77 doubtful. On January 1, 1918, 245 yeas, 143 nays, 47 doubtful.

On January 3, 1918, the House Committee on Woman Suffrage started a four-day hearing on a joint suffrage resolution of House and Senate; Mrs. Catt and Dr. Shaw were to be the NAWSA chief speakers, Miss Paul would speak for her Woman's Party, and full time would be given the antisuffragists, who were to be represented principally by a former Senator, Joseph W. Bailey of Texas. Mr. Bailey was florid and gallant; he loved the ladies, but he loved oratory better. He lavished affectionate phrases on a description of the way in which a drop of ink fouls a glass of clean water, then he concluded that woman's pure nature (the glass of clean water) must not be sullied by casting a single vote (the drop of ink).

A week later the effectiveness of this argument was tested. On January 10, 1918, a joint resolution of House and Senate for woman suffrage came to the floor of the House for debate and a vote. The galleries were packed with friends and foes. Tension was so thick that it seemed palpable. Enemies abounded, friends were ill and absent. One man was held up by a train wreck, another was in the hospital and had sent no request to have his vote paired. A third had fallen on the ice and broken his shoulder, but ordered himself carried in on a stretcher. A fourth had left his dying suffragist wife to come and vote for the cause she believed in.

Maud Wood Park, chairman of the Front Door Lobby, white with fatigue and excitement, counted 23 speeches in favor of the suffrage resolution and 17 against. When the roll call began the buzz of excited comment was so loud that voices could not be surely heard, and all 435 names had to be called again. The final score was 274 in favor of the measure, 136 opposed. Most of the rest were paired. The joint resolution had passed by a single vote.

It was the first victory on the national stage that the women had ever won. Some of them tried to control tears of excitement and gratitude, some frankly wept. Outside the door of the House

Gallery a woman's voice rose—"Praise God from Whom All Blessings Flow." Others took it up, and the famous old hymn that had become the suffrage song of victory rolled through the House corridors.

Heartening though it was, this victory did not mean the end. A joint resolution of House and Senate, to be legal, must be passed by both Houses; the Senate would have none of this one yet. A year and a month passed before a suffrage resolution came to a vote in the obdurate upper house. That time the lobby's preliminary count was very close; in the year that had intervened six more states had voted for suffrage and were making their voices heard in Congress. President Wilson, who was in Paris at the Peace Conference, had been won over to such an extent that he not only cabled his support to the suffragists but also cabled certain friendly Senators his hope that they would vote favorably.

The glowing effect of this aid was somewhat dampened by tactics on the part of Miss Paul's group, which, having developed its own ideas about how to win friends and influence people, had chosen the day before the vote to hold a demonstration in one of Washington's public squares, where they proposed to burn President Wilson in effigy. (The police stopped them.)

The news of this tactless maneuver appeared in the newspapers on the morning when the Senate vote was scheduled. It did not move a single Senator to vote in favor of the suffrage amendment, but one or two who in the suffrage files had been marked "possible" declared themselves so disgusted with the demonstration that they would make doubly sure no woman should ever vote. That Senate vote was lost.

The 65th Congress went out of office on March 4. The 66th was called into special session on May 19. President Wilson, still in Paris, conveyed his message to Congress by cable, and in it recommended that the suffrage amendment be passed. The Senate was still sticky, but in the House new members had been elected, 117 of them, of whom many came from the new suffrage states. With unexampled speed woman suffrage was given first priority. The advocates of the bill made their speeches. Even Representative Nicholas Longworth of Ohio, who had stood in opposition long and wittily, turned his coat and announced that he was "now convinced that the time has come when we ought to give suffrage to the women of the country." He added (making the best of his necessity) that it "could only have been granted through the medium of the Republican Party."* The bill was passed 304 to 90.

The Senate again proved harder to convince. Like the House it had a crop of new members; there the Republicans were in power. Senator Borah of Idaho, Senator Wadsworth of New York, Senator Brundage of Connecticut led the still bitter opposition. But the final narrow vote went at long last to the women; it went exactly as the Front Door Lobby had happily tallied it in advance studies.

"The yeas are 56 and the nays are 25. A quorum being present and the joint resolution having received the affirmative vote of more than two thirds of the Senators present and voting it is declared to have passed the Senate in accordance with the Constitution of the United States."† So stated the president pro tempore of the Senate on June 4, 1919. He was "pro tem" because Vice-President Marshall who customarily occupied that post had never been converted to suffrage; this time the best he could do was to stay away from his Senate chair.

After forty-one years the Senate of the United States had finally passed the Susan B. Anthony amendment. Susan Anthony was dead. So was Lucy Stone, so were Lucretia and Lydia Mott, so was Elizabeth Cady Stanton. Celebration was left to the second generation of suffrage leaders and the third generation. But they had sung their praise to God at the moment a year earlier when the favorable House vote had first breached the long Congressional opposition. Now they rejoiced, but with the mental reservation

* Maud Wood Park, *Front Door Lobby*. Boston: Beacon Press, 160, p. 255.
† *Ibid.*, p. 360.

that there was still a job ahead: the dog's job of getting the amendment ratified by thirty-six state legislatures.

The Catt strategy of simultaneous effort at state and national levels had worked thus far. The national legislative body had yielded. Now the suffragists must go straight to the state legislatures.

The hope was, of course, that the legislatures of states in which women already had the vote would rally at once to the cry for ratification. Enthusiastic optimists even dared to hope that they would rally without being urged. But Carrie Chapman Catt had long been a realist. The federal amendment was passed by Congress on June 4, 1919. Telegrams went out at once from Mrs. Catt and Alice Paul, leaders respectively of the right and left wings (the National American Woman Suffrage Association and the Woman's Party), to the governors of the forty-eight states asking them to make sure that their state legislatures ratified the amendment. Illinois and Wisconsin, which had legislatures in session, and Michigan, which at once called a special session, ratified on June 10; Kansas was the fourth, then came Ohio; New York followed on June 16.

Then the response began to slow, in suffrage as well as in non-suffrage states. The tale of the thirty-six state conventions that ratified the suffrage bill between June 4, 1919, when the Senate voted to submit to the states the amendment that the House had passed sixteen months earlier, and August 18, 1920, when the last-ditch opposition crumpled in Nashville, where the legislature reluctantly made Tennessee the thirty-sixth state to ratify, is full of curious inconsistencies. If they prove anything, it is how small and awkward the local women's forces still were and how important were the state variants in this least monolithic of democracies.

Montana ratified on August 2; Wyoming, which had been first to give its women the vote, as far back as 1869, could not be hurried to confirm that action for the women of other states until more than half a year after Congress had acted. California did not act until November 1. Washington, a suffrage state since 1910, waited nine long months, until it became thirty-fifth on the list. It was a bad augury to have women who had won the vote in their own states remain indifferent to the national call or to prove themselves unable to move their own legislators. Apparently a consciousness of national responsibility developed in them very slowly.

The danger—and it was a real danger—was that if the essential thirty-sixth state could not be reached quickly and moved to agree, the long fight might be prolonged past all patience. (This is what would happen later, with the Child Labor amendment that has never been ratified.) When January, 1920, arrived, only twenty-two states were on the "yes" list. The opposition, almost as well organized by this time as were the crusaders, and intent on doing everything in their power to stave off what they called the "menace of woman suffrage" as long as possible, counted on holding twelve states in the solid South plus one in New England—Connecticut or Vermont. They lost Kentucky to the suffragists, and West Virginia, which in March of 1920 became the thirty-fourth state to ratify. The others in the South the antisuffragists held, and they held both New England states, if only by the fact that Governor Holcomb of Connecticut and Governor Clement of Vermont were known antisuffragists who had entered into a compact not to call their respective legislatures into the special sessions that would be needed.

When, in March of 1920, laggard Washington became the thirty-fifth state to ratify, Mrs. Catt called a council of war to decide which state still holding out should be the center of a final and decisive campaign. Meanwhile, opposition forces had tried to insist that amendments to the federal Constitution could not be ratified by state legislatures alone, but must also be subject by referendum to a review by the voters. This legal quibble went to the Supreme Court which, fortunately for suffragists, ruled on June 2, 1920, that referenda on Constitutional amendments were invalid, and that the Constitution itself had settled that question long since.

Coming after the affirmative action of the state of Washington, this decision left Connecticut, Vermont, and Tennessee as possible candidates for the honor of becoming the crucial thirty-sixth. The first two had refused to act, and continued to refuse. Tennessee had a referendum provision in its constitution that had seemed to make its action impossible, but this was now abrogated by the Supreme Court's June decision. Tennessee was a possibility, but an unwilling one. However, by this time the pressure from women wanting to get the long fight done and the ballot in hand was so great that the Wilson administration itself found it expedient to intervene. On June 24, 1920, the Department of Justice ruled that the Supreme Court's decision of June 2 made it possible for Governor Roberts of Tennessee to call a special session of the legislature to consider the suffrage amendment. President Wilson followed this at once with a telegram urging the Governor "very earnestly," and as a "real service to the party and to the Nation" to call such a session.

Caught between clashing political loyalties within the Democratic Party, Governor Roberts shrugged his shoulders, armed himself with three separate legal opinions (one from his own Attorney General) that ratification by special session would be legal, and called the session for August 9: this is a date which in Nashville brings tropic temperatures.

Despite the climatic handicaps (this was, of course, before the advent of air conditioning) suffrage leaders and suffrage opponents poured into the Hermitage Hotel in Nashville. Mrs. Catt arrived with an overnight bag in hand, expecting a short session. For once, her temperamental optimism had got the better of her judgment: she was kept there two weeks. For once, the National Association and the Woman's Party worked in reasonable harmony, a harmony made the more noticeable by the fact that in the antisuffrage forces appeared two former members of the National Association's

Board, Laura Clay and Kate Gordon, who had resigned to join the opposition on the issue of state's rights.

The antisuffrage forces included a strange assortment of people from every Southern state and many states in the East. Some of them were honest opponents: others, predicting dire fate for any legislator who dared to vote for suffrage, were there to buy votes with money or whiskey. Scenes more riotous than any suffragists had ever witnessed raged in the hotel lobbies and the corridors.

The first polls of the legislature showed enough votes in favor of ratification to win in the House, but then Mrs. Catt and her aides watched these votes begin to melt away "under a barrage of threats and actions whose blatancy could hardly be paralleled. Legislators who had expressed favorable sentiments toward woman suffrage were threatened with the ruin of their business and political careers, some were all but kidnaped, and they were all systematically plied with liquor." On the night before the session was to open, Mrs. Catt saw the state's lawmakers, both suffrage and antisuffrage men, "reeling through the halls in a state of advanced intoxication—a sight no suffragist had before witnessed in the sixty years of suffrage struggle. . . . The legislature was drunk!"

Next morning the Senators were sober enough to pass the ratification measure by a vote of 25 to 4, but then it went to the House. There the opposition forces invoked "every caveman's prejudice," including what Mrs. Catt called "Negrophobia." Groups that the shocked suffrage leader identified as liquor, railroad, and manufacturing lobbies were spending sums of money which, in retrospect, can only be considered as compliments to the strength and moral purpose of the women's vote.

Thanks in part to the argument from the Democratic high command that the Party would be held responsible by the country if Tennessee failed to ratify, the bill finally passed by the hairline vote of 49 to 47. The last two "ayes" came in a stillness so profound that one could almost hear the turn of a head. The first of them was cast by Harry Burn, twenty-four years old, youngest member of the legislature, and the son of a farm woman who had written him, "Vote for suffrage, and don't keep them in doubt." The last affirmative vote, averting a possible tie, came from a personal friend of the Governor who had been expected by the suffragists to vote "No."

What followed was pure political melodrama. Thirty-eight members of the losing minority, determined to exploit that near defeat and to bring up the measure for a reconsideration that might reverse the legislature's decision, were persuaded to cross the state line into Alabama. Here they hoped to prevent a quorum until they could rally their forces and undermine the majority. The move, promptly ruled illegal, failed.

These legislative twistings and turnings help to explain why Secretary of State Bainbridge Colby, having been told that his office had received an official copy of the ratification document at 4:00 A.M. on August 26 and sent it to the legal branch to make sure it was correct, would think it well to hold a private signing ceremony at 8:00 A.M. With the certified copy of Tennessee's ratification certificate before him, he put his official signature on an official Proclamation of the Woman Suffrage Amendment to the Federal Constitution. This was a notice to the public, made before any bright minds could think up another objection, that the final step had been taken.

The Anthony Amendment was now part of the law of the land. When Secretary Colby laid down his pen, the seventy-two-year-old fight was over. The women had won. The struggle that had begun in Seneca Falls in 1848 was ended in Washington in 1920. Twenty-six million women had been given the vote.

What happened next held to the suffrage pattern of a constant touch of anticlimax. With three of her lieutenants, Marjorie Schuler, Harriet Taylor Upton, and Charl Williams, Mrs. Catt hurried to Washington, hoping to see the final legal act with their own eyes. They arrived only a few hours after the official document representing Nashville's surrender had reached the State Department, and went at once to the big suffrage headquarters house on Rhode Island Avenue. Here they telephoned to Secretary Colby, who reported in a pleased voice that the vital paper had reached him, and he had already signed it.

The telephone receiver fell from Mrs. Catt's hand; almost in a Victorian swoon, she dropped back against the wall. Her companions simply looked at each other. Seventy-two years of work for the right to vote, and a thoroughly nasty struggle at the end. Then the vital document signed, without ceremony, and with no suffragist present to witness it.

Mrs. Catt, with Maud Wood Park and Helen Gardner, who had hoped to represent at the signing ceremony the thousands who had worked so hard and so faithfully, picked up their handbags and went down to the bulbous old State Department building on Pennsylvania Avenue. Here they could at least see with their own eyes the document that symbolized such mountains of effort, such arguments and wranglings, such insults, such staunch and indomitable spirits. The memories that lay closest to the surface were of those incredible last days and nights in Tennessee, in their experience the absolute nadir of political life. But these leaders were not women to brood over disgraceful scenes. They thanked Secretary Colby sincerely for his quick signing, then Mrs. Catt and Mrs. Gardner went to the White House to present their thanks to President Wilson for his support.

They found Mr. Wilson shrouded in a blanket, unable to rise from his chair. Physically an invalid, mentally he was a bitter and defeated man. He had lost the fight to get the United States into the League of Nations; his party was facing the probability of losing in the next election. Nevertheless, the old Democrat had lent a sustaining hand when the suffragists needed it most, and for that his visitors expressed deep gratitude.

Then they went back to New York to be greeted by brass bands at Pennsylvania Station, with Governor Alfred E. Smith, Senator Calder, and a huge group of cheering women, who welcomed them with arms full of blue and golden flowers. No anticlimax here, but a rapturous and abiding sense of victory. Escorted by a detachment of U.S. Marines, played up Fifth Avenue by the band of the 71st Regiment with flags flying, cheered by shouting citizens crowding the sidewalks, they led the last of the great suffrage parades in triumph up the center of New York City.

The whole country rang with enthusiastic congratulations. Bit by bit, admiration for the women's gallantry and persistence had grown, and as the Tennessee story was spread by newspaper men, indignation also grew. When the women's victory was certain, bells were set ringing in St. Louis, and whistles blowing. Men and women on Chicago streets added their cheers. Boston rang the church bells that had rung in 1776, and Massachusetts women with a sense of history swarmed to Faneuil Hall to celebrate this new political victory: their victory.

A ridiculous anticlimax followed in Nashville. The Tennessee legislators who had fled to Alabama drifted back to the capital, held a rump session, and passed a resolution rescinding the ratifying action of their soberer brothers. But the leaders of both parties took instant alarm. A Presidential election lay only three months ahead. Twenty-six million women of voting age had been enfranchised. By the mere fact of existing within the body politic they exerted far more political pressure than did a drunken group of die-hards fumbling in a moonshine state. William Howard Taft, Republican, the Chief Justice of the Supreme Court of the United States, thundered forth his comment that the rump session was a "disgraceful and anarchical method of opposing legitimate action," and that the Tennessee legislators involved are "willing by a scaly trick to involve the country in dangerous uncertainty as to the result of a presidential election."

Fortunately, it was not necessary to corner the cave dwellers and make them retract. The state of Connecticut, where legislators were believed eager to ratify but could do so only when a governor, previously unconvinced, called a special session, was at long last spurred into action. To make sure that no Tennessean dithering could be suspected of them, they ratified the Nineteenth Amendment three full times. Whether Tennessee or Connecticut may claim the honor of being the thirty-sixth state where ratification proceedings crowned seven decades of feminine striving for voting rights is a question that got lost in election clamor.

Such a story should end with rewards and honors, nationally bestowed. A woman like Carrie Chapman Catt, with her political genius and her long political experience, should at least have been made a Senator, a Cabinet member, or a chairman of one of the great national parties.

But it did not work out that way. The professional politicians who had watched the New York campaign and the final Congressional vote and ratification drive were, with mingled fear and admiration for this new force, ready to yield at least token posts. What was offered Mrs. Catt her biographer does not say, but Gertrude Foster Brown, who had led the New York State Suffrage Association in 1915, was invited to become New York State's Secretary of State. Pleased at the gesture, recognizing both the honor and the emptiness of the post, she refused with thanks, on the ground that she wanted to return to private life.

This may have been a major blunder. Mrs. Catt, moved by the same traditional reasoning, went back from the final ceremonies of rejoicing to her home, Juniper Ledge, in the Westchester County hills. There she announced that she would spend a year making jelly, canning fruit, planting trees, and working in her garden. She would soothe her soul with what had been the domestic tasks of her childhood. It was a dream filled with nostalgia, but the cost of it to women would be heavy.

The reasoning of both leaders was similar and understandable, but it nullified many of the arguments they had used so effectively. It is only fair to say for them that in the first place they were bone-tired, weary of the hard years of suffrage discipline, sick of the sight and sound of political maneuverings. As Mrs. Catt was to write three years afterward,

It is doubtful if any man, even among suffrage men, ever realized what the suffrage struggle came to mean for women before the end was allowed in America. How much time and patience, how much work, energy and aspiration, how much faith, how much hope, how much despair went into it. It leaves its mark on one, such a struggle. It fills the days and it rides the nights. Working, eating, drinking, sleeping, it is there.

In the second place, these leaders wanted to make it quite plain to their followers and associates and to the world that they had not undertaken the years of fighting for woman suffrage in the hope of personal gain for themselves. To profit individually by taking a political post, actual or nominal, seemed to them ignoble. They preferred to withdraw with honor from the political scene, to return to their own private lives and turn to other tasks that the winning of the vote made possible. It was a mid-Victorian, sentimental, highly feminine bit of reasoning. Noble if you like, but illusionary. Both of them had been spending years to get women out of that unrealistic domestic trap, yet in their triumph and their fatigue they fell straight into it.

There was a third element, which Mrs. Catt, rarely bitter, would make public in 1923 when her *Woman Suffrage and Politics* was published. American politics, she said, "was an age-long trap for woman's suffrage." She added, "Many men expressed disappointment that women did not at once enter the party campaigns with the same zeal and consecration they had shown in the struggle for the vote. These men forget that the dominant political parties blocked the normal progress of woman suffrage for half a century. The women remember."

To the shrewder of the professional politicans this attitude must have been, while puzzling, a signal for rejoicing. If this was the way the leaders of twenty-six million new voters were to behave, perhaps their followers would not be so difficult to control. Perhaps women, voters or not, were going to continue being women, and subject to all the masculine skills of management that for a moment they had seemed determined to set aside.

There had been an earlier signal. In 1919 the National American Woman Suffrage Association had formed the League of Women Voters. This new organization was, in suffragist minds, to have an educational mission. Members were to study political theory and fact, and in Mrs. Catt's words: "To finish the fight and to aid in the reconstruction of the nation." Or, as the constitution of the NAWSA put it, "To increase the effectiveness of women's votes in furthering better government."

Education, reform, these women would support as wielders of the dearly bought vote. But *not* as active political figures, *not* as active participants in party government; rather as studious observers from the sidelines, as objective critics. It is arguable that this was perhaps a great mistake. This was the threshold into reality that they failed to cross, and it was to cost women much of the power they thought they had won. Together with Mrs. Catt's unexpected glorification of domesticity, it was a strange omen for the future.

8. WHAT THEY WON
—AND WHAT
THEY LOST

"They've taken a notion to speak for themselves,
  And are wielding the tongue and the pen;
 They've mounted the rostrum, the termagent elves,
  And—oh horrid!—are talking to men!"
                                    Maria Weston Chapman (1806-1885)

The Nineteenth Amendment, which Susan herself had framed back in 1875, reads as follows:

1. The right of citizens of the United States to vote shall not be denied or abridged by the United States or by any State on account of sex.
2. Congress shall have the power to enforce this Article by appropriate legislation.

The language is definite and leaves no room for doubt or equivocation. Susan had learned hard lessons and had put them in precise words. Little was said, but since those words were chosen it had taken forty-five years to make them official. Much was hoped, but she who had started the amendment on its way did not live to see it made law. Nevertheless, she had known exactly what she wanted, and the first step was now completed.

In the passage of this Amendment by the Congress and its subsequent ratification by thirty-six states, the women of the United States won the right to vote in any kind of public election: local, county, state, or national. Or to put it in the negative form, they won the right never to be kept from voting on the ground that they were women, never to be publicly disgraced and punished for casting a ballot in an election as Susan B. Anthony had been, half a century earlier.

They had won the right to be people, political people, voting people in a democracy where government draws its strength from the consent of the governed. They could now give their consent officially, or withhold it. Their opinion had value. Henceforth they would legally be people in the eyes of the federal government as men were people; in the states, the federal government's word about voting rights set the legal pattern for even the most backward.

The women had won their long campaign for the ballot. At the same time, the brighter of them knew that the ballot was only the beginning. The vote was to them a tool. With it in hand, they could more effectively work for all the other points of equality. But they would have to work.

In the long battle women had won other gains. Most of them were better educated than their mothers had a chance to be. They had a better knowledge of government and how it functioned, an experienced skill in organization, a sense of feminine solidarity and of their power, as women and as citizens, to get what they wanted if they wanted it badly enough and worked for it hard enough. The years to come would tell how well they would remember and apply the lessons they had learned.

What tasks the newly won vote set for the suffragists was made quite clear in a book that the New York organization published in 1918, just after they had won the vote in that state. Gertrude Foster Brown, who wrote it, called it *Your Vote and How to Use*

It. Mrs. Catt provided a foreword in which she said gravely,

Citizenship has been very lightly regarded by our country in the past. It has been given to the immigrant without any ceremony, in the midst of the sordid surroundings of a local court-room; it has come to the boy of twenty-one without any special preparation on his part; it has often been bought and sold. It now remains for women to give it the importance it deserves. . . . The ballot should be regarded as a sacred trust. Every man and woman who grows up under the protection of our flag should feel the obligation to give of his and her best to make our democracy a better expression of our ideals.

In this simple primer its author said flatly that

there are certain problems of government today, and certain departments of politics, which have to do with things which are of special interest to women. The protection and care of human life has always been woman's great business in life. So a book on civics must include an outline of what the state is doing for its children, for its poor, for working women, for public health and recreation. In short, for the same things in government with which she is concerned in her individual capacity as a woman. . . . It is natural [Mrs. Brown went on] that men should have given the greater care in government to business and material affairs. To counter-balance this, woman's work and votes are needed for the human side.

But the way was not going to be easy. A few of the suffrage leaders remembered that the Negroes, too, had won legal equality, through the tortuous Fourteenth Amendment and the subequent Fifteenth that should not have been needed had the Fourteenth been less foggy. Yet the Southern states had effectively subverted the federal pattern and warded off any real equality for Negroes. Would women meet any such barrier? Black women surely would, not because they were women but because they were black. But if color had proved a bar that could outpower the law, how about sex? Would white women meet state barriers against voting, just because they were women?

There is no available evidence that many suffragists asked themselves that question then. No such depth of antiwoman sentiment existed which could be compared with anti-Negro sentiment.
Comparisons between the handicaps of color and those of sex
were not often made publicly; the younger women appeared un-
aware of the lessons that such comparisons might have offered.

What the leaders did ask each other was a set of different questions.

Given the kind of opposition that the Nineteenth Amendment
had generated, could it be possible that its enemies would not
rest content with Congressional passage and state ratification, but
would take the provision to the courts? Even before the ratification wrangle in Tennessee, Mrs. Catt, remembering the amount of
money that had been spent by the opposition and the kind of
pressures that had been used in attempts to defeat the Amendment, faced this question. To handle it, she gathered a long list
of decisions that had been rendered decades earlier when the
Fourteenth and Fifteenth amendments, also controversial and
bitterly fought, had been brought before the courts. These she took
to Charles Evans Hughes, a leading member of the New York bar
and an active political figure. She told the bearded lawyer that she
was expecting trouble, and she suggested that precedents established in the older struggle might be useful. She asked Mr. Hughes
to act as counsel for the suffragists if the Nineteenth Amendment
was attacked in the courts. Impressed by her foresight, her reasoning, and her research, the famous attorney agreed to accept the
Susan B. Anthony amendment as his client.

Mrs. Catt's apprehensions were to prove fully justified. Once
ratification was completed, the antisuffrage forces did turn to the
courts. First they brought a test case in Maryland in which they
tried to blot the names of two women out of the registration books
on the ground that they were there illegally. The court ruled that,
on the contrary, the passage of the Nineteenth Amendment had

rendered those names legal on the books, as elsewhere. The case went to the Court of Appeals where the ruling of the lower court was upheld. Then another case was filed and appealed. Again the suffragists won. For two years the antisuffragists kept the Amendment in litigation; for two years Mrs. Catt and her counsel Mr. Hughes watched over its fate. At last two cases were carried up to the Supreme Court of the United States. The second decision came down in February, 1922. In both decisions the Amendment was clearly sustained at the highest possible level. Only then did direct opposition fade. The attackers cut their losses and sought more subtle means.

Collateral gains made themselves felt slowly. For the time being most of the suffragists felt the effect of a sure victory as one of enormous personal relief. It was as though a tight corset that had previously enclosed the entire body of women now had its stays cut open; the bodies of all of them could now expand to their natural shapes. Mrs. Catt allowed herself a year's holiday, though her definition of a holiday included speeches and an enormous correspondence. Auburn-haired Alice Paul, mesmerist of the Woman's Party, said years later that to her the Amendment was like a loosing of chains (she had been among those who had chained themselves to the White House fence, which may explain the simile); once they were removed and the chafing healed, the victim ceased to remember how she had felt when she was still bound.

Women who were less articulate simply put away their suffrage leaflets, their banners, their speeches, their lists of people to be argued with; they hung hammocks on the front porch and set about getting reacquainted with their families. Local headquarters of the National American Woman Suffrage Association were closed, official papers were sorted and offered to the Smithsonian Institution, to the Library of Congress, the New York Public Library. Housewives who had achieved a sense of political responsibility joined the local League of Women Voters, then went home and cleaned out the attic. Working women, professional women could now turn their full attention to jobs, careers, purposes from which they had been diverted to help with the suffrage campaign. The campaign was ended.

The fervor, however, would be a long time dying. For a while there were anniversary celebrations and anniversary measurings of what the vote had or had not accomplished. Like war veterans, the women reached back for the companions with whom they had worked, but who were now being swept into other channels by other demands. Memories of the fight stayed vivid. Even now, forty-odd years later, newspaper death notices still describe certain women as famous figures in the long suffrage fight. Bloodless it may have been but victims it had surely had, and now it had veterans. It was a war, it was a victory.

Mrs. Catt was already planning future work, but for the moment she was willing to bask, and to let her followers bask, in the glow of achievement. Her speech to the victory celebrants in New York City emphasized the emotional quality of the struggle, the sense of comradeship it had created within the women themselves, the responsibilities and the opportunities that had come with victory. "For many years," she said to them, "we have marched up the long hill together, you and I. Now we will all go our separate ways, holding in our hearts tender memories of our comrades in the great war. I have lived to realize the great dream of my life—the enfranchisement of women. We are no longer petitioners, we are not wards of the nation, but free and equal citizens." The applause was deafening, and honest tears of joy came with it.

Certain collateral gains—that feeling of ability in public affairs, that sense of feminine solidarity, those organizational and political skills that the suffrage fight left with its participants as a legacy— took tangible shape in the form of the League of Women Voters and in the establishment of Women's City Clubs in many places, including New York. The League was, of course, the deliberately created heiress of the National American Woman Suffrage Association. It was brought into being at St. Louis in March of 1919, when the old organization held a Jubilee Convention that was expected to be its last, and it was baptized in 1920 at its first convention, held jointly with the final one of the suffrage association. The Women's City Clubs were more individual and set up by local groups eager to bring local government nearer to their ideal. Some of them are still active; others were to die in the financial pinch of the depression that lay ahead.

The League was the dream and, to a considerable extent, the creation of Carrie Chapman Catt, who combined many of the instincts of a military commander with those of a first-rate civilian administrator. She had analyzed the strengths and the weaknesses of her followers too well to have any illusions about the likelihood that they could hold to an agreed course of action in a field so unaccustomed for women as was politics unless they had a sound and active organization to furnish them with programs, support, and continuity. She had built the scattered and frequently warring suffrage forces into an organization that for skill and efficiency had not been matched among women's voluntary groups. Like hundreds who recognized its peculiar virtues, she could not bear to see the members become scattered and ineffective the moment the vote was won. Trained women now had the vote. They would now get at the long-planned reforms. Outside the suffrage forces, the ignorance of the untrained concerning the duties expected of a citizen in this democracy was little short of abysmal. There would be action; there must also be education.

Mrs. Catt had therefore proposed in her opening speech at St. Louis that the NAWSA found a League of Women Voters to "finish the fight," and that they then "use their new freedom to make the country safer for their children and their children's children." She had urged a program of nonpartisan political leadership and education, with an expansion of the suffrage schools for citizenship that had been important factors in the fight for the vote and could be even more important in training new citizens. She hoped that the new League would avoid both religious and race bias, that it would work to free women from whatever legal discriminations against them still remained in state and national laws, that it would aid the women of other countries to obtain equal rights. Nor were women to be the only benefactors of League effort. A determined fight against "the world's oldest enemy, corrupt reaction" in government was to infuse its efforts with new energy.

The essence of the League, its pride and at times its stumbling block, lay in that word "nonpartisan." To work for political purposes outside the political parties was a new and revolutionary idea. It startled some of the suffragists who, having worked with or against political parties during the suffrage fight, had taken them for granted as the mechanisms that made political action possible. It shocked the parties which, though notably lagging in their support of suffragists, had assumed that they would reap the benefit of the woman's vote as soon as the women got it. When the argument for and against the League's involvement with parties raged hottest, Mrs. Catt, sitting in the role of Solomon, said firmly,

There are two kinds of partisanship: one kind has led the world onward, the other kind blinds the sight and paralyzes the judgment. In the League of Women Voters we have an anomaly; we are going to be a semi-political body. We want political things, we want legislation, so we are going to educate for citizenship. We have to be non-partisan and all-partisan. Democrats from Alabama and Republicans from New Hampshire must work for the same things.

She encouraged women as individuals to join the party of their individual choice, while in their work within the League they would take no party stand.

This was in the minds of many an ambivalent, not to say a schizophrenic attitude. It has brought down on the League wave after wave of criticism from disappointed politicians who wanted to organize all women for their own purposes. It lost the League many potential members. At the same time, it has proved to be a continuing source of League power and a source of strength to the parties insofar as they profit from League training of women who choose to work as party members. Whether it has redounded to the political credit of women is still a question. By and large their record in politics is not yet recognized as notable. How much of this failure, if failure it is, can be laid at the door of the suffragist disillusion with parties, of Mrs. Catt's consequent insistence on making the League nonpartisan, is still a question.

Realist that she was, Mrs. Catt suggested a five-year trial of the new organization. The League has now gone on for more than forty years, sometimes flourishing, sometimes feeble, but always with an enviable reputation for educating new voters as they come along, for taking hold of grubby local problems as well as glamorous wider ones, for training its people to think and to act as citizens who are both intelligent and concerned.

The experience that active suffragists had gained in handling themselves in public, knowledge of the practical side of American politics including its grimier aspects, self-confidence on platforms, skill in analyzing situations and deftness in running meetings were to prove useful tools in many other organizations. They represented woman's new maturity. Thanks to better education and a wider experience, she had moved a long step in advance of the sewing circle, the church missionary societies, the Browning societies of the nineteenth century. She could now play an honorable and useful part in the Citizen's Union, the Foreign Policy Association, the International Institute of Education, and scores of voluntary organizations yet to come.

Women who had engaged in the long battle for the vote had gone through an extensive if informal educational process in facing the actual world. Beginning as strictly private individuals, they had learned how to conduct themselves in public meetings, how to speak on public platforms, how to lead conferences, how to handle discussions, how to persuade, and how to order. They studied Robert's *Rules of Order* by day and some of them slept with it under their pillows at night, hoping that its recommended processes would seep into their unaccustomed minds by a kind of osmosis. (By 1962 those who lived in New York would have the booklet printed in Spanish, to serve the incoming Puerto Ricans.) Many of them had, over the years, become crisp, businesslike, and efficient women who knew all about local, state, and national conditions, the need for better labor laws, for better education and better working conditions for their fellow women and for their children.

It is arguable that the long struggle for suffrage was in itself a valuable education, that if the vote had been won with more ease and less struggle the women would not have emerged from the long campaign so ready to meet the challenges they found awaiting them. Experts now watching women of emerging nations who get the vote painlessly note that they tend to lack both the zest for it and any knowledge of its uses and possibilities.

Yet a seventy-year stretch of work is long. If the women were inherently as able as they showed themselves in the latter years of the suffrage fight, why did victory come so slowly? What were the forces that opposed them? And in the long run, was the long fight worth the doing? Was what they won worth the pain of winning?

It is forty-odd years since women began legal voting in this country, and some of the answers to those questions are still tentative. One can say with a fair degree of certainty that the fight was so long in part because the women were slow in pinpointing their goals and agreeing on procedures, in part because the enemies were formidable. The latter changed with the years.

In the early days the strongest opposition forces were laws that had come down from Blackstone's code, inherited custom, and the long habit of assuming that the proper place of a good woman was solely in the home. Women's attitude was in those days moral. Their understanding of political power grew with the crosscurrents of the Civil War; with it grew their ambition. Once the Negro was given the vote, they were told to wait for their own citizenship rights a little longer. This time they rebelled, and in 1878 Susan B.

Anthony started on her single-minded campaign for woman suffrage.

Within the suffrage forces ambition and honest difference of opinion on strategy and tactics proved repeatedly divisive. The split between those who favored state campaigns and those who were sure that concentration on a federal amendment was the way to suffrage salvation runs through the whole fabric, from the days of Miss Anthony, Mrs. Stanton, and Miss Stone to the rival dominance of Mrs. Catt and Miss Paul. The suffragist-suffragette differences that followed, beginning in 1913 and lasting even past 1920, proved perhaps the bitterest of all.

Meanwhile, outside the suffrage ranks new and strange enemies rose up to combat the idea that women should have the vote. These were given a respectable public image by the organization of a group of avowed antisuffragists, ranging in type from Senator James Wadsworth of upper New York state to the society leader who always appeared with Parma violets pinned to her coat and hands clothed in white kid gloves. Senator Wadsworth set the tone for a whole group of conservative politicians whose ideas had been formed and hardened early. They were born in the Victorian era, they liked it, they intended to stay there, and to keep every one else there as long as they could. They had political and economic power and did not intend to share it with anybody, least of all their mothers, their wives, their sisters.

The general attitude of this group was well illustrated in a speech with which, on June 4, 1919, Senator Wadsworth opened the Senate hearing on the suffrage bill. First he attacked the tactics of the suffragists, saying that they had no "regard for the spirit of our institutions" and that to them "The Constitution of the United States means nothing more . . . than that it shall be used as a vehicle to pick up a set purpose." Then he moved to tie the fear of woman suffrage with fear of every other reform that was in the making. "We are whittling away the responsibility of the individual citizen. We are teaching more people every year that the Government owes them a living; we are teaching more people every year that the Government should and can do things which they as individual citizens can do for themselves; we are urging 'the easiest way.' " What this diatribe, which has gone on echoing in Republican oratory ever since, had to do with giving the vote to women is not quite clear, but that Senator Wadsworth was a dedicated and wily opponent he made abundantly plain.

As for the women applauding Mr. Wadsworth who belonged to antisuffragist organizations, they were a queer and mixed lot. The outer shell was composed of ladies who, for one reason or another, thought that women should not vote, and said so on every occasion. Many of them were illogical; more than one was an able and articulate woman who ran her home, her husband, and the lives of her friends with recognized skill, who should have been prime suffrage material. The antis argued, and many honestly believed, that suffrage would put an intolerable burden on women, already overworked in their homes and with the care of their children. It was true that there were then few washing machines, no dish-washers, no vacuum cleaners, that many women were almost literally tied to the black iron cookstoves of the day. But the more articulate antis were not in this position. Women of means, their households were adequately staffed, their white gloves immaculate when they appeared in public to bemoan the threat of overwork that suffrage offered to their poorer sisters; many of the poorer women would happily have left the black iron cookstove long enough to go into the voting booth if the law had let them.

When the antisuffragists decided to start a propaganda magazine called *The Woman Patriot*, they celebrated their first appearance with an editorial from that famous old publicity genius, Marse Henry Watterson of the Louisville *Courier-Journal*. Summoning his considerable skill in diatribe, Marse Henry blasted at the suffragists with his own version of the charges which by now had become traditional. "The soul of Susan B. Anthony" he asserted, "goes marching on toward the feminist goal of blatant infidelity, rejecting the religion of Christ and Him crucified . . . in favor of the heresies of Voltaire, Paine, and Ingersoll, along with the Free Love of Mary Wollstonecraft, Victoria Woodhull and Ellen Key. . . ."

Certain powerful friends and supporters of the antisuffragists were more dangerous than Marse Henry. As early as the first Kansas campaign the devoted suffrage workers had suspected the presence of powerful liquor interests, but could not prove this. Not until 1918 was the proof produced. Then a Senate Judiciary Committee, investigating charges of propaganda carried on for both German and Bolshevik interests by the organized brewers during World War I, turned up evidence of what had happened years before.* The files of Percy Andreac, publicity man for the brewers, included a letter claiming that the brewers were "in a position to establish channels of communication with the leaders of the anti-suffrage movement for our friends in any state where suffrage is an issue." In Nebraska, said a brewers' organizer, suffrage had been defeated in 1911 at tremendous expense. In Wisconsin they had met "women's suffrage in about six different forms . . . which were all defeated." In South Dakota, "So far . . . we have defeated women's suffrage at three different times." In Iowa, "We are of the opinion that woman's suffrage can be defeated, although we believe that the liquor interests should not be known as the contending force against this campaign." The Lieutenant Governor of Wisconsin told a leading suffragist that he had seen the brewers' lobbyist "sit in the gallery of the Senate and tell his man with his hands how to vote."

Backed by repeated evidence such as this, Mrs. Catt wrote bitterly about a

clever, insistent, reactionary minority that for years has controlled through the brewing and whiskey interests, through enormous contributions to both parties, through its purchase of votes and its absolute dictatorship over men in high places, the politics of the

*"Brewing and Liquor Interests, and German and Bolshevik Propaganda," Report and Hearings of the Subcommittee on the Judiciary, United States Senate, 65th Congress, 1st Session, volume I, p. 1032.

nation. This minority shows itself in railroad management, in the great cotton industries North and South, in the packers trust, in the U.S. Senate."*

However dubious their methods, the interest of the liquor people in opposing woman's suffrage was understandable. No business welcomes the existence of political power among its avowed enemies, and to give such power to enemies not yet possessed of it must have seemed to them madness. Susan B. Anthony made no secret of her aversion to alcohol; neither did Carrie Chapman Catt. Nor were they exceptional. In the minds of many nineteenth century American women there was no doubt (indeed there was ample proof) that liquor and sin went hand in hand. The common alcoholic drinks, in town and countryside, were beer and whiskey; the common drinkers frequently became riotous. Temperance advocates were advocates of quiet homes where the head of the house came home sober. They wanted to do away with alcohol in the name of the moral code, the gentle wife, the helpless children, and of American civilization in general.

It is therefore not surprising that in the minds of men who owned big breweries, who treasured the handsome horses that drew brewery wagons, who made whiskey in licensed distilleries or in unlicensed mountain stills, the women who sought the vote represented a threat to thirst, to business, and to profits. They would, or so the liquor men thought, extend the system of local licenses, dry up the states, dry the whole country if they could. They had done enough damage with Carrie Nation and the WCTU. Give them the vote and they would be twice as dangerous.

To a certain extent the liquor men were right. In a democracy any citizen is more powerful with a vote than without it. Yet it is ironic that the liquor industry continued to spend for the purpose of forestalling woman suffrage funds that might have been more

* Catt and Shuler, *Woman Suffrage and Politics; the Inner Story of the Suffrage Movement.* New York: Chas. Scribner's Sons, 1923.

effective against the passage of the Eighteenth Amendment directly forbidding "the manufacture, sale, or transportation of intoxicating liquor" within the United States. If the liquor barons had correctly assessed the growing strength of their avowed enemies, men as well as women, they might have wasted less effort on what proved, from their point of view, to be a side issue. But a curious blindness pervaded the whole affair. Mr. Charles Merz of *The New York Times*, writing in 1932 about "The Dry Decade," observed that the belief that the "women vote" brought in prohibition was so deep-seated as to amount to a dogma. The only factual basis he could find was the rather slim reasoning that in seven Western states that had adopted prohibition before 1917 women were voters; ergo, they must have brought it about.

The apparent alignment of other businessmen against the suffrage amendment was less comprehensible. Railroad men, cotton kings, the packers' trust had no direct reason to fear women who voted. Indeed there was every reason for cherishing them, if only in their role as customers.

The crux of the difficulty seems to have been that suffrage for women meant change, and change was always chancey. Senator Wadsworth's aversion to change was the voice of big business. He and his supporters liked none of the reforms that were in the air after 1900, not the new federal income tax, or direct election of U.S. Senators, or the creation of a Federal Trade Commission, a Federal Reserve System, a Tariff Commission; not a move toward antitrust legislation, or toward improvement in wages or conditions of labor. The industrial overlords liked the *status quo,* in which they knew how to make money, and they were against anyone or anything that threatened to change it.

Meanwhile, of course, the position of women in American economic life was changing, and with it their relationship to business, big and little. The industrial revolution that had, during the seven decades of the suffrage fight, transformed the United States from an agricultural country into one in which industry had gained a statistical lead, had brought millions of women out of their homes and into working and earning in factories and offices. Once out, they felt a new freedom. The suffrage campaign had, in point of fact, moved more slowly than the working revolution. The women won their civic rights after many of them had won their working rights.

None of these victories came without its costs. The women won —they also lost. It is not easy to separate losses that can be attributed to the eroding effect of the suffrage battles from those that would have come inevitably with the growth of factories, offices, communication facilities with their constant demand for malleable and disciplined help. Life changed, society changed, standards changed, and because the suffrage campaign had been so much emphasized, suffrage became the scapegoat that was blamed for all these changes.

In an earlier chapter it was observed that the fight for woman suffrage was essentially a middle-class battle, waged by women properly brought up according to the standards of their day, whether Victorian or Edwardian. The effect of suffrage, once won, went rippling through this social structure like a stone thrown into quiet water. It affected woman's political influence directly. Indirectly, it colored the esteem, or lack of it, in which she was generally held, it cost her small vestigial courtesies, certain political illusions, and most of all, the unquestioning reverence of the young.

Until she got the vote, woman's political influence like her influence in many other fields was indirect. She might be able to persuade men to pass a law or to elect a representative of her choice, or she might not. This indirect influence was highly praised by romantic novelists and by antisuffragists. It was thought to be woman's special gift, a dower bestowed on the weak.

Old status symbols proved remarkably resistant to change, but observers noted that the cherished word "lady" began to lose caste and become quaint. Meanwhile, the word "woman," which replaced it, took on a new set of illusions and started to develop new myths.

This is not to say that the suffrage leaders themselves desired such changes. Their own high ideals were as firm as was their distress when the next generation failed to live up to them. Let no one mistake their moral configuration: they were indubitably ladies, metaphorically as well as literally, and in parades they did ride white horses. They did think themselves engaged in a moral crusade, they did expect to raise the moral tone of politics from New York to San Francisco.

The word "moral," as they used it, had wide implications. If, as they thought, women possessed by nature a real "moral" superiority over men, this referred to a strict code of behavior. It upheld what was then known as the sanctity of marriage. It frowned on sex irregularities in any form. It frowned on gambling, on drunkenness, sometimes on smoking, on lying, bribery, and corruption, on pool rooms, and in some ultrastrict circles on dancing and card-playing.

That ladies did not indulge in any of these "vices" may have been a myth, but all through the campaign that myth had played an important part in suffrage thinking. Susan B. Anthony had been quite sure that there was a real moral difference between the sexes, and that superior virtues lay with the women; so had Carrie Chapman Catt; so, although a shade less volubly as became a younger woman, had Gertrude Foster Brown.

The changes of which these women were a moving part proved hard on them. After 1915 their belief in the moral superiority of women began to falter. Skirts that had swept the ground during the nineteenth century shrank upward. Ankles appeared. Women were pictured with a glass of wine in the hand, then with a cigarette. Even in matters as fundamental as sex relations there were changes, excused, perhaps, as exceptions, but admitted, however regretfully.

In the political field, the argument that dealt a hard blow to feminine claims to moral superiority went something like this: men knew politics to be a dirty game. If women now wanted to come down from their Victorian pedestals and engage in the dirt, the dust, the rabbit-punching of the political arena, perhaps they were not as untouchable as they had appeared. That they probably never had been was beside the point. It was a matter of symbols. For women to demand voting equality meant that the symbol goddess-on-a-pedestal was developing political clay feet. Perhaps, in the Irish phrase, she was "no better than she should be." Perhaps she could even be used in political bargaining, as men could be used.

If women newly become voters lost among the politicians a certain old-fashioned moral glamor, they themselves lost, as they ventured into the political world, a host of political illusions. Having spent years of hard, grinding effort in the attempt to raise the moral tone of politics, they were not prepared, as more of them made their way into the political arena, to find conditions none the better for their entry.

What they had had in mind was the older ideal of representative government in which they desired to play an honorable part. What they got was the right of entry into a political world where certain manifestations appalled them. That world was growing bigger, the power of the individual vote was shrinking (they themselves were cutting it in two) and becoming less personal. Some of them were convinced by their own experience that the fate of the country was being handed over to private business interests more interested in making money than in upholding abstract and noble aims. Mrs. Catt, who wrote *Woman Suffrage and Politics* after the fight for suffrage was over, described "those invisible influences that were controlling elections; that invincible and invisible power that for forty years kept suffragists waiting for the woman's hour: ... the power that made Republican leaders hesitate to fulfill their promises to early suffragists, that restrained both parties from endorsing woman suffrage."

But representative government in the older sense of the term was long gone and democratic government, with all its faults of commission and omission, was there for them to enter and take part in. Could they afford to shrink from it now that they had won a place in it?

If, with the ending of the fight, women lost certain political illusions and a ringing clarity of faith in democracy, they also lost certain psychic treasures, such as disinterested friendship and the sense of participation in a great crusade. Many of them, especially those who lived in sparse communities, had been very lonely people. For a while that loneliness had been warmed and illumined. Suffrage had given them friends, an inspiring cause to work for, a sense of participation in a movement larger than anything in their meager lives. When the long campaign ended, color and excitement departed. Many of the lonely ones, newly timid, went back to their loneliness. The impatient ones scattered.

For a while the sense of sisterhood held. Those who made their way into professions, or into business, or into social work or the labor union organizations could always be called on to give time or money or a vote for this reform or that if it roused echoes of suffrage ideals. Some of the suffrage leaders enlisted in organizations that were the immediate successors of the suffrage organizations: the League of Women Voters, the Conference on the Cause and Cure of War, the International Council of Women, the International Suffrage Alliance. Along with these there developed the great flock of women's voluntary organizations that still grows and gives women an outlet for their idealism as well as for their energies.

But none of these had the enduring quality of selfless devotion to high and unpopular purpose that infused the suffrage fight. They did not impel sacrifice or the willingness to suffer the stings of opposition. Socially approved, they did not inflict martyrdom, and martyrdom for a cherished cause has a heady quality that mere good works cannot supply.

The most serious loss, however, was the loss of the young. This was borne in on the suffragists very slowly. They had always been sure that they were working not only for their own right to vote, but for the rights and the welfare of future generations of women. And so they were, but the first of the future generations seemed little interested. Born and brought up during the last decades of the suffrage struggle, these young had also been brought up during the first World War. The loosening of standards that had been symbolized by those ladies of 1910 who ventured out to make speeches on street corners was followed by further loosening on the part of ladies who, in 1917 and 1918, went through the wartime shock of contact with soldiers whose ways they could not anticipate. Or as Dr. Kinsey would describe it a decade later, that was the exposure "of millions of American youths to cultures and people whose sex codes and practices differ greatly from those in which they had been reared."

Important as such confrontations might be, the suffragists' loss of the next generation was not solely oriented in war. Nor was it simply the usual healthy rebellion of the young against their parents. It also had in it an important factor of disappointment and disillusion. Suffragist mothers and aunts, swept into hyperbole by their own enthusiasms, had talked too high and promised too much. Too little of what they said would happen came true. The vote proved to be not the key to heaven, not even the key to a good, sure job. That it was a privilege the young admitted. More impressively, it was dinned into them as a duty, and in the roaring twenties duties were not what they sought.

The counterreaction of their elders was one of shock and disbelief. Was it for these pert flappers that they had campaigned the country, sacrificed their sleep, listened to endless legislative oratory, incurred the boredom if not the displeasure of their loving husbands? They could not understand why young women showed so little interest in their exploits and in the possibilities offered by the newly won position of women. They could not bring the picture into focus, could not admit, even to each other, that in their moments of high fervor and country-wide campaigning they had in fact had such a glorious time that they possessed no real claim to the thanks of children who had been left at home. They could not see that in the eyes of the young they had enjoyed all the fights and won all the victories; that what was left for the next

This careless acceptance of the long battle and the hard-won and potentially fruitful victory was a bitter blow to the older suffragists. They had assumed that victory would be followed not only by applause but by gratitude. They had seen independence and the right to vote in classic suffrage terms that would make it possible for women to reform political ways of which they disapproved. Or perhaps it is fairer to say that they were moving in the current of thought of their time, and honestly believed that a kind of earthly paradise was within reach if only a little more education could be dispensed, a little more sense of responsibility instilled. That this did not at the moment seem to be working out, and that the young apparently did not care, was a wound that did not heal.

Carrie Chapman Catt, long after she had seen suffrage victorious, said in private conversation that she was greatly disappointed that younger women were doing so little with the political rights so hardly gained for them. Gertrude Foster Brown went even further. She was railing one evening at the young females of the younger generation for whom she and her suffrage companions had done so much, and who showed so little sense of their obligations as new voters and new citizens. She mentioned their flagrant drinking of illegal cocktails, the freedom with which they smoked long cigarettes in longer holders, the shocking shortness of their skirts, the uncorseted abandon of their gymnastic contortions on the dance floor. She thought these flappers were a disgrace to the female sex, and she said so in no uncertain terms.

Stopping just long enough to catch a breath, she was startled to hear her husband say gently, "You did all this, you know. You wanted independence, you wanted rights. Now you've got 'em, and you can't complain if women don't choose to use them as you thought they would."

For a moment Aunt Gertrude sputtered; then there was a long silence.

"They will subdue politics to their hearts' desire, change it as men would never dream of changing it, wreck it savagely in the face of our masculine protest, and merrily rebuild it anew in the face of our despair."

Floyd Dell

On August 19, 1920, the women in only seventeen states had the right to vote. On August 20, the great change became legal. Three months later the women in all forty-eight states faced their first national elections.

This dramatic shift posed several questions, all of them widely debated. How many women would vote? Which candidate would they vote for? Could they cast a ballot without changing their minds and defacing it? Would they?

The candidates offered them were hardly inspiring. The Republican choice was Warren Gamaliel Harding of Warren, Ohio, a handsome, amiable politician who liked nothing better than sitting on his front porch and saluting the ladies. His Democratic opponent was James M. Cox, a somewhat livelier newspaper editor, but hardly better known. Most women had not heard much of either of them. Few saw any compelling reason to confer on either candidate their first precious vote.

Apparently the men had similar doubts, for although Harding and normalcy won by five million votes, less than half the potential voters had bothered to go to the polls. Newspapers tried to find out how the women had voted, whether it was the effect on them of Mr. Harding's handsome face that had won him the election. They got little satisfaction. The raw figures showed that whereas twenty-five million votes were cast in 1920, only seventeen and a half million had been cast in 1916, but that told very little. Once a ballot went into the box, who could tell whether John or Susie had put it there?

What could be told was the existence of a wide public apathy. National interest in the exercise of political choice by ballot had fallen to a state that sounded dangerously low. Suffragists felt apologetic about the women; at the same time, they asked each other what was the matter with the men. The League of Women Voters set up an extensive "get out the vote" campaign for 1924, including citizenship schools to teach the new women voters their balloting duties.

That year three candidates were running, Calvin Coolidge of Vermont and Massachusetts on the Republican ticket, John W. Davis of West Virginia and New York for the Democrats, and Robert La Follette of Wisconsin for a newly born and short-lived Progressive Party. Eager to stir up enthusiasm, to urge the country out of its passive attitude toward democratic rights, the women wrote, they talked, they did their best to persuade their fellow citizens, men as well as women, that if the Republic was to be maintained the casting of a ballot was a duty as well as a privilege.

Their efforts were poorly rewarded. The net gain in votes cast was just one per cent.

If the earnest new voters could not stir up what, in indignation and concern, they called the "slacker vote," they could at least do something about the places where votes were cast. Before the wartime prohibition act and the Eighteenth Amendment had gone into force it had been not uncommon for polling booths to be set in saloons. Now that liquor selling was illegal, they appeared in barber shops and poolrooms, and sometimes in speakeasies. Few of these were places that ladies could enter with ease. Suffragists asked earnestly that the polling places be cleaned up. Political leaders agreed without argument, and moved the voting process into schoolrooms, settlement houses, and other neutral places.

For years this housekeeping effort was almost the only political credit that women got. It became a journalistic cliché that the first effect (some said the only effect) of feminine voting was a clean polling place. However, the women were in fact busily at work on reforms that had been discussed and planned during the long suffrage fight.

Theirs was a very different world from the one Elizabeth Cady Stanton, Lucretia Mott, Susan B. Anthony had protested against. Vast changes had come, but inevitably. Yet they had had a tremendous effect. Between 1848 and 1920 gold had been discovered in California and silver exploited in Colorado. Indian wars had been ended; the whole vast stretch of Western territory had been settled and cut into states. A civil war had split the country in two, with a healing that was still incomplete. Only twenty-three million people lived here in 1848. By 1920 the population had more than quadrupled; the number of females had quintupled. Thirty million immigrants had brought with them more than numbers; new concepts of living and governing came with them from Eastern Europe and Asia. Only a handful of the girls had gone to college in 1848, whereas in 1920 some 238,000 were enrolled in institutions of higher learning; indeed, they made up almost half the college population.

They were better educated, they held more and better jobs. In the agricultural world of Seneca Falls so few women had occupied places in the paid working force that the census takers did not even bother to count them. By 1920, 8,636,512 women were working at paid jobs. That their working numbers had enormously increased may be attributed in part to forces outside their control. But if, as some say, they went into offices and factories like sheep, they did well there. No longer could a visiting Miss Martineau observe that American women of good family who must work could not, by custom, do anything but sew or teach school. Industry and commerce invited them in, the worlds of retail trade and communications found them useful, the telephone system discovered they were indispensable. They had made their way into medicine, the federal and state civil service, even into architecture, the law, and the ministry.

These invasions took problems with them and created other problems. On entering a working world made for and by men, the women found—not surprisingly—that conditions were better suited to males than to females. This was not only in detail, not only a matter of the kind of toilets and dressing rooms provided (or not provided), but also a concern or lack of it for the health and safety of women workers, the hours and circumstances of their labor, the relations with their bosses and with their fellow workers.

The suffragists and their friends in the labor movement and in academic circles concerned with labor were painfully aware of these discrepancies. Sophonisba Breckenridge writing in 1933 about *Women in the Twentieth Century*, cites a 1910 report that

brought out the facts with reference to the dependence of great numbers of families on the wage-paid labor of women and girls as well as of men and boys, which destroyed the myth of the pin-money girl, emphasized the bargaining disadvantage as compared with the employer under which women and girls sought employment, and made obvious the relative inequality between men and women as wage bargainers. . . . The results of this bargaining weakness manifested themself in excessively long hours, in frequent employment at night which rendered enormously difficult the maintenance of home standards and of sound family life, in lack of Saturday half-holidays or Sunday rest, in conditions of work less than decent or morally safe, and in wage scales inferior to those of men workers even where skill or professional equipment might characterize their work.

The struggle to modify man's working world so as to meet the needs of women became a vital part of the suffrage and postsuffrage fight. Other earnest reformers kept an eye on what was happening to the home and the children. Those thirty million immigrants had brought their children with them, and many of them were lost and awkward in this strange and chaotic new world. Their standards of child care were the standards of the organized old world into which they had been born. Crowding into city slums in the new country, lonely on wide farmlands, they created new problems for themselves and their children that were intensified when the women took jobs outside the home. As early as 1912 the government was persuaded to set up the U.S. Children's Bureau to try to set standards for child needs and child care.

The 1919 Convention of the National American Woman Suffrage Association, which was also the first convention of the League of Women Voters, faced a vast program of recommended reforms prepared for the first voting years. It was accepted with an enthusiasm that still glows, forty years later, from the printed page. Officers appointed standing committees to study and report on specific changes needed in a dozen fields: American citizenship, protection of women in industry, child welfare, social hygiene, unification of laws concerning the civil status of women, food supply and demand, improvement in election laws and methods. They were also to look into "research," undefined but presumably connected with women's affairs. The new brooms were bent on sweeping clean.

The first program they evolved vowed support for a long list of legislative reforms. League members said they would support

collective bargaining; wages on the base of occupation and not of sex; a Women's Bureau in the Department of Labor [that one came almost at once]; a joint federal-state employment service; a child-labor law; wage-hour legislation; a minimum wage; a merit system in federal, state and local governments; maternity-infancy protective legislation; regulation of the meat-packing industry; laws to prevent food profiteering; pure-food laws; cooperative associations; social hygiene legislation; uniform marriage and divorce laws; independent citizenship for married women; equal interest of spouses in each other's real estate; mothers' pensions; equal guardianship by both parents of persons and property of children; jury service for women; compulsory education, including adequate training for citizenship in every state, for all children between six and sixteen, nine months of each year; education of adults by extension classes of the public schools.

The report of the League of Women Voters that lists these ambitious purposes adds "and forty-seven other specifics."

Notably, it said nothing general about "equal rights" or even about "rights." The right that years of struggle had taught suffragists to regard as of the highest importance they had won. Yet the program was clearly headed toward an equality of status except in certain labor sectors where, on the ground of physical difference, it asked for women better conditions than were provided for men. Otherwise, it listed the changes that would bring about a measure of equality in specific areas.

So effective were these reformers in their first enthusiastic years that the plea for a Women's Bureau in the Department of Labor was won almost before the program was off the press. Key measures followed in quick succession. The Sheppard-Towner Act, to promote welfare and hygiene among mothers and children, was passed in 1921. The Cable Act, on the very different subject of the independent citizenship of women, followed the next year and was signed by President Harding on September 22, 1922, only three months after it had been introduced into Congress.

The course of the Cable Act illustrated both the political strength of women at that moment and the difficulties attendant on altering an old legal status embedded in the country's dense structure of laws and habits. The Act was a nonpartisan measure, warmly advocated by both Republicans and Democrats in their 1920 platforms. Its declared purpose was to give married women their own citizenship, independent of that possessed by their husbands. It was particularly praised as putting an end to the hardships endured by American women who had married aliens.

Having been passed with too much warmth and too little debate, to right a specific wrong, the Cable Act resulted in the creation of other wrongs. Case after case was brought up in court and in 1924 the Immigration Act was amended; in 1930 the Cable Act was amended. Finally, in 1934 Congress made nationality rights as between the sexes equal and uniform in all essential respects.

Other reform measures concerned with the legal status of women were passed, until Mrs. Maud Wood Park, now president of the League of Women Voters, was able to report that "nearly two-thirds of our active federal program has been written off by Congressional enactment of fifteen measures." And in the states, "420 bills supported by state Leagues have become law . . . 64 bills opposed by state Leagues have been defeated."

It was a record to be proud of. Its rehearsal, even in brief, indicates the amount of active and intelligent work which women, conscious of their new power, could accomplish. It also hints at the extent to which the influence of women may be responsible for the trends that led the United States in the direction of a welfare state long before that term came into popular usage.

Obviously the women could not have accomplished this alone. Much of it was a correction of old wrongs that had dragged along far past their time, waiting for the surge of energy that would do away with them. Many men in high position were quick to recognize the economic realities that lay behind the needs that women voiced, and quick to act once the women had the vote. Earlier, they had been too busy about other things. Now, pushed by women who were in a position to make political threats as well as to bring up political support, they went to work.

The leading figures in that first decade of reforming effort came not so much out of New York as out of Chicago and Boston. Jane Addams had been running Hull House for many years, and with it a training school for social reformers that has not yet had the credit it deserves. The gentle scholar Edith Abbott, her raw-boned, kindly Nebraskan sister, Grace Abbott, (who followed Julia Lathrop as head of the new and much needed Federal Children's Bureau), the labor expert Nellie Schwartz were students at Hull House. The factory worker, Mary Anderson, who became the first head of the greatly prized Women's Bureau, Maud Swartz of the glovemakers' union, and red-haired Rose Schneiderman of the Women's Trade Union League, felt the Hull House influence. These were among the articulate and forceful ones who broke new ground.

They were creators of legislation and also administrators of the new organs of government which their industry, imagination, and ability to analyze the newly recognized social needs had brought into being. In this they were aided and supported by the nonpartisan political arm, which was the child of the National American Woman Suffrage Association. When Mrs. Catt in 1919, before the vote was won, had urged the organization of the League of Women Voters as a "semi-political body . . . nonpartisan and all-partisan," which would both educate for citizenship and work for needed legislation, she had suggested that it be set up for five years as a trial effort. It promptly became a power that carried reminders of the suffrage Front Door Lobby. By 1924 it had local organizations in 340 out of 433 Congressional districts.

The suffragists had no illusions about their numerical strength. They knew full well that while they themselves were a politically conscious group, eager to play a part in the political life of their town, their state, their country, they represented only a minority among women. When the vote came, they knew how to value it and to put it to work. They became, in the best American tradition, an active pressure group.

Like their fight for the vote, their struggle for reform was a political battle, waged with skill and effectiveness. Yet they did not always win. Their most bitter defeat concerned an amendment that would have given to Congress the "power to limit, regulate and prohibit the labor of persons under 18 years of age." This was passed by Congress in 1934 and sent to the states for ratification. Although a second section specified that the power of the several states would be "unimpaired by this article, except that the operation of State laws shall be suspended . . . to the extent necessary to give effect to legislation enacted by Congress," some states, and in particular the Southern states, still firmly set in the states' rights tradition, would have none of it.

To get a Child Labor Amendment through the Congress was a victory for the successors of the Front Door Lobby in Washington. To lose its ratification in the states, where it dragged on until 1938, was a defeat for women lobbyists in the states. They took it hard. Even the fact that Congress in that year passed a Fair Labor Standards Act, which covers many of the same points, did not heal the hurt. The Child Labor Amendment was a primary symbol of the kind of reform that women had urged for generations. To lose it was a blow to pride as well as to heart. It also gave a hint, perhaps, that the current which had been running so strongly in the channels marked out by the suffragists might be slowing, might even begin to drift in other directions.

If women did well in the first decade for the reforms in which they heartily believed, they did not do as well, then or later, in getting personal political power, either in the form of posts for themselves or of influence within the inner circle of the parties. This has puzzled many observers. It was, however, foreshadowed in two separate and somewhat contradictory statements made by Mrs. Catt when the suffrage fight was over. The first was her refusal to accept political appointment; the second, her urging of her followers to penetrate the core of politics.

Mrs. Catt was sixty-four years old in 1920, and age may have been a factor in her stout insistence on retiring. This free year made a great deal of sense to her—it took her out of the political world, put her in touch with the sound farm life she had known as a child, let her think in terms of a healthy reality. But it made no sense at all to the puzzled politicians. Having seen proof of her political sagacity, they had expected to find in her a hard, keen battler for one position after another. They did not understand her move back to the kitchen any more than they understood her failure to accept appointive office. Why did she have to disband that very able political machine, the Woman Suffrage Party of New York? Or the NAWSA? Why give up those hard-won positions of authority over an army of women, or yield the political bargaining power that went with the possession of a great following? Even less did they understand why Mrs. Catt and her disciples should turn their backs on the party system and set themselves to educating their sisters within the nonpartisan framework provided by the League of Women Voters.

Yet there is some curious quirk in the feminine mind that makes a great many women identify politics not as a way to earn a living or to exert political influence but as a joint endeavor for the common good. Women tend to see it as they see the Parent Teachers Association, or the Church Peace Union, or the Peace Corps: as a vast and vital effort for an unselfish cause. In the face of daily political tales in the newspapers they continue to see it that way.

The fact that this peculiarity exists in the most realistic of women does not make it easier for others to understand. For all her devotion to the nonpartisan League of Women Voters, Mrs. Catt herself recognized that participation in political life was essential. "For sixty years," the great leader told her followers, "we have been appealing to the political parties to give us the vote. I do not think we have won the vote in a single state where one or both parties have not given their consent—so powerful are they. Well then, is it our intention to remain outside of those parties as we have been for sixty years?"

The answer she expected she gave. The old campaigner went on,

The only way to get things done is to get them done on the inside of a political party. . . . You will be disillusioned, you will find yourselves in a political penumbra where most of the men are. . . . But if you stay long enough, you will discover a little denser thing which is the umbra of the political party—the people who are picking the candidates, doing the real work that you and the men sanction at the polls. You won't be welcome, but there is the place to go. You will see the real thing in the center with the door locked tight. You will have a long hard fight before you get inside . . . but you must move right up to the center.

Unfortunately, perhaps, for the future, Mrs. Catt at sixty-four years of age was not going to take her own advice and move up to the political center. The goal of her busy life was not political preferment but the improvement of the civil status of women, first insofar as their voting power was concerned, second in an improved knowledge of how to use that power effectively. Having played a key part in getting the vote for the women of the United States, she then turned to the plight of women in the rest of the world.

Her interest in foreign women dated from her early suffrage days, when she had persuaded Miss Anthony that an International Council of Women (founded by Susan), which was mildly interested in getting women the vote, was not enough, and had organized in Washington an international meeting that resulted in the formation of an International Woman Suffrage Alliance, composed of national suffrage organizations wherever they existed. Here the sole aim was to get the vote for women in as many countries as possible. Between 1904 and 1920 the number of such countries had grown from none to twenty-two, some of them with women in their local councils, their state legislatures, even their national congresses.

But there were weak spots in the global picture, and one of the most notable was the other half of the Western Hemisphere, Latin America. Only Uruguay and Argentina had sent delegates to the Geneva congress of the International Woman Suffrage Alliance in

1920; the lack of interest in the other Latin countries lay heavy on Mrs. Catt's mind.

Two years later the National League of Women Voters was to hold a convention in Baltimore. Why not invite the Latin women to come north? The idea was taken up with the Secretary of State, Charles Evans Hughes, whose friendship with Mrs. Catt dated at least from the moment when she had laid before him the threat that the suffrage amendment would be attacked through the courts, and persuaded him to take the defense. Mr. Hughes thought so well of her new idea that he agreed to transmit to the Latin American governments and to Canada an official invitation to appoint delegates to a Pan American women's conference, which would meet with the League of Women Voters' convention.

Twenty of the southern republics accepted; so did Canada. Mrs. Catt's biographer noted that the "leisurely Latin American women were greatly impressed as they watched the brisk way the League of Women Voters ran their convention, while the latter were overwhelmed by the oratory which flowed from inexhaustible reservoirs during the Pan American conference." The Latins found the North Americans matter-of-fact, hard-working, unglamorous, but "muy serias"—very serious. The Northerners found the Latins beautiful, charming, witty, but not very serious, either as to subjects or as to agreed hours for meetings, parties, conferences. They were not slaves of time, and they were fond of their independence.

Nevertheless, a sufficient current of mutual interest was established so that Mrs. Catt was invited to visit South America. In the winter of 1922-23 she went by ship down one side and up the other, crossing the Andes from Buenos Aires to Santiago by train, and using the long, dull journey across the pampas to catch up with her correspondence and write the articles she had promised for Susan B. Anthony's old publication, the *Woman's Journal*, now renamed the *Woman Citizen*.

When she got back to New York she told her friends that while she was sure women, north and south, must talk together, she was appalled at the extent of the gap between them. Mrs. Catt had an abiding faith in the educational value of meetings and conversations, but the difficulty was to find a safe subject of common interest. Political conditions, especially as they affected women, would have been her choice, but political topics could hardly be touched on without discussing dictators. Dictators, abundant in South America in the 1920's, could not be talked about openly without endangering lives. Freedom? Freedom might seem a common good, but it also came too close to the dictators for safety. Religion? The southern countries were officially Catholic, while the United States was mainly Protestant, and an avowed believer in the separation between church and state.

Finally, Mrs. Catt and her co-workers settled on the status of women and children as a safe subject of common interest. They framed a questionnaire that asked about the status of working women: who controlled the pay envelope, whether women could own and convey property; the status of children and which parent had legal control over them? What about illegitimate children? Did the father have any legal responsibility? Who was expected to pay for their support?

Replies came back slowly, but carefully framed. The great shock was to discover that instead of the simple North American distinction between a child born in or out of wedlock, some of the Latin countries had five or six different degrees or classes of illegitimacy, each one suitably provided with varying degrees of responsibility. It was Mrs. Catt's first contact with those realities in Latin life and the related subtleties of Latin law.

Her second contact came in 1924, when she was invited to lecture in Cuba. With Miss Hay, and this author as a translator more young than adequate, she embarked on a converted Liberty boat that smelled continually of cold cream. Miss Hay dozed her way south in the sunshine, Mrs. Catt spent each day on deck beside her, the chair strewn with serious magazines concerned with weighty problems. One magazine each day was her ration. Halfway down the Gulf Stream it was discovered that the famous leader did not, however, devote her full attention to the *World Review* but sometimes used it as a cover for a detective story. When her serious young translator raised an eyebrow, the old campaigner twinkled up at her. "It would never do," she explained, "for a suffrage leader to be caught with anything so frivolous, but for these travel days to Havana I have declared myself a vacation. My speeches are written, and for the moment I'm free. But I'm not telling the world about it."

The landing at Havana continued in the same seriocomic vein. On the gangplank Mrs. Catt and her companions were met by five different delegations, no two of which were on speaking terms. The translator was overwhelmed, but Mrs. Catt, true to her political training, solved the problems of protocol by accepting the escort of the official party that represented the Mayor of Havana.

In that handsome tropical city her progress from one public meeting to another, through the orphanages, the schools, the hospitals and the foundling homes she was invited to inspect (and expected to praise) was almost royal. Her fair skin and fine carriage made a particular appeal to that country of dark people. Her blue eyes sparkled, her white hair was as crisp as her starched petticoats. Tall, erect, magnetic, she was a superb mother figure, and the Cubans loved her. She was always introduced to a new audience by a long speech, and every orator called her "The Star of the West." In a curious and quite unconscious fashion she seemed indeed to shimmer.

These two trips to Latin America helped to usher modern woman into international work. Mrs. Catt had gone around the world spreading the suffrage message a decade earlier; her followers in the United States were now beginning to emerge from their local problems. Her zest for international co-operation led them not only into the widened work of the International Suffrage Alliance, but also into highly useful concentration on the causes and possible cures for war.

The phrase was provocative; so was the national situation. The United States, for the first time since achieving its independence, had fought in a major European war and by its fresh might determined the outcome. In the popular mind it had been "a war to end wars." Yet when the League of Nations was created, to lessen the danger of future wars by setting up mechanisms for the discussion and compromise of international disputes, the United States Congress refused to take this country into it.

Public reaction was divided on the part of the majority between apathy and puzzled concern. War was not, in those days, considered to be a field with which women had anything to do. They might agonize over it, might equip ambulance units and send them overseas as the suffragists had done, might bemoan their wounded and lament their dead, but no useful way had been discovered whereby they could effectively protest against war or even work to lessen its horrors. The Congressional refusal to enter the League of Nations was a blow to the best of them. In their dismay, their helplessness, and their frustration they turned, as by long habit, to Mrs. Catt. Nine of the foremost women's organizations agreed to form a special co-operating committee if Mrs. Catt would undertake to guide them into some form of effective protest.

She had just been asked to make, at a convention in Cleveland, what she thought would be her last speech concerned with woman's suffrage. That night she sat on the platform while Will Irwin, a returned war correspondent, told the audience exactly how World War I had looked to a close observer. When Irwin finished, Mrs. Catt rose to her feet, laid aside her prepared manuscript, and launched into a stinging demand that the people, and particularly women, force Congress to reverse itself.

"The people in this room tonight could put an end to war if they would set themselves to do it!" she proclaimed, while reporters at the press table felt chills go up their spines. "Let us put an end to this aloofness, this deadly silence! We can do it! This is an infinitely greater call than any of us will ever hear again. I say to you women in particular: You know that war is in the blood of men, they can't help it. They have been fighting since the days of the cave men, and to them there is a sort of honor about it. God is calling to the women of the world to come forward and stay the hands of men. . . ."

Charged with emotion as it was, and utterly sincere, the speech was like a trumpet call. Mrs. Catt had always believed that women had a far greater potential of power than they were willing to recognize or to exert. They had proved it in the suffrage fight. Let them prove it again in the vital struggle to abolish war.

With the enthusiastic support of her co-operating committee of women's organizations, Mrs. Catt called the first Conference on the Cause and Cure of War in January of 1925. So novel was its title, so well reasoned its theme and its agenda, so closely did it touch a deep and sensitive chord among Americans who felt that they had won a war only to lose a peace, that it commanded the best talent among diplomats, politicians, and statesmen. Speeches and discussions down in the Hall of Nations of the Hotel Washington were on a very high level, some of them above the heads of many participants. Local reporters, plunged into the intricacies of international affairs, were impressed but bewildered. They were not used to hearing talk like this.

There was evidence that the Conference made a deep impression on government circles and on Congressmen who had followed the Senate's lead in rejecting the League of Nations, and who now found themselves facing an intelligent and articulate scolding. Nor did the scolding end there. That first Conference was followed a year later by a second one, which carried the women's organizations into a steady campaign to rouse the United States out of its coma of "normalcy" and into joint action with other nations to put an end to chaos and establish world peace.

Did all this do any good? It won Mrs. Catt new rounds of criticism from the old antifeminist critics. More importantly, it kept the pot of public discussion bubbling about the League, the

World Court, and other aspects of that frail forerunner of the United Nations. There was no executive leadership in the country sufficiently able to break through the Republican opposition to the League of Nations, but the steady work of women in continuing to keep the subject alive proved a force that would pay off—after another war.

Women had called the Conference on the Cause and Cure of War; other women distrusted its discussions and its conclusions. These others, who were almost all members of so-called patriotic associations, usually identified themselves by their relationship to the veteran of some war, and might logically be thought to have had enough of war. Yet their sense of glory lay in wars, so they organized themselves into the Women's Patriotic Conference on National Defense, to hold yearly meetings in Washington.

Even before these two sharply opposed conferences were set up, the one to seek an end to war, the other to glorify it, American women were making their way into various new forms of participation in international affairs. The League of Nations had been established in 1920, seven months before the federal suffrage amendment was finally ratified. Though the United States did not join, Americans who were convinced of its importance began very early to seek places in the secretariat.

Urged on by liberals of both sexes, government officers accepted informal places within the League organization. By 1931 the American consul at Geneva, who could not, of course, be named as a delegate, was an "informal observer." Meanwhile collaboration with some of the League's agencies had become a commonplace. The government decided that its isolationist attitude would not be sullied by co-operation with the International Labor Office, and sent its own Labor representatives, some of them women, to meetings at Geneva.

With the working staff and the delegates appeared the amateur enthusiasts, come to express their personal admiration for the

League, and to prove that the position of the United States government did not necessarily represent the position of some of its important new citizens. A whole flock of lovely ladies descended on Geneva. Women of wealth and leisure, many of them former suffragists, found in the international world a welcome outlet for their energies. Some brought with them a suffrage sense of public obligation. Some were there because in certain circles this was the fashionable thing to do.

The League itself had a committee headed by Princess Radziwill that was deeply concerned with controlling, if not stopping, the cross-boundary traffic in women and children known then as the white slave trade. The lovely ladies did not limit their enthusiasm to such unpleasant matters. Declared emissaries of good will, dressing by preference in flowered chiffon and big, flowered hats, they found in Geneva a lush field for their talents as hostesses. They enjoyed the kind of masculine flattery provided by members of the diplomatic corps who kissed their gloved hands and sat at their tables (provided their cooks were good enough). For women who had previously prided themselves on attracting local legislators, foreign ambassadors in a foreign capitol were heady guests. Home in Minneapolis or Dubuque was never like this.

How much influence the ladies exerted in convincing Congressmen at home that the United States should have entered the League is a question, but any reporter who saw them there can testify to their enthusiasm. They expressed perhaps the froth of public opinion, but some were more intelligent than their rapid talk might indicate. They did back up their working sisters who had at heart weightier things than crème brulée. Also they wrote enthusiastic letters back home where the struggle for international collaboration went on despite Republican attempts to stifle it.

The real test of serious intent among the lovely ladies appeared within their own groups. In 1925 several voluntary associations of women came together to create an informal Joint Standing Committee on Women's International Organizations with an office in

Geneva, which formed a center of interest in the League of Nations. The International Alliance of Women was a member, so was the International Alliance of Women for Equal Suffrage and Citizenship, which Mrs. Catt had founded under the simpler name of International Woman Suffrage Alliance. Five years later the unofficial Joint Standing Committee became the official Liaison Committee of Women's International Organizations; in that guise it went so far as to forward recommendations to the League on such solid subjects as equal pay for equal work, nationality, forced and indentured labor, opium traffic, refugees, and disarmament.

So strong did this new wave of American interest in international affairs prove that in 1933, when Dr. Sophonisba Breckenridge published her scholarly study, *Women in the Twentieth Century*, she noted that most of the large American organizations of women "maintain some relationship with women's groups in other countries." She cited as examples the Woman's International League for Peace and Freedom and the International Policewomen's Association; the World's Christian Temperance Union (with members in fifty nations); the Inter-American Union of Women, which had sprung from that conference called by the League of Women Voters in 1922. She included religious organizations such as the International Union of Catholic Women's Leagues and the Jewish Women of the World; professional and working groups such as the International Council of Nurses, the International Federation of University Women, the International Association of Business and Professional Women's Clubs, the Medical Women's International Association. By 1964, the list would grow to fill a volume.

That sense of feminine solidarity, that ability to appear and to function in public, which had been concomitant skills and attitudes developed in the suffrage fight, were pushing American women to function on the world stage, as at home. Proud of being voting citizens in the United States, they felt able to speak their minds anywhere, and this they did.

They did not, however, do it alone or without healthy competition. By the time the United States had made up its mind to grant woman suffrage, twenty-six other nations had done so earlier. The fact irked Mrs. Catt as a patriot, while as a feminist it gave her cause for rejoicing. It seemed to have made very little impression on other Americans. Accustomed to being missionaries in many fields, instead of being missionaried to, few of them noted that the rest of the world was getting ahead of them. In the suffrage fight they had led the way. Their habit now was to go forth in the name of democracy to teach the rest of the world how to hold free and unhampered balloting, how to value the vote, and how to behave in a democratic society. It occurred to few of them that the technique of the secret ballot had been invented not in the United States but in Australia, and that many of the women to whom they went to teach the value of voting might have had the vote before their teachers. Even Mrs. Catt, for all her educated desire to find out the facts before coming to conclusions, was not free from the common American belief that the United States has most of the answers.

Meanwhile the women back home, in the states and in the national capitol, worked steadily ahead on their long task of securing equality of legal status between men and women. Year after year, in legislatures and in administrative offices, they continued to make their points. Year after year the old fabric of masculine dominance creaked and yielded a bit here, a bit there.

In 1929, the year of the great financial crash, this ancient web stiffened, and the women began to find the going harder. With the depression came the unemployment problem. As men lost their jobs, women found themselves scolded for working instead of being praised. Even the argument of family necessity failed to support them. Because they were more adaptable than men, because they would work more cheaply, the wife could find a job while the husband stayed at home. The family was upheld after a fashion, but neither its members nor the general public were grateful. Complaints rose on all sides that the women were depriving men of wages. Orators suggested that if only they would go back to the kitchen the economy would recover.

The idea was, of course, fallacious, but that did not alleviate the atmosphere of acute criticism and bitter complaint. Working women were become pariahs, and if one judged by the tone of magazine articles and newspaper editorials, most of them were frivolous parasites bent on self-decoration.

The advent of Franklin Roosevelt and his wife Eleanor on the national scene in 1932 did a great deal to clear the air of this miasma, only to fill it with another.

Eleanor Roosevelt was a new kind of woman in the White House. She had never been an active suffragist, and some of those who cherished suffrage memories held it against her that she, who had suffered none of the pains and burdens of the long campaign, should enter so effortlessly into its rewards. (Her excuse, if excuse were required, was that in the days of the great New York State campaigns she had been a young mother overborne by a tyrannical mother-in-law, and too busy bearing and bringing up children to march in parades or to manage suffrage offices.) Her immediate predecessors in the White House had been mostly the daughters of simple families with slender means, but Eleanor Roosevelt was born into a presidential family, educated in private schools, accustomed to wealth, skilled in social and sophisticated ways. It was the more remarkable, therefore, that she swung as if by instinct into the reform atmosphere with which the whole woman's movement, from Susan B. Anthony's days to those of Carrie Chapman Catt, and from Jane Addams to the New York factory laws, had been infused. That reform atmosphere, that convinced zeal for improvement of the country's social climate, became—when translated into political terms—the moving force in her husband's New Deal.

Which was cause and which effect, whether Eleanor Roosevelt followed where her husband led or influenced his leadership with her own ideas, is a question that deserves the attention of historians. Certainly her social attitude showed itself in many ways. The friends whom Mrs. Roosevelt chose to see during the hard years of her husband's governorship of New York—Frances Perkins, Molly Dewson, Elinore Herrick, Frieda Miller—were social reformers. They spoke her language and she spoke theirs. With their encouragement, and backed by the obvious political popularity of the New Deal reform measures, Mrs. Roosevelt was to grow into a leader who would in time take on the stature of a Carrie Chapman Catt and move into a position that Mrs. Catt never achieved, where she represented not only women but her entire country in the international arena.

By instinct, Mrs. Roosevelt analyzed problems, not politically, but in terms of human suffering and human need for kindness. Her approach to public as to private difficulties was that of the social worker, the mother, the teacher. One of her important early successes in Washington was with the women's press corps there. Until she came to the White House, an assorted body of newspaper women was called on mostly to report society events, clothes, food, and other phenomena of the capital's well-furnished and gossip-loving society. They had reported the activities of other "first ladies" in these terms. Mrs. Roosevelt was not interested. She was, however, interested in better schools, in reforming the terrible conditions then prevailing in Puerto Rico, in attacking the problems of agricultural surpluses, in hospitals, in efforts to raise the national standard of living, in economic problems, in decent treatment as between races.

As if by instinct she taught the newspaper women what kind of questions to ask in order to get from her the kind of information that she found valuable, interesting, and newsworthy. Gently, firmly, she managed to raise the intelligence quotient of the women's press corps without making them feel stupid. Like a mother bird, she kept pushing these hard-working fledglings out of the domestic nest into the modern world of women's new responsibilities. In the process she bound them to her for life.

With such a woman in the White House, the Roosevelt era became the climactic period of the woman's movement. Never before had women had such political recognition. Frieda Miller replaced the aging Mary Anderson in the Women's Bureau, reorganized it, and made a further name for herself and her policies in the International Labor Office. Dr. Martha Eliot with her long medical experience replaced Grace Abbott as head of the Children's Bureau. A woman, for the first time, made her way into the Cabinet.* Frances Perkins was a trained sociologist .A Lucy Stoner who kept her own name after marriage, she had done a brilliant job as Labor Commissioner of New York State. Her appointment as Secretary of Labor of the United States made her one of the many controversial figures in the Roosevelt Cabinets. Tall, abrupt, and handsome, given to wearing tricorne hats, she belonged to that exigent breed that does not suffer fools gladly; at times she let them know it.

The new President, handsome, charming, helpless in his lameness, surrounded himself with educated women as no President had done before, and they adored him. He needed their aid, and they responded wholeheartedly. He was at ease with them, he gave them their due measure of praise, and they served him without counting time. In return he gave them not only credit and opportunity, but he incorporated many of their ideas and their attitudes into the philosophy of his administration.

One result, perhaps minor, except for its contrast with the past, was that even in the delicate and difficult business of admitting that the "experiment, noble in motive" of prohibition had failed and should be ended, the women stood by him. There was a great deal of head-shaking among older suffragists who remembered the important part temperance had played among the early reformers,

---

*Anna Rosenberg, later head of the War Manpower Commission under Roosevelt, and Assistant Secretary of Defense from 1950 to 1953, sat with the Cabinet from time to time but was not actually a member of it.

and who regretted that attempts to confine the liquor trade had come to such a corrupt and disastrous end. But the evidence of that corruption was too visible to be disregarded any longer.

As early as 1929 a group headed by Mrs. Charles Sabin and including such socially famous names as Mrs. August Belmont, Mrs. Pierre S. Du Pont, Mrs. Archibald Roosevelt had helped to pave the way by forming the Women's Organization for National Prohibition Reform and making the dry side unfashionable. Repeal took on the same kind of smart approval the suffrage movement acquired when Mrs. O. H. P. Belmont and her society friends had enlisted in the woman suffrage campaign. This time women were not rebelling, but were doing what the men wanted. The reform, or counter—reform, would go through in four short years.

A month after Roosevelt's landslide victory the question of what he should do about prohibition was presented to Congress by Senator Blaine of Wisconsin. In February of 1933, before the new President was inaugurated, the Senate voted 63 to 23 to submit to the states for ratification a Twenty-first Amendment which provided for repeal of the Eighteenth. The House followed with a vote of 289 to 121.

The Anti-Prohibition amendment then started down the long road of state ratification, covering it faster than had the suffrage amendment. On December 5, 1933, Utah became the thirty-sixth state to ratify. The "experiment, noble in motive" left its traces in the shape of two amendments—one putting it in, the other taking it out—forever visible in the Constitution.

10. A DIFFERENT
WAR:
WIDER AIMS

*"Cram us with praise, and make us
As fat as tame things."*

Shakespeare

American historians are coming to regard World Wars I and II as separate phases of a single war, divided by a contentious and largely spurious peace. As far as women are concerned, the roles they played in the two wars and the effect those roles had on them were so diverse as to make that theory highly questionable. So much had their position and their attitudes changed between 1917 and 1941 that they seem to have been surrounded by actively different worlds.

In World War I the United States government flatly refused to accept the services of any woman in the Armed Forces except as a clerical aide in this country. In World War II they were not only accepted as members of the Armed Forces and workers in factories, but were urged to participate. Their performance was more co-operative, more spectacular, more exhausting than in World War I. Its postlude for a decade was, in feminist terms, curiously dis-appointing.

Women came up to the edge of that war in a state of despair mixed with doubt and uncertainty. The trauma of the economic depression, in which they had been stripped of their new sense of achievement in a man's world, accused of taking men's jobs if they went out to earn, and of failing to pull their weight if they didn't, had bitten deep. They had seen their men helpless to continue the old pattern of family support, made into failures by obscure economic forces that cooled factory chimneys, shut office doors, and abolished millions of jobs. The trouble was harder to understand because economists talked about the depression in terms that seemed to them sensible, and to the jobless public seemed idiotic. The American dream itself, on which women like men had staked their faith, wobbled on its foundations. The slogan that had moved mothers and grandmothers to the long, hard campaign for women's rights began to sound tinny. Why work for "rights," why work for equality of opportunity if all opportunity was vanishing?

Yet when Japan attacked and the government made it quite plain that it would need the services of women as well as men, despair and doubts were put aside; not, however, without leaving traces. When the need would end, so would the confidence.

Meanwhile, the Army enlisted WAACS, and put them into khaki and Army dormitories. The Navy enlisted WAVES and dressed them in blues designed by Mainbocher; the Marine Corps and the Air Force followed suit. By May, 1945, there were 266,184 women in the four military services, and 11,000 in the Coast Guard. Women who found no place in the Armed Forces flocked, regardless of social class, into factories as a patriotic duty, worked on night shifts, graveyard shifts, found their difficult way home in crowded public transport at unholy hours. Women were called into the hard-boiled masculine world of the shipyards, where no woman had worked before; shipyard owners ordered special uniforms designed for them, special shoes and steel head coverings: they had special showers installed and beauty parlor operators hired to keep up feminine morale while preserving physical safety. Women entertainers were sent flying in military planes to cheer the troops in whatever part of the world they were fighting. The women bloomed. Having been treated during the depression as a useless and bothersome surplus, they enjoyed finding themselves valuable again. They felt themselves needed and they responded to need as women alway do. From a feminist point of view, their wartime position was a great gain. This time they were not asked to stand aside while men sponged up both the suffering and the glory. This time they were accepted as part of the totality.

For American men and women the war lasted from December 7, 1941, until September 2, 1945.

And then came another great change, this one more disturbing for women than for men. The slump of the 1930's had cast down both sexes, and both had been raised up again to usefulness by war. The demands of peace in 1945 tripped the women again, while exalting the men. The men turned back toward home; filled with dreams of a warm, affectionate, and undemanding welcome, they were eager to get out of uniform and back to their old civilian jobs or into new and better ones. The women who had been enlisted also turned home, but toward what? Those who had been doing men's work suddenly found themselves, as members of the labor force, not only unwanted but unpopular. The war was over. The need for their services in factories and workshops and shipyards was over, or so it seemed.

The men began to show signs of resenting women in the jobs that, before the conflict broke, had been their own. They wanted their wives at home, and other men's wives out of the way, out of the competition of the labor market. Economists and labor leaders sharpened this demand by predicting a new depression which, they said, would throw eight million men out of work and plunge the country into a worse state than it had endured in 1938. The prophecy proved absurd. But who could be sure, in 1945? What woman had the knowledge and the courage to laugh off the voices prophesying doom? The trauma of depression, soothed by war activity but not yet cured, had gone too deep. The undertow was too strong. In surprisingly large numbers the women yielded to popular clamor, left their jobs, and went back to their kitchens.

Six million of them had come out of those kitchens to do war work. When the war ended, more than half put down their tools, took off their uniforms, dropped their titles, and went home. The Women's Bureau reported that whereas nineteen and a half million women were at work in April of 1945, only sixteen million were working in April, 1947. The war had ended. The need for women in men's jobs was over.

The retreat, in the beginning at least, had no leader to stem it. Mrs. Catt was old and fading, and so was her power to inspire. Mrs. Roosevelt was, while her husband lived, primarily the hand-maid of his policies and his needs. The older leader had come through the war with remarkable stamina and had lent her support to a Women's Action Committee for Victory and Lasting Peace that several of the old suffrage stalwarts had founded. This was considered as a successor organization to Mrs. Catt's earlier Conference on the Cause and Cure of War.

These women wanted to make sure that, once the war was won, the United States would not retreat from the international arena into an outmoded isolationism, would not fail to join the projected United Nations as it had failed to join the League of Nations. In January, 1944, Mrs. Catt had come out of her big white house in New Rochelle to speak for this point as part of a public celebration of her eighty-fifth birthday. She made a speech over radio, she appeared with Mrs. Roosevelt before newsreel cameras, she spoke again (as did Mrs. Roosevelt and the actress Helen Hayes) at a luncheon given for her by old friends in the Women"s Action Committee.

But the famous voice had lost much of its timbre, the famous face had developed a small tic at the corner of the mouth. Her time was running out, and she knew it. Her days were mostly spent in watching the progress of the war and in meditating on the quality and effect of the peace that would follow. Her years on the Council on the Cause and Cure of War, her travels across the world, her conversations with responsible statesmen in many countries had given her an intimate knowledge of the way decisions were made and of how people reacted to them. No one was more aware of the drag and the undertow that followed a great surge of effort.

She had three more years to live, but they were tired years. Her fame around the world was still strong. Her correspondence would have supplied a dozen stamp collectors with foreign treasures. When she died, in her birth month of January, 1947, Carrie Lane Chapman Catt would be eighty-eight years old, and honored the world around. She would be buried not beside either husband, but in Woodlawn Cemetery, New York, where in 1928 she had bought a plot big enough for two graves, had buried her friend Mary Garrett Hay, and later had put up a plain stone on which she had had incised the simple statement, "Here lie two friends, for thirty-eight years united in serving a great cause."

In that penultimate period her friend and biographer, Mary Gray Peck, wrote the story of Mrs. Catt's life and in it gave, very gently, a picture of the great suffragist's last despair.

She had hoped that with the release of the full capacities of womanhood the democratic way of life might cleanse itself of its evils, banish war and create a world society "with liberty and justice toward all." There had been a chance for it at the close of the First World War, but it was lost. Would the second chance be seized after the Second World War? . . . She had given everything she had to the setting free of the maternal spirit which was the profoundest social movement of her life—perhaps of any time. She believed there was something elemental in the rise of great women to prominence in the nations now fighting for freedom. In the darkest days this world has ever seen, knowing that her work was done, it comforted her to reflect upon the new and benignant power free women were carrying forward into the future.

Fortunately, she was spared the sight of what that freed maternal spirit did with the benignant power thus won for them. She never knew that in her own country, at least, too many of the freed women went back home the moment the war was over, pulled the blankets over their heads, and subsided into a synthetic domesticity.

The death of the famous old leader marked the formal end of an epoch that was almost finished when the war began. The National American Woman Suffrage Association she had served brilliantly was formally dissolved after she was buried. Its leaders had expected to close the organization's books in 1920. Then they found certain bequests left by will to the suffrage cause that had, for one reason or another, not come due or not been paid. Legally, they must stay longer in existence. Every year since that time they had held a Board meeting. Not until January, 1950, could they disband.

From the residue of funds left in the treasury they voted to give $5,000 to the International Woman Suffrage Alliance that Mrs. Catt had headed; $1,000 to the Susan B. Anthony Museum being set up in Rochester, New York (it seemed only proper that the money of her niece, Melissa Dickinson, should help there); and $25,000 to the League of Women Voters as a "living memorial to Mrs. Catt." They decided that the records of the Leslie Commission were to be destroyed, and with them a handful of Mrs. Leslie's securities that had proved worthless.

On February 23, 1950, the officers surrendered the Association's Charter. *The New York Times,* with its instinctive sense of history, carried the story. Almost a hundred and two years had elapsed since that July day when Elizabeth Cady Stanton and her friends had gathered around that table in Auburn, New York, to frame the Declaration of Women's Rights that the meeting in Seneca Falls a few days later would immortalize.

Whether another Carrie Chapman Catt could have stirred women to a better postwar performance is a vain question. There was no other Mrs. Catt. There was Mrs. Roosevelt, and while she roused hearty and sometimes worshipful admiration she did not operate on the levels that inspired other women to go and do likewise. She performed splendidly in her own person, but she led no crusades aimed to galvanize women into a consciousness of their public responsibilities as citizens.

Lacking leadership, pushed by popular pressures of various kinds, the women slumped into the curious and discouraging decade of the 1950's. It is perhaps too early to analyze the causes of that retreat into sentimentality. The bare figures tell quantitatively what happened. In March, 1940, nine months before Pearl Harbor, 13,480,000 women over fourteen were counted as included under that technical phrase "in the labor force." This meant that 28 per cent of all the women in the country were at work in the period when the United States, only partially recovered from the depression, was not actually at war but engaged in activities that justified its title, "the arsenal of democracy." Five years later, in April of 1945, when the United States was not only the arsenal for her allies but also the factory and the fighting force for democracy, there were 19,570,000 women, 37 per cent of the total in the country, "in the labor force."

Then, with victory, these figures began dropping. Within two years (in April, 1947) 3,250,000 women had gone home, leaving only 30 per cent at work, scarcely 5 per cent more than were working before the war began. In numbers, the sentimental slump did not last very long. By April, 1950, even before the Korean war, the trend had begun to reverse itself, though the percentages climbed more slowly than had the numerical totals. By April, 1960, there were 23,239,000 women at work, 36 per cent of the total. Two million more women worked in service occupations than in 1940, and a million and a quarter more in the professions.

Attempts to find out why women went back to work are hardly more successful than efforts to divine why they dropped their tools after 1945. The reasons generally given for the return to the bassinet swing from private emotional woes to economic imperatives. "My husband wants me at home," was what one heard most of those women say. Sometimes the phrase means, "I worked only because I needed the money. I'm happier at home, and glad to get back." Sometimes it meant, "I'm sorry to leave my job, but I must —he wants it that way." In that highly emotional year, "He" was all powerful. The independent woman had, for the moment, abdicated.

These elemental and understandable factors do not, however, explain the qualitative slump that accompanied the quantitative retreat. They do not explain why women in positions of responsibility that called for executive and managerial skills increased in number very slowly. The proportion of women professional workers in the total number of women working was no greater in 1960 than it had been in 1940. Not enough of them were going into jobs requiring mathematical skills, not enough into the upper reaches of teaching. College presidencies, a prime target of ambitious and scholarly women before 1930, actually lost women. The qualitative as well as quantitative lag worried those who, believing that women had infinite innate abilities, also knew that they must have the same high degree of education and training that men have in order to fit within the upper layers of the modern world. It seemed curiously significant that "feminism" became a dirty word while "momism," however ridiculed, continued to flourish.

Other forces were at work behind the scenes that saw a commercial importance in woman's return to the hearthside. The huge and complex industrial plant of the United States, with all its ramifications, must be converted from the satisfying of wartime demands to the locating and filling of peacetime needs. Customers were the first requirement, and research teams sent to locate them came up with all sorts of factors influential in the growth of the nation, including the marriage rate, the marriage age, the national rate of accession of newborn babies who would, in a determinable number of years, become new purchasers.

It gradually became clear that the greater good of industry in its customer-seeking phase demanded early marriages, early babies, and as many of them as possible. This became the postwar pattern of American life. Woman was the keystone, but as a customer and a creator of custom. A slogan was invented, "Never underestimate the power of a woman," and that power was alleged to be great.

The phrase took on prestige; it was hailed in all sorts of places. Powered by Madison Avenue advertising forces, a new wave of sentimental illusion spread across the country. The postwar world of the United States was pictured, for a moment and in certain circles that found the idea profitable, as a women's world. Woman could sway industry, she could sway Wall Street, she could sway commerce.

Much of this illusion failed to stand close scrutiny. It was true that the number of women's names on the stockholder lists had increased; it was also true that for various reasons many men were putting their investments into their wives' names. But a sample study of corporation reports showed that ownership and control were two different things. The fact that so much corporate stock was reported as registered in feminine names had little effect on the structure of corporate responsibility or decision. Stockholders in great numbers the women were, but only rarely did the name of a woman appear in the ranks of top management or on lists of directors. Of twenty industrial corporations—public utility, railroad, oil, motors, food products, and so on—chosen at random in 1960, listing 419 officers and 298 directors, only two names of women appeared, and both for internal reasons. One was an assistant secretary and one an assistant treasurer. No wise man would underestimate the power of a woman, but there was as yet little evidence that he would welcome that power within the doors of the board room or at the executive desk in the president's office.

However, that glimpse of reality discouraged no one. The game of glorifying women in fancy while denying them position in fact went on. Businessmen and their advertising advisors hired profes-

sors of psychology to find out the lowest common denominator of
what made women tick. According to them, the desire of every
war-weary young housewife was to have a new home, and if not
that, at least a dream kitchen equipped with newly designed and
arranged stoves, sinks, refrigerators, cupboards, to which were
added electric diswashers and clothes washers, and a multitude of
smaller electric gadgets.

These toys were expensive; they rapidly became status symbols.
A curious split in aim followed. The first drive for these improve-
ments was pitched on a labor-saving note. Home economics experts
at Cornell University made time and motion studies of a housewife's tasks, and worked out the most effective pattern for placing
the standard kitchen items in relation to the room and to each
other.

But these first postwar designers were still thinking in terms of
war workers. Soon, the new cooking centers began to feature
charm, to be advertised not as the place where mother could get
through her household tasks as rapidly as possible, but as the center
of the home where she was to spend most of her life. It was grand-
mother's black iron cookstove all over again, but now granddaugh-
ter, her outside working life behind her, was supposed to love her
elaborate new toy and to tie herself to it by choice.

Fortunately the facts of postwar life have proved woman richer
in aim and more varied than the spinners of illusion believed. Not
all women dived back into the home, and many of those who did
came up to the fresh air again, sputtering. Two million of them
went back to work in the three years between 1947 and 1950.

But enough concern had been aroused so that in 1961 President
Kennedy appointed a National Commission on the Status of
Women to study and report. Subdividing their task, working with
a set of seven committees, the Commission had as basic resource
the 1960 census figures and the work done over years by the Wom-
en's Bureau of the Labor Department. In October, 1963, only a
month before the President was killed, the Commission produced

a report that "considered women in the content of the total American society." This covered seven phases of the life of modern women, the circumstances surrounding and affecting her, and the facilities available to her.

It takes only a little reading of this crisp report to recognize that in its picture of "96 million women . . . from infant to octogenarian, from migrant farm mother to suburban homemaker, from file clerk to research scientist, from Olympic athlete to college president," the governing element is not illusion, but fact. What most interested the Commission was not woman as spender of the family purse, or woman as voter, but the extent to which "greater development of women's potential and fuller use of their present abilities can greatly enhance the quality of American life."

Yet even in terms of this broader view the elements of reaction, retreat, and disappointment appear. The careful chapter on "Women as Citizens" notes sadly that although the nation now has 3.75 million more women than men, "in terms of registration and election-day turnout, their failure to use their vote converts them into a minority."

In the wave of sentimental regression that followed World War II, men appeared larger than life and women smaller. Those who had been genuine feminists knew all too well what the battle had cost: they held their memories dear, but they almost ceased to mention feminism. Those who were younger, and had heard about the movement from their elders, developed a resentment against it. They professed to be sick of the sound of feminism, of the problems it raised, the responsibilities it imposed, the decisions it implied. So did the public, which had always thought feminists and suffragists a little queer.

But if women in the United States sought a rest from their victories, women in Asia, South America, Africa began to sniff freedom's intoxicating breezes.

In this they were aided and abetted by forces and organizations that the older suffragists had set in motion years before. The long wave of feminine demand in other countries that Miss Anthony and Mrs. Stanton had stirred back in 1888, that Mrs. Catt had encouraged in her journeying around the world, was piling up. The International Council of Women was now a going concern, as was the International Woman Suffrage Association, which as early as 1915 had claimed twenty-two national branches.

But it was the creation of the League of Nations in 1920, the American suffrage year, that transformed the feminist battle into an international crusade. The very Covenant of the League gave women the promise of a real equality. Fifty nations signed it and their expressions of adherence to its articles were at the very least expressions of intent more emphatic than fifty nations had ever voiced before. Also, they were taken as facts back home.

Regions of the world that had seemed to slumber began to stir. The fifth International Council of American States, meeting in Santiago de Chile in 1923, seized the honor of being the first inter-governmental body to take action against discrimination on account of sex. In Havana, in 1928, the same body decided to establish an Inter-American Commission of Women, which would study the status of women in all the American republics and would work for women's civil and political rights.

In 1933, in Montevideo, the Council of American States adopted a convention on women's political rights. Two years later the League of Nations adopted and approved that convention. And in Bogotá after the Second World War, at a turbulent conference in 1948, the same Council adopted two inter-American conventions, one concerning the granting of political rights to women and the other civil rights.

As the second war, which had interrupted many normal activities and initiated many abnormal ones, drew to a close, the older generation of leaders in the United States were disappearing. The best of the younger ones had joined forces with Mrs. Roosevelt in New Deal reforms (many of them stemming from earlier suffrage aspirations) or had moved into the sphere of international activity.

When plans were announced from Yalta on February 13, 1945, for a meeting to be held to frame the charter of a new international organization to be called the United Nations, such women sprang into action with so much enthusiasm that even the State Department welcomed them. Entrusted with the task of developing public support for this new international venture, it drew women's organizations into its campaign. A woman's name, that of Virginia Gildersleeve, the able Dean of Barnard College, appeared on the first list of delegates. Letters came pouring in from individuals as well as from groups, asking for representation, seeking the right to take part in debates, for the right even to have a gallery seat in the San Francisco Opera House where the Conference was to meet.

The very visible groups of American women who won the right to attend the charter-making conference at San Francisco now looked forward to playing a part not only in national matters but in the affairs of the world. With their bright eyes and their determined voices, they saw themselves as public opinion in person, each possessed of a vote, each able to exert pressure large or small on the body politic, including the Senate—which held the fate of the nation and of the United Nations in its reluctant hands.

In its decision to include women as members of its national delegation the United States was by no means alone. A recommendation came asking, in substance, that the projected Economic and Social Council set up "a special commission of women to study conditions . . . with special reference to the discrimination and limitations placed on them on account of their sex." This novelty was proposed by women delegates whose nations had been members of the League, and backed by precedents established in the work of the Inter-American Commission of Women, which had repeatedly made recommendations welcomed by the League.

The Charter as framed at San Francisco set the modern tone. In the Preamble the peoples proclaim their determination "to reaffirm faith in fundamental human rights, in the dignity and worth of the human person, in the equal rights of men and women. . . ."

Article I states that one of the purposes of the UN to is promote and encourage "respect for human rights and for fundamental freedoms for all without distinction as to race, sex, language or religion. . . ."

The acceptance of this charter by member countries included the recognition that women's rights had entered a new phase. It had become an international movement, and in that field American women were almost as ignorant and untried as they had been twenty-five years earlier.

They gained experience fast. The first American appointed as delegate to what was known as the UN Subcommission on the Status of Women (later to become a full Commission) was Dorothy Kenyon, a graduate of Smith College and an experienced lawyer. She had served a term as Judge of the Municipal Court in New York City, and was a witty and persuasive speaker for liberal causes. With the official backing of Rachel Nason, who represented the State Department in this new international adventure, and the aid of the Secretary-General's office whose task it was to guide procedures, keep track of arguments, see that minutes were taken, and in general gear the activities of the delegates into the still amorphous routine of the UN secretariat, Judge Kenyon undertook the pioneer task of presenting and protecting the still tender and sometimes unformulated attitude of the United States toward women and the "discrimination and limitations placed upon them."

In the matter of woman's nationality American policy was clear; the much-amended Cable Act provided ample precedent. But on equal pay for equal work the Congress had taken no action; hence no policy existed. The State Department could make no guiding statement. Judge Kenyon, knowledgeable in labor matters, eager in the new game of scoring points against her Soviet opponent, seized the initiative. On the strength of a telephone call to Washington, she framed and brought in a resolution asking equal pay for equal work before Mme. Popova could get clearance from Moscow for the same idea.

The work of the Commission, and indeed its very existence, have not gone without criticism. There are those who argue that the Charter of the United Nations itself should be enough. There are others who would rest their faith on the great Declaration of Human Rights passed in 1948. It is one of the paradoxes of the UN that after such firm declarations of intent and purpose, an immense effort must be put forth to make them come true.

In the antiseptic governmental phrase, they must be implemented.

The Commission on the Status of Women is, in substance, part of the machinery of implementation. There are some who feel that in continuing a Commission devoted solely to women's affairs the UN is in fact denying its own assertion of equality, and setting women in a position of special privilege. Thus far the women themselves have held to their special position and continued to push for resolutions, conventions, expressions of principle that mirror what they still conceive to be their limited situation and aim to correct it.

As the work of study, analysis, classification, and recommendation went on, the matter of equal rights, appearing more and more complex, was subdivided into more and more sections. The General Assembly itself has accepted three highly important conventions—one on the Political Rights of Women (in 1952), one on the Nationality of Married Women (in 1957) and the third on Consent to Marriage, Minimum Age for Marriage, and Registration of Marriage (in 1962). The Commission meeting called for Teheran in the spring of 1965 had before it informative material on the subject of the Access of Women to Public Services and Functions. In addition, the Economic and Social Commission has passed a long series of resolutions brought to it from time to time by the Commission, resolutions that are expressions of desire, attempts at setting standards, statements signifying that it is politically expedient for one nation or another to appear before the world as upholding this or that noble banner in the cause of women. Some of these may sound as obvious as shouts for Mother, and against Sin, but they do testify to the change in woman's position that has been accomplished in a century. None of them would exist if American women had not won the vote.

Perhaps the most spectacular tribute to the sweep of the woman's movement is implied in the fact that whereas only twenty-five countries allowed women to vote when the UN charter-making conference was convened in 1945, there were in August of 1963 a hundred and four countries where they could vote; only ten remained in all the world, developed or underdeveloped, where they had no voting rights and were not eligible for election. Two were those small and obdurate European conservatives, Switzerland and Liechtenstein.

The work of women in and around their specific Commission is only a small part of their preoccupation with the United Nations. Within the UN complex their place is, in theory at least, on a par with that of men. They may be named as delegates of their governments, once in a while they are named as heads of national missions. One woman, Mme. Pandit of India, has served as President of the General Assembly. They form an important sector of the staff of the Secretariat; no woman yet has been named as Secretary-General, nor as one of the Secretary's deputies.

The Liaison Committee of Women's International Organizations laid the foundation for expressions of opinion by feminine pressure groups at the League of Nations. With the creation of the United Nations, the work of these organizations in the charter-framing stage gained them recognition as prime representatives of public opinion whose influence was great and whose co-operation was desirable. There was therefore set up a special category of Non-Governmental Organizations, which were given "consultative status with the Economic and Social Council." More than three hundred such organizations are listed, of which a sizable proportion are concerned with women's interests. The rubric NGO is recognized; a newer one, WINGO, stands for Women's International Non-Governmental Organizations.

Skeptics, of whom this author is one, sometimes wonder how much reality underlies the expression of good intent and the recommendations of noble sentiment into which the UN Commission on the Status of Women puts such hard work. What is there about woman's position in this diverse and complicated world on which women delegates from Argentina, Australia, China (or that part of it resident in Formosa) and Colombia, Czechoslovakia and Finland, France, Ghana and Indonesia, Japan and Mexico, the Netherlands, Peru, the Philippines and Poland, Sierre Leone, Spain and the USSR, the United Arab Republic, the UK and the USA—all of whom attended the 1963 session—could possibly agree?

These strangers, with their strange names, have met in some twenty-six plenary sessions. Here, for example, is the 1963 list of subjects they discussed in the seventeenth session; it is taken from the official agenda.

Political rights of women, the progress achieved, the status of women in the few non-self-governing territories which remain in the world.

Access of women to education—the activities of UNESCO which are of particular interest to women, the education of women in those rural areas which cover so much of the earth's surface.

Economic rights and opportunities for women: the activities of ILO which have a bearing on the employment of women; the access of women to training and employment in the professional and technical fields; the age of retirement and the right to pensions.

Advisory services in the field of human rights, and United Nations assistance for the advancement of women in developing countries.

The status of women in private law, particularly a Draft Recommendation on Consent to Marriage, Minimum Age for Marriage, and Registration of Marriages [out of this the Commission hopes to get a Convention which the whole Assembly will adopt]. Also the legal conditions and effects of the dissolution of marriage, the annulment of marriage, and judicial separations.

The Nationality of married women (on which the Assembly has already taken action).

If, as it is sometimes alleged, the most important American contribution to the process of welding the world's nations into a commonly recognized civilization is the creation and manufacture of desired gadgets, from the bobby pin to the bulldozer, here is one field where this assertion can be refuted.

11. WHERE WOMEN ARE NOW: MEASURES OF A WAY STATION

"Today's woman, armed with her ballot, her diploma, her union card, faces a dizzily complex world; inevitably she is often confused and paralyzed by it. So, one might add, is her male opposite. . . ."
Eleanor Flexner—*Century of Struggle*

The emancipation of women may have been, as Professor Edward Samuels of Northwestern University avers, "the most momentous fact of the nineteenth century," but the nineteenth is long gone, the twentieth is more than half over, and emancipation is still a process rather than an achieved fact. Spotty in its implications and responsibilities, only half accepted, opening doors to some women and having no perceptible effect on others, it is complex and hard to assess.

Many yardsticks have been applied in an effort to measure the present level of feminine emancipation, but for our purposes the best way to start is to go back to that Seneca Falls Declaration of Women's Rights and see how far the situation it mirrors compares with the one in which we now live. The contrast marks the distance women have come in legal and political standing, and in terms of economics, education, morals, and self-confidence—the distance in their right to be people.

It will be remembered that the women's Declaration of 1848 was shaped in three parts: first, a prologue based on the older Declaration of Independence, then a list of particular charges against man, whose history is declared to be "one of repeated injuries and usurpations . . . toward woman, having in direct object the establishing of an absolute tyranny toward her," and then a series of twelve resolutions.

The charges against "man the usurper" are given in detail. (1) "He has never permitted her to exercise her inalienable right to the elective franchise." "Never" began to break apart in 1869, when the territory of Wyoming gave women the vote, and it disappeared in 1920 when the Nineteenth Amendment was ratified.

The second charge is allied to the first. (2) "He has compelled her to submit to laws, in the formation of which she has had no voice." This is still true, in that a great body of law that preceded woman suffrage continues valid. The plaint has, however, lost a good deal of its force as women have taken part in the long process of modifying specific state and national laws that had militated against them.

The third charge moves to ground that even then was less certain. (3) "He has withheld from her rights which are given to the most ignorant and degraded men—both natives and foreigners." But which rights? Did this refer to voting, or to the ownership of property, the right to sign contracts, or to govern the upbringing of children? Its meaning was not spelled out. In any event, most of the legal rights she then lacked she now possesses.

The accusations speed up. (4) "Having deprived her of this first right of a citizen, the elective franchise, thereby leaving her without representation in the halls of legislation, he has oppressed her on all sides." He may still oppress her on all sides, and in a variety of ways. The newspapers are not empty of tales of beatings, cruelty, desertion, even wife murder, some of which reach the courts and some of which do not. But the implied cause of this oppression, the lack of a vote and therefore of "representation in the halls of legislation," is long gone. Representation in Congress she has in full. She can even sit in Congress, if she can get elected (ten women sat in the 89th Congress, eleven in the 88th, seventeen in the 87th). She can, and does to a small degree, sit in the state legislatures and in town councils. If she still finds herself oppressed, it is not for lack of legal recourse.

(5) "He has made her, if married, in the eyes of the law, civilly dead." In 1848, that was a slight exaggeration, but only slight. Married women actually were nonentities under the law. They could not administer their own property, or even will it as they chose. They could not enter into contracts, sue or be sued in their own names, engage in business, or keep what money they earned if their husbands chose to take it. Painfully, slowly, under the spur of women's demands and with the support of men whose consciences were touched, much of this injustice has been cleared away in the individual states, where the law on such subjects still resides. But remnants of the old English common law still stain the total picture: a number of states continue to limit a wife's right to serve in a position of trust; a few restrict her right to take part in a separate business. Five of them insist that she ask the court for permission to do this; one would make the personal property of a married business woman liable for her husband's debts unless he files a certificate of exception with the town clerk. The President's Commission on the Status of Women took note of these antiquated situations in their 1963 report; in several of the states corrections will be pushed.

The sixth charge (6), "He has taken from her all right in property, even to the wages she earns" reiterates in more specific terms the same complaint, and is subject to the same comment.

The seventh carries a deeper sting of indignation, a personal sense of outrage. (7) "He has made her, morally, an irresponsible being, as she can commit many crimes with impunity, provided they be done in the presence of her husband. In the covenant of marriage, she is compelled to promise obedience to her husband, he becoming, to all intents and purposes, her master—the law giving him power to deprive her of her liberty, and to administer chastisement." Here the record is less clear, and varies in the states. Generally speaking, a woman who commits a crime in her husband's presence is no longer immune from punishment. As for being beaten, the modern view is that a wife has just as much right to protest to the police as has anyone else.

The tale of mid-Victorian outrage and inequality went on. (8) "He has so framed the laws of divorce, as to what shall be the proper causes, and in case of separation, to whom the guardianship of children shall be given, as to be wholly regardless of the happiness of women—the law, in all cases, going upon a false supposition of the supremacy of men, and giving all power into his hands." Just what the "happiness of women" would have required of the divorce law in an age when divorce itself was very rare is not specified. The point of stress then was the guardianship of children. Now divorce in many states is far easier than it used to be, and most of the states put the guardianship of a minor child into the hands of both parents, giving the mother equal rights with the father. Still, there are six (Alaska, Georgia, Louisiana, North Carolina, Oklahoma, and Texas) that continue to declare the father "the preferred natural guardian."

The next charge speaks up for the rights of spinsters. (9) "After depriving her of all rights as a married woman, if single, and the owner of property, he has taxed her to support a government which recognizes her only when her property can be made profitable to it." This was taxation without representation, a theme that having sparked the American revolution was still full of fire. It also had to do with woman's rights to hold and to will property, a matter so charged with pressures, even in those days, that New York State moved to correct it shortly after 1848, with other states following as pressures reached them.

At that point in the Declaration the field of protest changes from the political and legal to the economic. (10) "He has monopolized nearly all the profitable employments, and from those she is permitted to follow, she receives but a scanty remuneration. He closes against her all the avenues to wealth and distinction which he considers most honorable to himself." And what were these "most honorable" occupations in 1848? The next sentence implies the answer. "As a teacher of theology, medicine, or law she is not known."

In the wide field of woman's employment, of labor laws, of demands for equal pay for equal work, of the value of woman's work to herself and to the nation the changes have been tremendous. Far from being barred, as they used to be, from "nearly all the profitable employments," women now work in every one of the 479 individual occupations listed by the Census Bureau. They function in all the professions, even including the teaching of theology, medicine, and law.

They do not yet earn as much as men do; the mass figures for this comparison are not cheerful. Men with incomes, however acquired, get on the median average more than three times what women get ($4,189 a year as compared with $1,262). The remuneration is on the average still "scanty," but it is improving. The new federal law prescribing equal pay for equal work should help.

In 1848 there was little she could do and little she could earn. Moreover, she could see almost no opportunity to improve herself, her occupation, or her wages for (11) "He has denied her the facilities for obtaining a thorough education, all colleges being closed to her." This too was a slight exaggeration; Oberlin, at least, had opened its collegiate department to women a decade earlier, but no other college had been as hospitable, nor would be until Elmira opened its doors in 1855.

In this field of complaint the changes have been as great as in the area of employment. Far from being barred against her, most colleges are now wide open to her. A plethora of women's colleges and state universities welcome her, an increasing number of men's colleges will accept her if she can meet their standards. All she must do is to prove herself as good a student as men are. The chance of equality is there if she will reach for it.

The present protest is that she does not seem to reach for it hard enough. In the autumn of 1962 there were 1,039,000 students enrolled in American colleges; 58 per cent of these students were men, only 42 per cent were women, and this despite the fact that the country has more women than men (three and a quarter million more). This may represent merely an educational lag, or echo the older view that women are not worth educating. In any event the situation, while far better than it was, is not yet balanced. In Mrs. Stanton's day and among ambitious women the desire for a thorough education was considerable, but opportunities were lacking. Now opportunities are ample, but the desire seems weak.

In the field of religion, the complaints of 1848 were loud. (12) "He allows her in Church, as well as State, but a subordinate position, claiming Apostolic authority for her exclusion from the ministry, and, with some exceptions, from any public participation in the affairs of the Church."

The church in 1848 loomed as a major force. It was mostly Protestant, with heavy Puritan overtones. Those preachers in London who, eight years earlier, had refused to let Mrs. Stanton, Lucretia Mott, or any other woman take part in their meetings were all too typical of a widespread attitude among clergy and conservative laymen.

In comparison, women nowadays have much less reason for complaint. In Protestant churches they are no longer excluded from the ministry, nor "from public participation in the affairs of the Church." They still walk softly here.

The next point of complaint, the double standard of morality, is more difficult to assess. What Mrs. Stanton and her friends charged was that man (13) "has created a false public sentiment by giving to the world a different code of morals for men and women, by which moral delinquencies which exclude women from society, are not only tolerated, but deemed of little account in man."

What "moral delinquencies" had they in mind? Gambling? Drinking? Smoking? Wife beating? Wife desertion? Adultery? Perhaps all of them. But then what?

Their aim to reform in this matter was on a high level; in modern terms it appears to have little connection with reality. Resolution (6) of the twelve that were to follow the fifteen complaints of the Seneca Falls ladies demands that "the same amount of virtue, delicacy and refinement of behavior that is required of women in the same social state, should also be required of man, and the same transgressions should be visited with equal severity, on both man and woman." The ladies were reformers to the core. In their legal, political, and economic demands they wanted women raised to the same level as men. In the realm of morality, however, women saw themselves in the ascendancy, and the elevating process was to be applied to men.

What they surely did not contemplate was that the leveling process might work another way; that men might stay about where they were, in moral codes as well as in political and economic dominance, whereas women, in making their way upward toward the masculine haven of voting power, fine jobs, and good wages, might also find their Victorian moral standards dropping toward the masculine floor. Some "moral delinquencies" which in 1848 were "deemed of little account" in men have now won a certain degree of tolerance in women.

To cap all this (remember the Seneca Falls meeting was held in a church) come two final charges: (14) "He has usurped the prerogative of Jehovah himself, claiming it as his right to assign for her a sphere of action, when that belongs to her conscience and her God."

The prerogatives of Jehovah, like whatever prerogatives man still assigns to himself, are not much weighed or discussed these days.

The last charge was bitter. In substance, it summed up the net effect of those injustices, the key complaint underlying all the rest.

(15) "He has endeavored, in every way that he could, to lessen her self-respect, and to make her willing to lead a dependent and abject life."

Some men may still hold to this course; one school of thought charges that the members of the advertising world, with clients in the worlds of production and distribution, are doing it deliberately, because they make money at it. At the same time, "a dependent and abject life" is hard to reconcile with statistics that show how many young women are choosing to support their husbands while the latter work for advanced academic degrees. One can hardly describe the twenty-four million women in the labor force as abject or dependent. The forty-six million not counted there may be both, but they do not look it.

Whether most women felt "dependent and abject" in 1848 is a matter of opinion. It is, however, entirely probable that had the protesters been less passionately indignant, had they asked then a single redress such as the vote rather than making a shotgun attack against discrimination, their protest would have had less impact. Only by massing their charges and scattering their shots could they gain attention and win sympathy. Only later could the target be narrowed to a single point, and that point won.

The twelve "Resolutions," which followed the fifteen charges, were presumably meant to correct the listed injustices, but most of the force had gone into the attack. The women resolved (3) "that woman is man's equal, was intended to be so by the Creator, and the highest good of the race demands that she be recognized as such." They wanted women (4) "to be enlightened in regard to the laws under which they live." They saw (7) no reason why women speaking on public platforms should be frowned on, whereas women singing, acting, walking tightropes in circuses were applauded. They wanted (12) both men and women to bend "untiring efforts . . . for the overthrow of the monopoly of the pulpit, and for the securing to women an equal participation in the various trades, professions and commerce."

In one way or another, and with changes in phrase and emphasis as the years went on, this complex is what women worked for during the next century. In one way or another, this is what their grandmothers, their great-aunts, their aunts, and their mothers won for them: the right to vote, and to be represented in Congress through the exercise of that vote; to be citizens on their own account; to get a good education, and a job if they want it; to handle property, to control their wages, to act as guardians of their children. In other words, to be recognized as people. These rights, with some minor qualifications, they have won. These the women of other nations possess, in some measure, when they come as representatives of their governments to the United Nations; they are determined to improve that measure, as far as or further than the American standard.

It is true that for most American women political life is still sticky, and that, despite interested efforts on the part of two recent presidents, few make their way onto the upper levels of power and influence. A federal commission concerned with their status suggested that too few "possess the practical experience obtained at middle and upper levels of administrative and executive responsibility . . . they therefore lack the public visibility."

There may be some truth in this, though women seem to have plenty of public visibility if one consults billboards and display advertising. But if it is true that in political circles they are still shy violets, why? This is 1966; what have women been doing ever since 1920? What good, in terms of the world about them, is all this fine health, this splendid education, this open door to opportunity for which their mothers and grandmothers clamored? Are they still preoccupied with consuming? Still trying to justify their old devotion to domestic monopoly in a world so tangled that it deprives them of household help when they need it most, and adds onto their long lives a brace of years when they are too old to have fun or be useful?

The recognition that "woman is man's equal" they do not have, nor do many women continue to clamor for so dubious a prize. Better education has brought into play better logic, and one begins to hear that equality cuts both ways; if woman is to be man's equal, man must be woman's equal—not only sharing shirts and slacks with her, but bringing up the children, doing the darning, acting as Den Mother, quieting quarrels and looking beautiful on five minutes' notice.

In the face of this logic and the absurdities it engenders the old claim falls to the ground. To replace it comes a growing recognition that despite the images presented by current fashions men and women are inescapably different, and that the differences bring enrichment to both. Skills, attitudes, and qualities are not identical but complementary, and the best basis for their use lies in encouraging development and collaboration for both sexes.

Slowly but surely women are learning. The hard-won vote has lifted them out of a deep feeling of uncertainty and lack of competence in a man's world to a point on level ground where they begin to take a hand in that world, with no apologies to be made and no quarter asked, where they are truly people. Small straws point to big changes. The young Radcliffe student who recently became the first woman ever to be chosen as managing editor of Harvard's student paper set the new shape of things straight. "Life is competition," she said. "I would feel guilty living comfortably."

The amount of progress that appears in this quick comparison between 1848 and 1966 is stupendous, and even more so when one looks closely at the actualities that lie beneath the generalities. Having come so far, women might be expected to stop pushing. But to ask this is to expect them not to be human. And it was at a great cost that there was won for them the right to be people.

DECLARATION OF WOMEN'S RIGHTS
SENECA FALLS, NEW YORK, 1848*

Declaration of Sentiments

"When, in the course of human events, it becomes necessary for one portion of the family of man to assume among the people of the earth a position different from that which they have hitherto occupied, but one to which the laws of nature and of nature's God entitle them, a decent respect to the opinions of mankind requires that they should declare the causes that impel them to such a course.

"We hold these truths to be self-evident: that all men and women are created equal; that they are endowed by their Creator with certain inalienable rights; that among these are life, liberty, and the pursuit of happiness; that to secure these rights governments are instituted, deriving their just powers from the consent of the governed. Whenever any form of government becomes destructive of these ends, it is the right of those who suffer from it to refuse

*From *History of Woman Suffrage*, Vol. I, pp. 70-75.

allegiance to it, and to insist upon the institution of a new government, laying its foundation on such principles, and organizing its powers in such form, as to them shall seem most likely to effect their safety and happiness. Prudence, indeed, will dictate that governments long established should not be changed for light and transient causes; and accordingly all experience hath shown that mankind are more disposed to suffer, while evils are sufferable, than to right themselves by abolishing the forms to which they were accustomed. But when a long train of abuses and usurpations, pursuing invariably the same object evinces a design to reduce them under absolute despotism, it is their duty to throw off such government, and to provide new guards for their future security. Such has been the patient sufferance of the women under this government, and such is now the necessity which constrains them to demand the equal station to which they are entitled.

"The history of mankind is a history of repeated injuries and usurpations on the part of man toward woman, having in direct object the establishment of an absolute tyranny over her. To prove this, let facts be submitted to a candid world.

"He has never permitted her to exercise her inalienable right to the elective franchise.

"He has compelled her to submit to laws, in the formation of which she had no voice.

"He has withheld from her rights which are given to the most ignorant and degraded men—both natives and foreigners.

"Having deprived her of this first right of a citizen, the elective franchise, thereby leaving her without representation in the halls of legislation, he has oppressed her on all sides.

"He has made her, if married, in the eye of the law, civilly dead.

"He has taken from her all right in property, even to the wages she earns.

"He has made her, morally, an irresponsible being, as she can commit many crimes with impunity, provided they be done in the presence of her husband. In the covenant of marriage, she is compelled to promise obedience to her husband, he becoming, to all intents and purposes, her master—the law giving him power to deprive her of her liberty, and to administer chastisement.

"He has so framed the laws of divorce, as to what shall be the proper causes, and in case of separation, to whom the guardianship of the children shall be given, as to be wholly regardless of the happiness of women—the law, in all cases, going upon a false supposition of the supremacy of man, and giving all power into his hands.

"After depriving her of all rights as a married woman, if single, and the owner of property, he has taxed her to support a government which recognizes her only when her property can be made profitable to it.

"He has monopolized nearly all the profitable employments, and from those she is permitted to follow, she receives but a scanty remuneration. He closes against her all the avenues to wealth and distinction which he considers most honorable to himself. As a teacher of theology, medicine, or law, she is not known.

"He has denied her the facilities for obtaining a thorough education, all colleges being closed against her.

"He allows her in Church, as well as State, but a subordinate position, claiming Apostolic authority for her exclusion from the ministry, and, with some exceptions, from any public participation in the affairs of the Church.

"He has created a false public sentiment by giving to the world a different code of morals for men and women, by which moral delinquencies which exclude women from society, are not only tolerated, but deemed of little account in man.

"He has usurped the prerogative of Jehovah himself, claiming it as his right to assign for her a sphere of action, when that belongs to her conscience and to her God.

"He has endeavored, in every way that he could, to destroy her confidence in her own powers, to lessen her self-respect, and to make her willing to lead a dependent and abject life.

"Now, in view of this entire disfranchisement of one-half the people of this country, their social and religious degradation—in view of the unjust laws above mentioned, and because women do feel themselves aggrieved, oppressed, and fraudulently deprived of their most sacred rights, we insist that they have immediate admission to all the rights and privileges which belong to them as citizens of the United States.

"In entering upon the great work before us, we anticipate no small amount of misconception, misrepresentation, and ridicule; but we shall use every instrumentality within our power to effect our object. We shall employ agents, circulate tracts, petition the State and National legislatures, and endeavor to enlist the pulpit and the press in our behalf. We hope this Convention will be followed by a series of Conventions embracing every part of the country."

NOTE ON SOURCES

The official *History of Woman's Suffrage*, which is the primary and indispensable source for everyone interested in the subject, was written at various times and by several persons. Susan B. Anthony and Elizabeth Cady Stanton started it in 1880. Susan had saved letters, clippings, speeches, pamphlets, pictures as their work went along, and trunks full of this material were waiting in Mrs. Stanton's storeroom for sorting and for use. With the assistance of Matilda Joslyn Gage, the two pioneers wrote the first three volumes in six years of hard work. This brought the story up to 1886. The last three volumes were in part the work of Ida Husted Harper, who helped Miss Anthony to finish the fourth one in 1900, and then worked on the fifth and sixth. The last she finished, with the aid of Nettie Rogers Shuler, in 1922. Better than any other single source, these volumes give the facts and the flavor of the years, the people, the events.

Other illuminating books are:

Beard, Mary R. *Woman as a Force in History*, a Study of Traditions and Realities. New York, 1946.

Herold, J. Christopher. *Mistress to an Age, a Life of Madame de Staël*, Indianapolis, 1958.

Martineau, Harriet. *Society in America*, London, 1837.

Wollstonecraft, Mary. *A Vindication of the Rights of Women*, ed, by George E. G. Catlin, London, 1929.

For People and What They Did

Anthony, Katherine. *Susan B. Anthony: Her Personal History and Her Era*. Garden City, New York: 1954.

Blackwell, Alice Stone. *Lucy Stone, Pioneer of Women's Rights*. Boston: 1930.

Breckenridge, Sophonisba P. *Women in the Twentieth Century, a Study of Their Political, Social and Economic Activities*. New York: 1933.

———. *Marriage and the Civic Rights of Women*. Chicago: 1931.

Brown, Gertrude Foster (Mrs. Raymond Brown). *Your Vote and How to Use It*. New York: 1918.

Brown, Raymond. *How It Feels to Be the Husband of a Suffragette*. New York: 1916.

Catt, Carrie Chapman, and Shuler, Nellie Rogers. *Woman Suffrage and Politics: the Inner Story of the Suffrage Movement*. New York: 1923.

Flexner, Eleanor. *Century of Struggle, the Woman's Rights Movement*. Cambridge: 1959.

Irwin, Inez Haynes. *The Story of the Woman's Party*. New York: 1921.

National American Woman Suffrage Association. *Victory. How the Women Won It, a Centennial Symposium, 1840-1940*. New York: 1940.

Newcomer, Mabel. *A Century of Higher Education*. New York: 1959.

Park, Maud Wood. *Front Door Lobby*. Boston: 1960.

Peck, Mary Gray. *Carrie Chapman Catt, a Biography*. New York: 1944.

President's Commission on the Status of Women. *American*

Women. Washington: 1963.

Sach, Emanie. *The Terrible Siren, Victoria Woodhull (1838-1927).* New York: 1928.

Shaw, Anna Howard. *The Story of a Pioneer.* New York: 1915.

Stanton, Theodore, and Blatch, Harriet Stanton (eds). *Elizabeth Cady Stanton, As Revealed in Her Letters, Diary, and Reminiscences.* (This reprints Mrs. Stanton's own autobiography, *Eighty Years and More.*) New York: 1922.

Stein, Leon. *The Triangle Fire.* New York: 1962.

Young, Rose. *The Record of the Leslie Woman Suffrage Commission, Inc., 1917-1929.* New York: 1949.

INDEX